GOING HOME TO GLORY

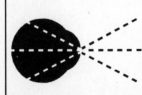

This Large Print Book carries the
Seal of Approval of N.A.V.H.

Going Home to Glory

A MEMOIR OF LIFE WITH
DWIGHT D. EISENHOWER, 1961–1969

David Eisenhower with
Julie Nixon Eisenhower

THORNDIKE PRESS
A part of Gale, Cengage Learning

GALE
CENGAGE Learning

Detroit • New York • San Francisco • New Haven, Conn • Waterville, Maine • London

GALE
CENGAGE Learning™

LIBRARY OF CONGRESS CATALOGING-IN-PUBLICATION DATA

Eisenhower, David, 1948–
    Going home to glory : a memoir of life with Dwight D.
Eisenhower, 1961–1969 / by David Eisenhower with Julie Nixon
Eisenhower. — Large print ed.
        p. cm.
    Originally published: New York : Simon & Schuster, 2010.
    ISBN-13: 978-1-4104-3438-8 (lg. print : hardcover)
    ISBN-10: 1-4104-3438-9 (lg. print : hardcover) 1. Eisenhower,
Dwight D. (Dwight David), 1890–1969. 2. Eisenhower, Dwight
D. (Dwight David), 1890–1969—Family. 3. Presidents—United
States—Biography. 4. Ex-presidents—United States—Biography.
5. Eisenhower, David, 1948– I. Eisenhower, Julie Nixon. II. Title.
E836.E383 2011
973.921092—dc22   2010044443

Published in 2011 by arrangement with Simon & Schuster, Inc.

Printed in the United States of America
1 2 3 4 5 6 7 15 14 13 12 11

To Jennie, Alex, and Melanie

CONTENTS

■ ■ ■ ■

PART I:
GENERAL
EISENHOWER

■ ■ ■ ■

1
GETTYSBURG

GOING HOME

In the late afternoon of Inauguration Day, January 20, 1961, Dwight and Mamie Eisenhower drove north to Gettysburg, Pennsylvania, in the 1955 Chrysler Imperial that Mamie had purchased for Ike on his sixty-fifth birthday. The outgoing President and First Lady, their personal servants, Sergeant John Moaney and Rosie Woods, and chauffeur, Leonard Dry, sat together in the roomy car. There was an eerie loneliness about the absence of motorcycle escorts and caravans of Secret Service and press cars. A single Secret Service vehicle with driver and agent led the Chrysler. When the Eisenhowers approached the entrance to their Gettysburg farm, the Secret Service honked the horn and made a U-turn, heading back to Washington.

The Eisenhowers' itinerary had been published in newspapers. Despite a blizzard the night before and below-freezing temperatures, friendly groups in twos and threes lined the road between Washington and Frederick, Maryland. Near Emmitsburg, on Route 15, the crowds grew larger. The nuns, priests, and students of Mount St. Mary's and St. Joseph's colleges, bundled in overcoats and scarves, congregated along the road bearing "Welcome Home" signs.

In Gettysburg, a festive mood reigned. Over sixty civic organizations prepared for celebrations scheduled the following evening in the town square welcoming the Eisenhowers home as private citizens. Henry Scharf, owner of the Gettysburg Hotel and host of the "Welcome Home Day" celebration, was pleased that Eisenhower had selected Gettysburg to retire. The Eisenhowers would not only mean tourism, but also add to the historical stature of the community. Scharf, like the majority of the townspeople, had a sense of history about Gettysburg. His study at home was packed with books on the Civil War, World War II, and the American Revolution. By the untidy appearance of his study, one judged he used those references constantly, and he did. He was convinced Eisenhower's decision to retire to Gettysburg was an affirmation of the town's historical uniqueness.

As Scharf said to his wife, Peggy, "This is the greatest thing to happen to this town since the battle. This man is beloved by everyone, including his opponents. He is the best-loved president since Lincoln."

But there was a difference. While in office, Lincoln had been one of the most maligned presidents in American history. His stature had grown with the passage of time and he was linked to Gettysburg by his unforgettable address at the dedication of the National Cemetery. Eisenhower, on the other hand, was perhaps the most popular president while in office, but his reputation might not grow like Lincoln's, might in fact diminish.

Earlier that morning, Scharf's daughter, Elise, scurried about her Alexandria, Virginia, apartment collecting a few necessities for the journey to Gettysburg along the precise route the Eisenhower party would take. Not only was Elise needed at home to assist with the multicourse dinner arrangements; she also eagerly anticipated a chance to see the Eisenhowers close-up and perhaps even to chat. Elise admired President Eisenhower and had seen him from a distance on the few occasions her father's staff had been involved in catering functions on the grounds of the Gettysburg farm. She had gone along as a member of the kitchen or grounds crew, just for a glimpse. Now, as far as she and several thousand other Gettysburgians were concerned, the Eisenhowers were becoming neighbors. Nobody planned to bother them or to ask them to appear at social gatherings and club functions. Everyone expected that eventually the Eisenhowers would take some active part in the community, but no one would impose.

The weather was ominous. Elise worried that she would be blocked by the accumulating snowdrifts, which were paralyzing the capital city and the roads leading to southern Pennsylvania. Snow had fallen heavily the night before, and the entire Potomac Basin was frozen. Temperatures had plummeted. As the ceremonies inaugurating John Kennedy as the thirty-fifth president drew to a conclusion, Elise called the Maryland State Police to learn the status of the northbound roads. She found out that nothing could be guaranteed after three o'clock but that if she left immediately, she had a reasonable chance of getting home.

Additionally, she reasoned, if she could reach Route 15 at Frederick, the remainder of the road running through Thurmont and Emmitsburg would be kept open for the Eisenhower motorcade. Elise set off on her uncertain trek and eventually joined up five minutes behind the bittersweet Eisenhower procession.

Every mile, Elise saw evidence that the Eisenhower motorcade had passed through minutes before. She saw discarded signs reading "Welcome Home," and the dispersing throngs who moments earlier had braved the cold to ease Eisenhower's transition to private life. In Emmitsburg, Peggy passed the congregation of nuns packing up blankets and signs outside of St. Joseph's College. Upon arriving in Gettysburg, she learned of improving forecasts for the 21st, calling for frigid weather but gradually diminishing snowfall. The ceremonies set for the next day were on.

At dinnertime, my grandparents drove directly to our home, a former schoolhouse that stood on the corner of their farm. My three younger sisters, Anne, eleven, Susan, nine, Mary Jean, five, and I, now a grown-up twelve years old, had watched the inauguration at home in Gettysburg. I remembered thinking that it should have been the Nixons moving into the White House — and then thinking that being twelve and fourteen years old, the ages of Julie and Tricia Nixon, would be a terrible time to have Secret

15

Service agents. I would miss the men on my detail, but not their constant guarding of Gran One, Gran Two, Gran Three, and Gran Four, the official Secret Service names for my sisters and me.

Everyone now seemed animated and happy, in sharp contrast to the air of numbing tension in the White House several weeks earlier. Relaxed, Granddad listened intently to every word spoken and seemed to say less than usual. He basked in the attention, joking lightly. Characteristically, he wandered frequently into the kitchen to supervise dinner preparations by Sergeant Moaney and his wife, Delores, who had arrived at the farm earlier in the day. Moaney had joined Granddad's staff as his orderly in the early months of the war in Europe and Delores had become my grandparents' cook after the war.

My father, John, broke the spell of gaiety toward the end of the evening, standing up from the dinner table to speak. He reviewed briefly Granddad's accomplishments and then spoke of the years before the fame. As a small, tight-knit family of three, the Eisenhowers had seen much of the world. They had lived in Paris and in Washington both before and during the Depression. They then went on to the Philippines and four years of service under General Douglas MacArthur. The war had dispersed the family, John going to West Point, Mamie returning to Washington, and Dwight Eisenhower going on, in Douglas MacArthur's words, to "write his name in history." Dad recalled that the decision to run for president had been difficult, but in the end, Dwight Eisenhower had returned from his NATO command to lead the country through eight years of peace and prosperity. Dad spoke of the experience of a lifetime he had had serving his father in the West Wing.

"Leaving the White House will not be easy at first," Dad said. "But we are reunited as a family, and this" — Dad gestured to all of us seated, and outside toward the farm — "is what we have wanted. I suppose that tonight, we welcome back a member of this clan who has done us proud." Dad raised his glass in a toast.

Too moved to reply, Granddad simply held his glass high and joined in the "hear, hear."

It had been a long day. Earlier, Eisenhower had transferred power to John F. Kennedy. That morning, after coffee at the White House and a brief pause at the North Portico for the benefit of newsmen, photographers, and television cameras, Eisenhower and Kennedy had driven off to the Capitol wearing top hats in place of the homburgs that Eisenhower had sought to install as a tradition at his inaugural in 1953. The tradition, *Time* noted, "will end with his [Eisenhower's] administration."

Slowly the black limousine bearing the oldest and second-youngest presidents in U.S. history had rolled toward the gleaming Capitol building, past the crowd estimated at nearly a million people lining Washington's broad boulevards and gradually filling the newly installed tiers of spectator's stands. In December, Eisenhower had ruefully likened the stands appearing around the White House and along the inaugural parade route to "scaffolds." By that comment Eisenhower might have been mindful of his inauguration eight years earlier. After he and Harry Truman exchanged only a few words during the entire ceremony, Truman's departure, in Eisenhower's mind, had taken on the character of a hanging. But in January 1961, Harry Truman, busy making the rounds of inaugural parties, appeared to have forgotten the affair. On the 19th, Truman told reporters he had "no advice" regarding Eisenhower's retirement, adding that as far as he was concerned, Eisenhower was "a very nice person."

Eisenhower was being handled gently, even affectionately, as he went through the ritual of laying down power. Since November, Kennedy had been at his cordial best. Before the inaugural ceremony, Eisenhower and Kennedy had chatted amicably in the Red Room. For his part, Kennedy was almost alight with the intense media excitement over his ascension to power.

Eisenhower had been busy in January preparing his final messages to the American people. In his eighth State of the Union address, he declared the state of the union to be sound. He reminded the country that for eight years Americans had "lived in peace." Eisenhower listed his administration's measures that had ensured the peace: the ballistic missile program, strong support for foreign aid, a series of alliances ringing the Sino-Soviet landmass, and efforts to open talks between East and West. Two weeks later, in his farewell address to the nation, Eisenhower had expressed forebodings about the domestic implications of a permanent state of mobilization without war, warning that a "military industrial complex" could undermine democratic self-rule.

But Eisenhower's message fell on deaf ears. The inaugural coincided with a period of turmoil. Nikita Khrushchev in early January issued an ominous declaration. Aimed partly at China, partly at the United States, he endorsed "wars of national liberation," a program of Soviet support for insurgencies and sabotage worldwide against the remnants of Western colonialism. In Laos, North Vietnamese battalions operated with Pathet Lao units in a battle against pro-Western forces for control of the strategic Plain of Jars. In Cuba, Fidel Castro paraded Soviet-built tanks and Cuban militiamen through downtown Havana, proclaiming his preparedness against a rumored invasion from the north. In France, voters approved a referendum endorsing Charles de Gaulle's program to end the war in Algeria, setting the stage for France's capitulation to the rebel forces. Throughout Belgium, half a million workers, teachers, and businessmen protested the government's austerity program, enacted because of the wrenching loss of the Congo and the end of colonialism in Africa.

Kennedy disagreed with Eisenhower's optimism about the state of the union and now it was his turn to speak. In January, the president-elect had proclaimed before the Massachusetts legislature that his government would "always consider that we shall be as a city upon a hill — the eyes of all the people are upon us." Now center stage, on the threshold of assuming the presidency, Kennedy wanted to convey a sense of urgency, to "rekindle the spirit of the American revolution," and to ask for greater exertions by the American people. In New York on September 14, he had declared his presidency would be "a hazardous experience," predicting, "We will live on the edge of danger."

Minor mishaps enriched the pageantry of the Kennedy inaugural. Cardinal Cushing's invocation was interrupted by a short circuit in the electric motor powering the heating system that warmed the seated dignitaries. Mamie Eisenhower first noticed the smoke and for several awkward moments the assembled officials on the platform scurried about in confusion. The winter sun's glare temporarily blinded poet Robert Frost at the lectern, and forced him to recite from memory a poem he had published in 1942 titled "The Gift Outright," rather than the poem he had written for the inaugural.

Following the administration of the oath, Kennedy delivered the most memorable inaugural speech since Franklin Delano Roosevelt's in 1933. The young president achieved eloquence, an inspirational quality, a tone of defiance and resolve. He repudiated the confident premise of the Eisenhower administration. "Only a few generations," he declared, "have been granted the role of defending freedom in its hour of maximum danger. I welcome this responsibility."

Kennedy drew attention to his youth and to his awareness that this was a moment of transition from wartime to postwar leadership.

We dare not forget today that we are the heirs of that first revolution. Let the word go forth from this time and place, to friend and foe alike, that the torch is passed to a new generation of Americans — born in this century, tempered by war, disciplined by a hard and bitter peace, proud of our ancient heritage — and unwilling to witness or permit the slow undoing of those human rights to which this nation has always been committed, and to which we are committed today, at home and around the world.

To Khrushchev's promise to subsidize "wars of national liberation," Kennedy replied:

Let every nation know whether it wishes us well or ill, that we shall pay any price, bear any burden, meet any hardship, support any friend or oppose any foe to assure the survival and success of liberty. This much we pledge and more.

Implying years of inaction under Eisenhower, he cried: "But let us begin . . . let us begin anew."

The *Los Angeles Times* noted about Kennedy: "He is wrong in implying the beginning came with him, but he is right in suggesting that the perfecting of mankind is tedious and unpredictable." But *Time* magazine had applauded Kennedy's "lean, lucid phrases," noting his message had "profound meaning for the US future."

Fourteen years later, author Robert Nisbet, criticizing the liberals' fondness for crisis, wrote that "crisis is always an opportunity for a break with the despised present, liberation from the kinds of authority which are most repugnant to bold, creative and utopian minds." Kennedy was now president. The "despised present" was the Eisenhower administration and the "liberation" from constraints had been accomplished by the inaugural ceremony.

Naturally, feelings about the speech ran

high and negative among Eisenhower's associates, friends, and family. From the Capitol, Eisenhower motored to a farewell reception at the F Street Club hosted by former chairman of the Atomic Energy Commission Admiral Lewis Strauss and attended by the Nixons, my parents, John and Barbara Eisenhower, and former members of the cabinet. During one of the toasts that dwelled sentimentally on Eisenhower and the departed administration, my mother whispered to Nixon seated to her right, "Wasn't it sad?" Nixon shrugged.

Milton Eisenhower, Eisenhower's youngest brother and closest confidant, lacking the heart to attend either the inauguration or the F Street farewell, watched the ceremonies on television in his home on the Johns Hopkins University campus, where he was president. Once a delegate to UNESCO, he had long believed the United States could "change history" by working toward mutual understanding among peoples. As Milton later recalled, the unilateral character of Kennedy's speech "hit me like bricks."

At Washington's Jefferson Hotel, Eisenhower staff members, including appointments secretary Tom Stephens, Mamie's aide Mary Jane McCaffrey, the President's secretary Ann Whitman, and White House speech-writer Kevin McCann, watched the speech and parade on television. They drowned their sorrow and remorse with martinis. As McCann recalled, "The world was coming to an end."

On January 21, the Eisenhower family packed suitcases and drove the several miles from our home into Gettysburg for the welcome ceremony. The severe weather might force us to stay at the Gettysburg Hotel.

In the frigid (14 degrees) night, more than two thousand people crammed into floodlit Lincoln Square to witness the remarks. Judge W. C. Sheely delivered the welcome on behalf of Gettysburg, Cumberland Township, and Adams County. The Gettysburg High School Band played "The Battle Hymn of the Republic." An honor guard comprised of one Army and one Air Force ROTC detachment from Gettysburg College rendered the ceremonial salute.

My sisters and I had taken places among a crowd of grade school classmates. I had seen my grandfather many times on television, as he returned from trips overseas, or addressed Congress or the United Nations. I had seen documentaries about his role during World War II, and I had ridden with him in the presidential limousine through parades and motorcades, but I had never watched him as part of a crowd. The connection between the man on a television screen and the man I knew had always been somewhat abstract. I had never comprehended the barriers between Granddad and others, or experienced them as others had. I realized that if I ran forward that night to the podium, a policeman would restrain me and that I would wreck the decorum of the ceremony. This tugged at me slightly. Yet looking around me, all the people I knew seemed to regard the sight of Granddad on the platform addressing the crowd, waving, being blinded by cameras, ringed by police, as perfectly natural. This, I thought, either set me apart from my friends or set me apart from my grandfather. It occurred to me I had not fully appreciated that familiar and now suddenly distant bald, silhouetted figure being serenaded and honored by my friends.

After the speeches, minutes before the banquet was scheduled to begin, Elise Scharf slipped into the second-floor suite where the Eisenhowers were due to arrive for a cocktail with her parents and a few of the local sponsors of the event.

Mamie Eisenhower was the first person to enter the room. Elise was startled. The former First Lady seemed surprised to see Elise and said nothing. Suddenly Dwight Eisenhower stood a foot away. "Hi! I'm General Eisenhower," he said, extending his hand. Eisenhower's face was ruddy and smiling.

Elise froze. She was speechless. After shaking his hand in confusion, she wandered back into an old kitchen, then a bedroom, where she found a solitary and forlorn-looking Secret Service agent standing watch. He was Dick Flohr, dispatched by President Kennedy as a courtesy to stay for several days in Gettysburg to ward off the curious who might attempt to disturb the Eisenhowers in their isolation on the farm.

Flohr had been among the handful of agents with Granddad during his heart attack in 1955, and had protected him on the campaign trail in 1956. In time Flohr had accumulated a number of intimate experiences with the Eisenhower family. And after eight years of protecting President Eisenhower, agent Flohr's loyalty had become personal. He had traveled everywhere with the President and he loved him. In time he would serve President Kennedy loyally and faithfully, as he had Eisenhower.

"Why are you talking to me?" he asked Elise. She confessed that she did not know what to say to anyone if she were to go back in. "Young lady," he said reproachfully, "the greatest man you will ever meet is standing out there in the next room. You are wasting your time here. Go talk to him."

Elise still hesitated. In the adjoining living room, the gales of laughter and rapid conversation were deafening. But several minutes later she was standing next to Eisenhower. He turned and stunned her with his question: "You're in education aren't you?"

"I almost called you to hitch a ride; the snow was awful," she bubbled. There, she had broken the ice. It was a start.

"Well," he said laughing, "they disconnected me at noon!" He became serious and the two began to discuss one of Eisenhower's pet concerns, federal aid to education. As they talked on for what seemed to Elise to be ten minutes or more, she learned Eisenhower was skeptical of the clamor for federal aid to education. When the federal government begins to fund education, he argued, educational institutions will find they cannot live without the assistance they receive. Then, he added with dark emphasis, the government eventually tells educators what to do. Elise agreed. Whether for good purposes or for evil purposes, Eisenhower continued, the ability to control education has the potential to be used to promote mind control and that should be enough to recommend against letting any such thing take root. She agreed again. This man is wonderful, she thought.

"Driving up here I knew you were just ahead of me. I could see the nuns at St. Joseph's, the signs," she said.

"Wasn't that wonderful," Eisenhower said smiling.

As new friends, Granddad and Elise strolled together downstairs for the presentations, the dinner music, and songs by members of the Gettysburg College Choir. Henry Scharf served as toastmaster. At the end of the dinner he presented the Eisenhowers with a sterling silver wall plaque. Engraved on it was Eisenhower's response to the question of what he wanted Soviet premier Khrushchev to see in America during his historic 1959 visit: "I want him to see a happy people . . . doing exactly as they choose, within the limits that they must not transgress the rights of others."

AN ECCENTRIC REQUEST

On January 24, with an improvement in the weather, Eisenhower was able to fly to

Albany, Georgia, for a stag vacation starting at the plantation belonging to W. Alton "Pete" Jones, his future partner in the Eisenhower Farms. Granddad loved to hunt and he was a good shot. In Gettysburg during the pheasant and hunting season, he used to complain to his farm manager and lifelong Army colleague Brigadier General Arthur Nevins that as soon as the season opened, "the pheasants got news of it" and all the cocks took refuge in the adjoining national battlefield, where hunting was prohibited. But at the Jones plantation, for ten days he could shoot quail to his heart's content.

While Eisenhower vacationed in Georgia, the skeletal staff that had accompanied him to Gettysburg began collecting materials for the memoir Eisenhower planned to write on the presidency. Dad began gathering back issues of the Sunday editions of the *New York Times* and organizing presidential secretary Ann Whitman's files, which included Eisenhower's sporadic dictations in office diary form, important correspondence, and classified memoranda. For a month Dad would be working on his own, collecting news summaries and outlining chapters.

When Eisenhower returned from Georgia,

he left promptly with Mamie for Palm Desert, California, and the extended vacation he had planned the month before. A number of Eisenhower's friends arranged to be in California. Longtime friend and partner in the Eisenhower farm operation George Allen flew in to be nearby at his home at La Quinta. Ellis "Slats" Slater, retired President of Frankfort Distillers, flew to California from New York to join the crowd berthing five miles north at the exclusive Thunderbird Country Club. Radio personality Freeman Gosden played host at the Eldorado Country Club, where Texas oilman Robert McCulloch was constructing a home on the eleventh fairway for the Eisenhowers' lifetime winter use.

Every day, Eisenhower and his friends rose early to play golf at Eldorado, Thunderbird, or a neighboring club in matching foursomes. At noon the group broke up for lunch and naps and later assembled for shopping at neighboring stores during the late afternoon. In the evenings the friends assembled for dinner and bridge marathons. For days Eisenhower and his friends donned the uniforms of leisure and relaxed furiously with infrequent intrusions from the outside world.

After a complete rest lasting several weeks,

Eisenhower gradually began to open the door to visitors and old government colleagues. In March, former secretary of state Christian Herter visited for dinner and a long conversation. Subsequently former labor secretary James Mitchell paid a call on Eisenhower, as did former vice president Richard Nixon, who drove from Los Angeles to Palm Desert for an afternoon and evening of talks. Five months after the fact, Eisenhower and Nixon were still smarting from the razor-thin loss of the White House to Kennedy. The almost too-close-to-call election had been a referendum on the Eisenhower administration as much as it had been about Nixon and his campaign. Eisenhower had been disheartened by the loss and was still questioning why Nixon had not used him more in the final days of the campaign. At the same time, he knew his vice president had had much more at stake and had taken the defeat hard, especially in view of the disputed returns in Chicago and Texas. The morning after the election, Eisenhower had written from the White House:

Dear Dick and Pat:
. . . I want to express to you both the fervent hope that the two of you will not be

too greatly disappointed by yesterday's election returns. I know that whatever disappointment you do feel will not be for yourselves but for our country and for the jeopardy in which our great hopes and aims for the future have been placed.

On the personal side, you will unquestionably have a happier life during these next four years, especially because of your closer contact with your two beautiful daughters. Of course I have no indication of what your future plans may be — possibly you do not know yourselves. But wherever you go or whatever activities in which you may be engaged, you will have my best wishes.

I assure you that my official confidence in you, Dick, has not been shaken for a moment, and of course all four of you may be certain that the affection that Mamie and I feel for you will never grow less.

With warm regard,
As ever,
Dwight D. Eisenhower

Eisenhower surfaced for newsmen at the Palm Springs training camp of the newly formed Los Angeles Angels baseball team. He remained topical. On March 3, to his amusement, the ZengaKuren radical organizations, which had succeeded in forcing cancellation of his planned 1960 trip to Japan, announced a pledge not to demonstrate in the event Eisenhower returned, provided that he visit in the capacity of former president of Columbia University. On March 31, Che Guevara, Cuba's leading "banker," swaggeringly boasted at a press conference that he could beat Eisenhower at golf. In late March, Eisenhower and several friends flew to Baja for a few days of hunting and fishing in La Paz.

While in California, Eisenhower was not altogether free of the White House. Since the law regarding presidential papers vested him with full ownership, Eisenhower had ordered packed and removed every memorandum, letter, and minute of meetings even remotely connected with his conduct of office, and had had the materials sent to the site of his future presidential library in Abilene, Kansas. The classified materials he shipped to nearby Fort Ritchie, Maryland, for safe storage. Consequently, the Kennedy administration found itself lacking memoranda and wires on holdover matters, particularly in the field of atomic energy, where limited copies of the draft policies and memoranda existed. Back in Gettysburg, Dad took on the job of clearing Kennedy administration requests for documents through Granddad, and then locating them in the files stored at Fort Ritchie. Pursuant to an understanding reached between Eisenhower and Kennedy after their December 6 meeting, General Andrew Goodpaster, who had served Eisenhower as staff secretary, remained temporarily in his job, providing a daily presidential intelligence briefing. In time he would transfer his duties to General Ted Clifton and depart for Germany and the field command Eisenhower had promised him.

Meanwhile, Goodpaster remained in steady contact with Dad and other former White House staffers. He reported that he got along quite well with McGeorge Bundy, Walt Rostow, and other Kennedy appointees. As for the President, Goodpaster told my father that he would find John Kennedy a "fine fellow" to work with, cordial, intelligent, and humorous.

But Goodpaster had adjustments to make during his short tenure in the Kennedy White House. Working for Eisenhower, Goodpaster had arrived each morning prepared to deliver concise, military-style oral briefings to the President. In contrast, Kennedy, a voracious reader, asked Goodpaster to devise a digest format that enabled the President to read daily intelligence developments as if he were scanning a newspaper.

Upon assuming office, Kennedy made clear to Ted Clifton that there was "nothing Eisenhower wants that we will not provide." Kennedy offered helicopter transportation, limousine service when Eisenhower visited Washington, the use of Walter Reed Army Medical Center, and of Air Force One to transport him to California when Eisenhower left for his February vacation. Eisenhower accepted Walter Reed but declined the helicopter and limousine with thanks, as well as the Air Force transportation to California, which he felt would be "misunderstood."

Eisenhower had promised Kennedy at both the December 6, 1960, and January 19, 1961, meetings that he would support Kennedy on foreign policy with two caveats. He would oppose any move to recognize Red China and he would stop any efforts to rename Dulles International Airport, then under construction in the northern Virginia suburbs. Eisenhower also had a personal favor to ask of Kennedy. Through intermediaries, he requested that the Kennedy administration expedite a bill through Congress, drafted during the final days of the Eisenhower administration by congressional liaison Bryce Harlow, that would restore his five-star rank. Since five-star status brought with it certain perquisites in addition to those of former presidents, Eisenhower agreed to live within the budgetary limits of a former president. The arrangement permitted Eisenhower to retain the services of his chauffeur Leonard Dry, his valet Sergeant Moaney, and his principal office assistant, Colonel Robert Schulz.

In March, Kennedy summoned Ted Clifton to the Oval Office to review Eisenhower's "eccentric request." Kennedy observed at the outset that the restoration of rank involved forfeiting Eisenhower's title as "Mr. President." Kennedy could not conceive any hidden benefit Eisenhower might gain by becoming a five-star general and declining the presidential title. There would be neither monetary nor power gains.

Clifton suggested that perhaps simply the matter of the title was important to Eisenhower. After all, he explained, "Mr. President" placed Eisenhower in company with Kennedy, Truman, and Hoover. "General" was an independent title, unassociated with Kennedy, something of Eisenhower's very own. Clifton concluded, "Well sir, and if he is a five-star general, he needs no favors from you or the White House."

Enlightened, Kennedy ordered Clifton to go ahead. When the bill was passed without opposition in March, Kennedy directed Clifton that the announcement be made "without fanfare" and "on background" at the daily presidential press briefing. "Hold it up," Kennedy gestured in a reference to the commissioning documents, "but downplay it, no story."

On March 22, 1961, Clifton called Robert Schulz at the new Eisenhower offices at Gettysburg College to inform him that his boss was once again a general of the Army. As he signed the bill a day later, Kennedy penned a brief note to Eisenhower in Palm Desert officially informing him of the appointment. A day later, a red five-star pennant was run up the flagpole on the east grounds of the farm, marking Eisenhower's return to the ranks of the Army.

A quick check of history would have explained everything. Years earlier Truman's secretary of state, General George Marshall, had also puzzled friends and Truman by wishing to be known as "General" instead of "Mr. Secretary" after retiring from the cabinet. Marshall, reflecting Eisenhower's sentiment, explained that the military title meant more to him than any civilian title.

"I worked all my life to be 'General,' " Marshall explained. So had Eisenhower.

For several months, Eisenhower and Kennedy would exchange correspondence on a variety of routine items — the restoration of rank, the transition, a note of thanks from Kennedy for Eisenhower's strong statement pledging bipartisan support in foreign policy. But there was little possibility of a warm, personal, even advisory relationship. Despite the surface cordiality and the holdover of many familiar faces from the Eisenhower years, including John A. Mc-Cone at the Atomic Energy Commission, C. Douglas Dillon at Treasury, Allen Dulles at CIA, and J. Edgar Hoover at FBI, there was a natural antagonism between the administrations.

The Kennedy administration swept boldly into Washington "eager to be tried" and persuaded that the Eisenhower presidency had been a "great postponement." The elaborate organizational staff reforms of the Eisenhower White House were stripped away with an almost evangelical glee, in particular the downgrading of Eisenhower's cherished National Security Council (NSC), described in Arthur Schlesinger, Jr.'s chapter "The Hour of Euphoria" in his book *A Thousand Days:*

Mac [McGeorge Bundy] was presently engaged in dismantling the elaborate national security apparatus built up by the Eisenhower administration. . . . Richard Neustadt had taken great pleasure during the interregnum in introducing Bundy to the Eisenhower White House as the equivalent of five officers on the Eisenhower staff. After the inauguration, Bundy promptly slaughtered committees right and left and collapsed what was left of the inherited apparatus into a compact and flexible National Security Council staff. With Walt Rostow as his deputy, and Bromley Smith, a remarkable civil servant as the NSC's secretary, he was shaping a supple instrument to meet the new President's distinctive needs.

One of Kennedy's "distinctive needs" would be the counsel of an elder statesman. Because of the lack of rapport between Kennedy and Eisenhower, the role of elder statesman naturally fell to Harry S. Truman, although he, like Eisenhower, had difficulty warming up to the president whom he had snidely called a "spoiled young man." Nonetheless, Kennedy made an early gesture of goodwill, inviting Truman to stay overnight at the White House not long after the inauguration. As the story goes, after dinner the two men took a stroll along the ground floor of the mansion past the Diplomatic Reception Room and toward the movie theater. At the massive doorway leading to the East Wing, the two men paused at the spot where the White House renovation during the Truman years is officially recorded in gold-bronze lettering on the wall. A member of the mansion staff overheard Kennedy remark wryly to Truman, "The S.O.B. [Eisenhower] had a painting over it."

The story is a reminder that changes of administration in those days always touched off a remodeling of the White House to reflect the style and preferences of the new president. Paintings of presidents and first ladies adorn the White House on the ground floor, the first floor, and the presidential offices in the West Wing. The positioning of these portraits revealed the favorites of the current president. The least favored presidents and first ladies were banished to oblivion: at the very top of the Grand Staircase descending from the family quarters to the first floor, outside the doctor's office on the ground floor, or outside the library behind a partition that is drawn as tourists walk through.

The Eisenhower years highlighted Lincoln and Washington. The Kennedy-Johnson years would highlight Franklin and Eleanor Roosevelt, and Truman. The circle would come around again during the Nixon years when the Tom Stephens portrait of Eisenhower dominated the Cabinet Room and the J. Anthony Wills portrait of Eisenhower hung at the entrance to the East Room.

Certain concessions are made for the sake of avoiding pettiness. Eisenhower had inadvertently scarred the Oval Office floor with his golf cleats. He often wore golf shoes in the Oval Office so he could slip out for a quick session of putting and sand practice on the South Lawn. Kennedy decided not to repair the floor, as did Johnson. Nixon, however, had no fears about being accused of obliterating Eisenhower's mark in the Oval Office. At Pat Nixon's insistence, the floor was replaced soon after the 1969 inauguration, but the sentimental Nixon had the scarred portions of the old floor cut up into two-inch square pieces, mounted on small plaques, and mailed to Eisenhower's friends as mementos.

In the 1950s, Eisenhower had felt less need for the advice of his predecessor. Throughout his presidency, Eisenhower's relationship with Truman had been frozen in mutual antagonism. Truman never forgave Eisenhower's decision to run as a Republican in 1952 and Eisenhower had never forgiven Truman for certain statements Truman made in the campaign, which ended a long-standing and friendly partnership. By 1961, Truman no longer cared to remember that in 1947 he suggested to Eisenhower that he would serve as vice president if Eisenhower headed the ticket in 1948. The offer, which Truman now denied, is recorded in Truman's diary, which he presumably thought was destroyed. It was discovered in the Truman Library in 2003 in an obscure stack of books. In his diary entry dated July 25, 1947, Truman wrote, "Ike and I think MacArthur expects to make a Roman triumphal return to the U.S. a short time before the Republican convention meets in Philadelphia. I told Ike that if he did that," then Eisenhower should "announce for the nomination for president on the Democratic ticket and that I'd be glad to be in second place, or vice president."

In his own diary, Eisenhower had described the day:

Astounding talk at the White House at

3:30 this afternoon. I stick on my determination to have nothing to do with politics — but I can well understand the calamity that might overtake us if some utterly ruthless and ambitious person [a draft Douglas MacArthur for president headquarters had just opened in Washington] should capture public imagination at the critical moment. —

A cabin in the woods looms up daily as the perfect haven.

I wonder whether five years from now HT will (or will want to) remember his amazing suggestion!!

Five months later, on New Year's Eve, December 31, 1947, Eisenhower, mulling over the pressures on him to accept the Democratic nomination, wrote:

My amazing conversation in July with President T, while I realize he may have been talking under conditions as he then saw them — yet the suggestion that he might want to take the lead to ensure the defeat of one particular danger [Douglas MacArthur] he saw on the horizon was, to say the least, extraordinary. . . .

We end the year on a somber note —

but battles are not won by pessimism! We should cultivate the spirit of "Onward Christian Soldiers." . . .

A few hours later, he recorded:

January 1. This morning I called the President to wish him a happy New Year.

Only a few days ago, he said to me "Ike, no matter what you do or whatever your plans, let us both resolve that nothing shall ever mar our personal friendship. . . ."

SETTLING IN

In early April, the Eisenhowers returned from California to Gettysburg. Granddad and Mamie loved the farm, which they had purchased in late 1950. The residence they built on the property and moved into in 1955 was the first home they had owned after thirty-three Army moves. As often as possible in White House years, they had spent weekends at the farm.

It had been Granddad's dream for years to own a piece of land. As his farm manager, Brigadier General Arthur Nevins, recalled, Ike simply wanted the chance "to improve the fertility of the soil" of his 190 acres. He had chosen Gettysburg because he felt a connection to the area. His ancestors had settled near the Susquehanna in 1753. Young officer Ike Eisenhower and Mamie also had strong memories of their life in Gettysburg with their first-born son in 1917–18, when Eisenhower commanded a tank-training battalion on the southern edge of town. But perhaps the strongest draw to Gettysburg was that longtime friends, the high-spirited George Allen and his wife, Mary, owned a farm in Gettysburg and had been urging the Eisenhowers to join them.

Allen was an intimate friend of Roosevelt and Truman and author of the humorous book *Presidents Who Have Known Me,* published in 1950. My grandparents loved his yarns about Mississippi politics, football, and Washington. Like the Eisenhowers, he was drawn to Gettsyburg as a Civil War site. His father, who died when Allen was eight, had been a scout for General Nathan Bedford Forrest during the Civil War. His uncle, John M. Allen, had been an eight-term congressman from Tupelo, Mississippi, during Reconstruction. A plaque at the Allen homestead in Mississippi read: "This house gave nine souls to the Confederacy."

During the presidency, Eisenhower had left the day-to-day workings of the farm to others. Eisenhower arranged to lease his farmlands to Allen and businessman B. G. Byars of Tyler, Texas, in return for a nominal rental fee for use of the arable acres, while paying the Allen-Byars partnership to maintain his growing Angus herd. Under the direction of General Nevins, the farm had been transformed. When Eisenhower purchased it in 1950, the farmland had poor fertility and drainage, inadequate fencing, and had been suitable only for dairy farming and eggs for shipment to Baltimore. By 1961, the Eisenhower farm was a humming cattle-breeding complex equipped with corrals, cattle chutes, a platform scale, feed lots, and seventy-six head of Angus. Now, with the Allen-Byars partnership about to expire, Eisenhower looked forward to finalizing new business arrangements and to immersing himself in the farm operation.

Indeed, by spring of 1961, new acquisitions on the farm property had converted the sleepy dairy farm into an estate worthy of Eisenhower's earliest dreams as a boy. "Pete" Jones donated a skeet and trap shoot range, landscaped so that it was hidden behind a cluster of trees adjoining Confederate Avenue and the battlefield. A putting green was nestled below the residence next to beds of roses, daffodils, begonias, and gladiolas. Granddad had a small brick hut and patio constructed for his ritual steak barbeques, served up for large parties and special family gatherings. Gifts of trees and shrubbery comprised some of southern Pennsylvania's most unusual landscaping. Near the residence, there were rose bushes, a davidia tree, walnut and pecan trees, and two pink dogwoods. There was also a peach orchard near the horse corral and a cherry tree orchard near the barbeque pit. Fifty evergreens lined the avenue from Waterworks Road to the farm residence, a gift of the Republican state committees. My grandparents' prize object was an artifact of the Civil War — a rusty old pump near Sergeant Moaney's kitchen garden that, according to legend, had been used by General John Bell Hood's brigade encamped on the grounds during the Battle of Gettysburg.

I had been working on the farm since the age of ten. My tenth birthday, March 31, 1958, had been a grand occasion. Delores Moaney used to say, "Master David, when you are ten years old, you'll be all grown up." Birthdays and Christmases had in the past brought forth a cornucopia of toy soldiers, model airplanes, Davy Crockett rifles, and coonskin caps. But on my tenth birthday, when we gathered on the sunporch to open presents Granddad had presented me with a large, wine-colored family Bible with ten parchment pages to enter births, deaths, and marriages of my sons and daughters, their children, and their children's children. My parents, who knew I was an aspiring short story writer, presented me with a leatherbound folder engraved DDE.

In 1958, it was decided that I would start work as a farmhand for thirty cents an hour. My daily chore would be to weed and tend the large vegetable garden below the residence; my summer-long project was to paint the seemingly endless white corral-style fences on the farm property, beginning first in the barnyard, near the Quonset-hut shed and dog kennel. Because we were living in Alexandria at the time, Granddad arranged for me to stay with Navy Chief Petty Officer Walter West, who was supervisor of the fourteen acres surrounding the Gettysburg residence. He lived in a small, two-story frame house near Thurmont just off old Route 15, the main highway to Gettysburg.

In early June I had packed a duffel bag, hopped in the Secret Service sedan, and jauntily took off to begin my career. Each day, Chief West and I were up by six for a hearty breakfast cooked by his wife, who worked at nearby Fort Ritchie. By sunup,

49

the Chief and I were rumbling along in his pickup at fifty miles an hour. It was a fine drive — past Cunningham Falls and Camp David, then past the sprawling snake farm, a tourist attraction north of Frederick filled with exotic cobras and rattlesnakes. By seven, we were beyond Mount St. Mary's College and crossing the Mason-Dixon Line. Entering the heart of the Union, we left behind us the crumbling Maryland state roads and picked up speed on Pennsylvania's smooth and modern highways.

The workday began over coffee in the Quonset hut with the staff reviewing the assignments. We had one hour for lunch. At 2:30, a Secret Service agent and I exercised the horses Sporty Miss and Doodle de Doo. On these daily rides, we explored the Eisenhower and adjacent Alton Jones farm and occasionally ventured onto the bridle paths in the battlefield. By 4:30, after the horses were brushed and the farm tools packed, Chief West and I were in the pickup and headed back to Thurmont.

The Chief was a native Floridian with a deep tan, a military flattop, and forearms swathed with gaily decorative tattoos acquired during his years in the Navy. The Chief knew how to make hands "turn to." He was a hard worker and an undisputed authority at the farm.

The Chief talked a mile a minute, punctuating his vivid tales with expressive gestures. His favorite subject in late afternoon was fishing and returning to the St. Johns River in Duval County, Florida, which he claimed was the best bass and perch stream in the world. He had his retirement planned to the minute and hour. It would be June 1964, a year after the interstate under construction near Thurmont, two miles away from his front porch, would be complete. The Chief figured it would take about forty-eight hours to pack all of his belongings in the pickup truck, another twenty hours to reach Jacksonville and his small cottage on the St. Johns River. Chief West ventured only one opinion about politics that summer, saying once en route to the farm, "Shoot, David, a man's just gotta be crazy to want to be president, just crazy."

Every two weeks Granddad arrived at the farm and the place swarmed with aides, limousines, and police. We had a day's notice so all the equipment could be properly stored and projects rushed to completion before the Chief conducted a rigid inspection of the garden and fences. I trailed him with a notepad. Finding sloppy work or weeds, the Chief would stop and call out

51

"holiday." All holidays were to be squared away by quitting time.

The next day, when Granddad swept in, he carried out the same inspection. I usually awaited him at the garden. At attention, I answered questions about rainfall and the appearance of pests and certain kinds of weeds. Then I led him and Chief West through the rows of corn, peas, and tomatoes, then on to the corral and the north pasture to check the painting. Three years later, in 1961, I would be returning to work for fifty cents an hour and the routine would be much the same, but with two changes. First, the Chief was now working part-time, and second, the Secret Service had left.

Granddad's return to private life meant other changes for our family. My parents had moved into the house on the corner of the Gettysburg farm two years before, anxious for their children to be out of the glare of publicity permeating the White House. My father, still an aide to Granddad, had stayed in Washington during the week and commuted home on weekends. But now that Granddad was living next door to us, most of his prodigious energy would be unleashed around the farmhouse and inevitably radiate out toward his family. The most directly affected would be Mamie.

Since "the Great Divide," defined by Mamie as Granddad's fiftieth birthday, in 1940, she had experienced the gradual loss of power over her husband's affairs. Originally Mamie had handled all the family correspondence. Granddad's growing prominence, however, required secretaries, and eventually Granddad took over the entire burden of corresponding with the outside world except for items sent directly to Mamie.

Mamie entered her marriage with the money in the family, her father having semiretired at the age of thirty-six from his profitable meatpacking business. For the first thirty years of her marriage, Mamie had written the checks and balanced the books except for a small secret account Dwight Eisenhower kept, which consisted of poker and gambling winnings that he drew on to buy anniversary and birthday gifts for Mamie. As recently as their Columbia University years, Mamie had filled a pinchpenny purse with small change for Granddad's weekly lunch and incidental expenses. Now, thanks to a large income from Eisenhower's *Crusade in Europe,* his best-selling account of his war years, lawyers wrote the checks and balanced the accounts. Stubbornly, almost from force of habit,

Mamie kept a small account of her own for incidentals, and nightly recorded the checks and withdrawals. Now, a dozen years later, Mamie was reclaiming responsibility for many matters pertaining to the household.

Another change in Mamie's life was that during the presidency, the affairs of state had absorbed her husband's energies, freeing Mamie to see friends, watch television, play solitaire, and read. Now, in retirement, they spent evenings together. "Complicating things," Mamie recalled, "was that Ike never had the slightest notion how to live with women." She explained: "His mother would have been a good celibate. Ike grew up with six boys and no feminine influence. His idea of affection was a pinch and a kick."

Mamie's support system was Rosie Woods. Mamie recalled first seeing her future personal maid the way one remembers a first date. When Granddad was chief of staff after World War II, Mamie frequented a hairdressing shop called Ogilvie's, where the wives of official Washington gossiped and chatted in brocade satin surroundings over tea and coffee. The proprietor suggested to Mamie that she was in need of a companion.

With Ike's triumphal return from the war,

most of her friends had gravitated toward the war hero, leaving Mamie somewhat adrift in a sea of courtiers pursuing her husband. Almost in self-defense, Mamie decided Mrs. Ogilvie was right. She needed a companion to look after her, fix her tea, lay out her clothes, and be on hand.

"Fine," replied Mrs. Ogilvie. "I have the right person."

Rosie Woods, a wispy, bespectacled, soft-spoken Irishwoman in her sixties, had been "in service" for fifty years. Rosie's parents had migrated to the United States in 1880, bringing their children along one by one. Rosie began to work at fourteen in the purple velvet uniform of the governess–ladies' maid.

When Rosie and Mamie were introduced, they fell in love. Mamie thought instantly how much Rosie reminded her of her own governess as a child. Rosie later related that upon setting eyes on Mrs. Eisenhower, she knew instantly, "That's my madame."

Mamie prized Rosie's discretion and her ability to keep a confidence nurtured over long years of domestic service. Rosie was sweet, gentle, and deferential. When Rosie brought Mamie tea, often while Mamie sat in bed writing letters and watching television, Mamie would ask her to sit down with her. "Madame," she invariably replied, "I would rather stand."

Rosie became not only a confidante, but also an adviser. She was "hoity-toity," in Mamie's words, constantly on the lookout for people who might harm Mamie with malicious gossip or intrigue. More than once, she warned, "Mrs. Eisenhower, don't go with her — she's not a lady."

When Mamie was ill, which was quite frequently, Rosie would stay up all night within earshot should Mamie need tea. Mamie used to insist Rosie get some sleep. "Quite all right," Rosie would whisper. "Quite all right."

Now, during evenings on the farm, Rosie was always nearby to anticipate Mamie's every wish, be it a handkerchief or a chocolate.

Like the Moaneys, Rosie was a part of the family. Routinely, she, Sergeant Moaney, and Delores joined all of us on the sunporch to watch television.

One night that spring, as we watched, I was slightly startled by a low hum from Rosie's corner. The singers were rendering a version of "Danny Boy," a sentimental Irish folk song. As Rosie hummed the tune along with the singers, tears ran down her cheeks. Soon my grandparents turned and noticed.

"David," Mamie said gaily, "this is one of the wonderful songs of Ireland and it reminds Rosie of home." At that moment, Mamie and Granddad joined with Rosie in humming and singing the song, Granddad's atonal bass rumbling rather off-key, but adding resonance to the song.

Granddad adored Rosie almost as much as my grandmother did. At bedtime, Rosie tucked my grandparents under the sheets, drew back, and asked if all was well and anything more was needed. My grandfather would select the western he planned to read until dozing off into loud snores. When he wiggled his toes, Rosie would lift up the sheet and let it settle over his legs, sending a slight breeze over his face.

"Thank you, Rosie," he would chime.

"You're welcome, sir," she would reply, always blushing, and quickly she would slip off to her own room two doors down the hall.

Rosie would not stay for a long time in Gettysburg. She had suffered from cataracts for over sixteen years, and by 1961 she was nearly blind. Within the year, Rosie announced that she would not allow herself to be a burden, nor would she work any longer when she felt she could not earn her pay.

Breaking Mamie's heart, she retired to the home of a nephew in Arlington, Virginia, where she spent her days fussing over her grandnephews, buying them clothes, and enriching her clan with many stories of all the places she had been with the Eisenhowers in Europe and throughout America. Her life's greatest honor had been in 1951, when she met Pope Pius XII. She spoke endlessly about him.

A change for the grandchildren was the departure of the Secret Service detail. For eight years my sisters and I had been guarded by a group of men who had become friends. The Secret Service command post was a 1953 Pontiac station wagon, parked in front of whatever house we lived in at the time. In heat, rain, and snow, the Pontiac sat out front cluttered with coffee cups, radio equipment, newspapers, sports publications, and mysterious magazines with women in bathing suits — stored under the front seat. A sleek black government Ford sedan was the vehicle the agents used to tail us at a distance as we roamed through the neighborhood with our friends. In Alexandria, our home before Dad went to work at the White House, my sister Anne decided one evening at dusk to "run away." She left the dinner table and marched out the front door, down the flagstone walkway, past the Pontiac, then turned left at the first intersection. She pressed on for several blocks, casting frustrated looks backward at the agents trailing behind at forty yards in the black Ford, radioing information to the Pontiac. After twenty minutes she gave up and climbed into the front seat of the Secret Service car. My parents tactfully were waiting at the window, and gratefully welcomed her home.

Now our lives revolved around Granddad and Mamie at the farm. We joined them for dinner at least once a week. Whereas Granddad had always been a remote, though important figure in our lives, he now became a third parent, quizzing us about what we had learned at school, slipping out unannounced to sit in the bleachers at Little League games, attending Anne's piano recitals and Susan's horse shows. Granddad instituted an incentive system for school grades. He paid each of us five dollars for A's brought home on our report cards, three dollars for B's, and deducted one dollar for C's. My parents observed this with misgiving: on payday, our earnings were taken to be placed in a savings account.

Often we fished at a pond stocked with bluegills and perch. Occasionally before dinner, Granddad, my father, and I would shoot skeet or step out into the fields facing the Blue Ridge Mountains to the west to shoot target practice at tomato paste cans that Sergeant Moaney rigged on a cardboard plank.

That spring I found myself on a "marble regimen." It was an exercise designed to strengthen flat feet by picking up marbles with the big toe and index toe and depositing them into plastic cans. Flat feet were disqualification at West Point. Dad told me that Granddad had drilled him endlessly with marbles as a child to overcome his flat feet. It worked and he was accepted to the Class of 1944 at the U.S. Military Academy. The marbles regimen was simply "giving me the choice" should I decide to apply to West Point.

Life otherwise settled into a routine and the Eisenhowers found themselves adjusting to a relaxed pace and many quiet hours together on the sunporch. Typically, after dinner Granddad and Mamie settled down to television, which invariably brought on arguments. Mamie preferred romance and dramas with "grown-up" themes. Granddad liked westerns and musical comedies. When Granddad had his way, Mamie would play solitaire in an alcove on the southern end of the sunporch and listen to a large portable radio with the volume turned low.

One evening, caught in the middle of a friendly argument over what to watch, I divided the difference by sitting in an armchair within view of the television and within conversational range of my grandmother at her wrought-iron card table. Granddad sat in rapt attention watching an Indian raid on a defenseless group of Conestoga wagons, and Mamie wove three decks together in a sprawling game of solitaire. After a while, one of the bird dogs dragged a skunk by the sliding glass door and deposited it within two feet of Granddad's rocker.

"Smell anything, Ike?" Mamie asked amid the din of war whoops and broken radio reception.

"Nothing, dear," Granddad replied.

Within five minutes, the smell became unmistakable. Granddad remained glued to the set, Mamie fixed at her card table. The cavalry arrived and the show ended. Granddad stood up, stretched, yawned deeply, and sauntered off to bed, bidding us good night. Mamie folded the hand and rose.

Passing the buck, she kissed me on the cheek and said, "Check with Sergeant Moaney, dear, and ask him if anything is spoiled in the kitchen."

Granddad's favorite nighttime reading was either historical biography or the western pulp paperbacks he had relied on in the White House when he needed to relax. The bookshelves alongside his bed contained several hundred books. In Gettysburg, as in past postings, a staff member, usually secretary Rusty Brown or chief of staff Colonel Robert Schulz, was assigned a special responsibility to find the General a good supply of westerns, always with the proviso he wanted them without women. "Though Ike was sentimental," Mamie shrugged years later, "if they put a woman in his western he just closed the book — that's the way he liked history too, no goo — he believed in a man in men's company."

At night Granddad also took up studying things we grandchildren were learning in school. According to Mamie, "Ike was not going to let his grandchildren come home from school and teach him anything." Several nights, long past midnight, Mamie fell asleep while Granddad pored over texts of the "new math" then being introduced in public schools.

Meanwhile, Granddad and Mamie were rarely without weekend visitors. The guest book records each visitor to the farm. The signatures are usually embellished with a little comment summarizing the weekend's activity. On April 23, 1961, former head of NATO and master bridge player General Alfred Gruenther's guest book entry states: "Last hand — doubled by Bill. Perfect cross ruff succeeded. Bill in despair — also Pete." Next to his signature, businessman and investor in the Eisenhower farm W. Alton "Pete" Jones added: "sad sad sad."

As in the White House days, during the bridge games the wives retired to chat and play canasta. In a guest book entry dated April 26, they gently teased their ambitious husbands: "Ann Nevins, Bess Gruenther, Kate Hughes, Helen Titus. When you see a monkey climb a tree, pull his tail and think of me."

When there were guests, Sergeant Moaney would haul out the movie projector and show a film. Granddad and Mamie never watched movies dealing with the war, despite possessing a large collection of films and documentaries on the subject that had been given to them over the years. To see war films, I had to arrange for an afternoon showing in the den with drawn shades. And, as in the White House, Granddad wanted no part of "message movies." Instead he preferred light comedies, musicals, and westerns, movies for "pure enjoyment."

Granddad's favorite was a 1951 film titled *Angels in the Outfield,* starring Paul Douglas. Sergeant Moaney claimed to have run the movie for Eisenhower precisely thirty-eight times. *Angels in the Outfield* is a fairy tale about "Guffy McGovern," a tough, hardhearted, weathered baseball manager on the verge of losing his job as skipper of the Pittsburgh Pirates. His temper is irascible. His ball club, a collection of utility infielders and fading stars, is a steady cellar dweller. Then Guffy is visited by an angel who offers help on condition that Guffy control his swearing and fighting.

When a young Catholic orphan insists she sees angels standing behind the Pirates when batting and in the field, a female reporter scoops the story and it becomes a sensation around the league. Guffy, the reporter, and the orphan girl become acquainted and inseparable, and the Pirates start winning.

Amid stories that angels are helping the Pirates, Guffy becomes the target of a shifty-eyed columnist determined to prove that he has gone crazy. The columnist finally provokes McGovern into losing his self-control, and McGovern punches him out. The angel reappears to tell McGovern that all deals are off.

The Pirates reach the final game in a tie. McGovern decides to settle a long-standing feud with an aging right-hander on the club by awarding him the crucial start. The angel has told McGovern that the right-hander will soon be pitching for "the Heavenly Choir Nine," including the ghosts of Babe Ruth, Christy Mathewson, Walter Johnson, and Honus Wagner.

Bearing this secret, McGovern makes up with the pitcher. Pittsburgh wins a cliff-hanger. McGovern adopts the girl and marries the reporter.

At the conclusion of every showing, Granddad would sit silently, allowing his eyes to adjust to the light. "Wonderful show," he would say, almost inaudibly, rising from his chair and wandering off to bed.

THE LOYAL OPPOSITION

The Eisenhower farm, ideally located roughly between Washington, D.C., and New York, afforded Granddad and Mamie the ability to attend events in the capital and to see friends in New York. It also placed Granddad within easy reach of the White House and his successor, who soon found reasons to be in touch.

In April, Eisenhower was startled by the astonishing news of the debacle at the Bay of Pigs. The news of landings of exile forces in Cuba and of an attempt to unseat Castro came as no surprise, however. A year before, Eisenhower had approved a CIA project to train Cuban exiles in Guatemala for an operation to take back Cuba from Castro. The CIA proposal as of January 1961, when Eisenhower left office, had been to land a force of exiles on the south coast of Cuba in the Trinidad area, and secure a beachhead. The invasion force would then be joined by a provisional government that would forthwith be recognized by the United States. In turn the provisional government would seek U.S. logistical backing and expand the beachhead perimeter outward from Trinidad toward Havana and wage a campaign of "attrition." At their final transition meeting on January 19, Eisenhower had urged Kennedy to take immediate action against the Castro government, although he could not recommend the current plan until a provisional government could be formed without pro-Batista reactionaries.

By all accounts, Kennedy struggled with the plan to sponsor the exileled invasion of Cuba. Since he sought to identify himself and his presidency with the worldwide clamor for independence against colonialism and imperial domination, Kennedy had misgivings about overtly sponsoring an invasion, preferring to remove Castro clandestinely. Kennedy hesitated for several months. The earliest date for the invasion was postponed, and for weeks thereafter the inner councils of the Kennedy administration agonized over the plan, skeptical of success and fearful of failure and of not carrying through on a project drafted with the knowledge of Eisenhower and Nixon.

Kennedy decided on a compromise: he would approve the invasion but insist on steps to conceal the American hand. To avoid conspicuous American involvement, the landing site was shifted from Trinidad, which had been chosen because of the suitability of the beach, the proximity of a major town, and the easy avenue of escape in the event of failure, to a more remote location at the Bay of Pigs. Instead of an "invasion" by daylight, Kennedy ordered an "infiltration" by night. Instead of relying on military force and "attrition," success would depend on a spontaneous domestic uprising to bring down the Castro regime. Although undoubtedly a victim of conflicting and confusing advice, Kennedy never acknowledged the irony of his insistence that the invasion be an "entirely Cuban affair" while retaining in his hands the power to approve the operation, dictate when it would happen, choose the landing site, and order air support.

When the landings came on April 17, Castro's counterstrokes, swift and effective, contained and defeated the small force of exiles within forty-eight hours, inflicting a spectacular humiliation on the United States. The American hand was immediately apparent to the world. As resistance petered out and ship-to-shore communications became a "wail of SOS's," Kennedy commenced the painful task of containing the diplomatic and political consequences.

On April 19, the President reached Eisenhower by phone in Gettysburg and asked him to meet nearby at Camp David for a discussion. Although Eisenhower suspected Kennedy of attempting to diffuse responsibility and to associate him with the failed invasion, he readily assented.

Their meeting on the 22nd began on a bizarre note. Kennedy had not yet been to Camp David, and thus had not met the military personnel who administered the camp. In the three months since Eisenhower's last visit to Camp David, there had been few transfers. In their unguarded thoughts, the camp staff could have been excused for wondering who was host and who was guest. With Eisenhower acting as guide, the two men toured the compound.

At first glance, Camp David was a complex of modest cabins linked by macadam road and a flagstone walkway. But the big forest concealed a small self-contained city. There was a bowling alley maintained for the camp personnel and a movie theater. Next to the heliport was a large, unheated freshwater swimming pool, and next to it a practice skeet range. Below the main lodge, Aspen, nestled in a clearing, was a two-hole golf course. The camp was a wildlife preserve protecting a small herd of domesticated deer that often wandered out of the dense forest and up to the back door of the main cabin looking for food.

The Navy-maintained camp had been erected only twenty years earlier by Roosevelt's Civilian Conservation Corps and the one- and two-room cabins, though cozy, were rustic and sometimes drafty. They still bore the quaint Navy touches of FDR, who had named the compound Shangri-la. Granddad changed the name in 1953 to honor his father, David, and me.

As Eisenhower showed Kennedy the

Maple, Birch, and Dogwood cabins clustered around the cul-de-sac near the President's cottage, Aspen Lodge, he lingered over the points of interest: the wooden bench next to a goldfish pond that FDR had used for fishing when the pond had been a freshwater stream; the bomb shelter underneath Aspen. After Eisenhower introduced Kennedy to the staff, the two men returned to Aspen.

Seated by the picture window looking out over Eisenhower's putting green, with the eastern slope of the Catoctin Hills and the countryside of central Maryland beyond, the two men talked at length about the Bay of Pigs and Kennedy's first months in office. In an interview five years later with his former speechwriter Malcolm Moos, at that time University of Minnesota president, Eisenhower recalled the details of his conversation with Kennedy, seemingly remembering every word.

Eisenhower noted that at the moment the two men sat down alone, "the President seemed himself," no pretenses, openly shaken over the implications of his handling of the incident.

Kennedy: No one knows how tough this job is until after he has been in it a few months.

Eisenhower: Mr. President, if you will forgive me, I think I mentioned that to you three months ago.

Kennedy: I have certainly learned a lot since then.

Eisenhower had arrived rankled by reports emanating from Kennedy aides suggesting that Kennedy had been a prisoner of a preexisting plan with regard to Cuba, but alone together, Eisenhower recalled, "the President made no attempt to blame the previous administration." Eisenhower had emphasized at their final meeting in January that the ultimate decision regarding the Cuban operation would rest with Kennedy. Additionally, Kennedy had given Eisenhower no advance warning of the operation.

Kennedy: Well, I just approved a plan that had been recommended by the CIA and by the Joint Chiefs of Staff. I took their advice.

Eisenhower: Mr. President, were there any changes in the ultimate plan that the Joint Chiefs approved?

Kennedy: Yes there were — we did want to call off one bombing sally.

Eisenhower: Why was that called off?

71

Kennedy: Well, we felt it necessary that we keep our hand concealed in this affair; we thought that if it was learned that we were really doing this rather than the rebels themselves, the Soviets would be apt to cause trouble in Berlin.

Eisenhower then asked Kennedy how the American hand could have been concealed in view of the U.S. Navy ships involved, American weapons, and the elaborate systems of communications and B-26s involved in support of the operation. Kennedy did not reply.

Eisenhower: There is only one thing to do when you get into this kind of thing: make sure it succeeds.
Kennedy: Anything like it in the future will succeed.
Eisenhower: Well I'm glad to hear that.

The point of pride between the two men had to do with their differing views about the NSC and Eisenhower's elaborate staff system, which Schlesinger later said Bundy was "slaughtering" with such glee. Kennedy's most irritating campaign promise had been to restore Roosevelt's improvisational methods of organization, a promise that appealed to liberals who for eight years had lampooned the Eisenhower "staff system." Kennedy had further delighted nostalgic admirers of Franklin Roosevelt by stating he intended to function as his own secretary of state. Upon hearing the latter, Eisenhower had remarked to several people that Kennedy had thereby "proven his complete unawareness of the job."

Kennedy raised the question of process. "Well, just somewhere along the line, I blundered and I don't know how badly," he sighed. "Everyone approved — the JCS, the CIA, my staff."

Eisenhower questioned Kennedy on whether he had in fact gained the approval of the Joint Chiefs of Staff (JCS). As a former Army chief of staff and ex officio chairman of the Joint Chiefs under Defense Secretary James Forrestal, Eisenhower was familiar with the JCS habit of hedging approval with a misleading flourish of seeming enthusiasm. The test of JCS opinion lay in what they committed to in writing. And even their written approval had to be scrutinized carefully to sort out qualifiers, conditions, and alternatives.

Eisenhower drew Kennedy into a startling admission. The JCS had issued "guarded approval" of the plan Kennedy had inherited from Eisenhower in January. As for the later plan, drafted between February and April, which shifted the landing zone, H-hour, and canceled air support, the JCS had approved nothing. But the JCS purportedly had seemed enthusiastic.

Eisenhower took the opportunity to suggest a link between Kennedy's mishandled operation and his downgrading of the NSC. "Mr. President," Eisenhower ventured, "before you approved the plan did you have everyone in front of you debating the thing so you got the pros and cons yourself and then made your decision, or did you see these people one at a time?"

Kennedy smiled. "Well," he replied, "I did have a meeting but. . . . It was not my whole NSC."

Eisenhower listened intently. He had heard from reliable sources that Kennedy had succumbed to a last-minute appeal from Ambassador to the United Nations Adlai Stevenson to call off bombing strikes, Stevenson having denied to the United Nations that Americans were flying preliminary missions in support of the Castro forces. At Stevenson's promptings, hours before the landing, Undersecretary of State Chester Bowles and Secretary of State Dean Rusk reached the President and talked him into canceling the air strikes over the beaches as the Cuban brigade went ashore. In other words, the young President was guilty of the cardinal error of yielding to the last man he talked to, the very sin the NSC was designed to prevent.

The two men parted. Kennedy had observed protocol and had created the desired impression of joint responsibility. But Eisenhower had made his point: proper organization is a vital — *the* vital — element of success in any presidential undertaking.

Weeks later, Kennedy would invite Eisenhower to drop by the White House for a second meeting on Cuba and Berlin. Kennedy meanwhile had appointed General Taylor to head a commission to investigate the causes of failure in Cuba. Eisenhower suspected that the Taylor group had been assembled to "produce a corpse," a scapegoat for the Cuban affair, which Eisenhower predicted would be the CIA's Allen Dulles. Eisenhower had sarcastically referred to the Taylor Commission as "appointing the fox to investigate the chicken coop."

Kennedy must have known the antagonism Eisenhower felt toward Taylor for having published *The Uncertain Trumpet,* a critical look at Eisenhower's defense policies in the late 1950s. Taylor had taken issue with Eisenhower's "inflexible" deterrence strategy in Europe. In addition, Taylor's commission had been formally organized to study the NSC and national security policymaking bodies, a project Eisenhower deduced was a device to produce scholarship in support of Kennedy's preordained intention to dispense with the NSC system altogether. He nonetheless agreed to attend the meeting.

Eisenhower's meeting with the President was outwardly cordial but insubstantial. Eisenhower's feelings about leaving intact the NSC system he had devised were politely noted. Kennedy arranged to have Taylor brief Eisenhower on Cuba and NSC matters.

These meetings between Eisenhower and Kennedy were a civilized affirmation of their mutual wariness. As his assistant Kevin McCann later explained, Eisenhower respected but did not particularly like Kennedy and vice versa. Following the Camp David meeting, Eisenhower privately spoke more openly about the immaturity of his successor. He complained about Kennedy's indifference about the balance-of-payments question, his thirst for power, and ridiculed the hyped accounts of Kennedy's personal "self-confidence." To intimates, Kennedy spoke of his respect for Eisenhower's vote-getting ability and his skills as a general, but of his distaste for Eisenhower personally. Arthur Schlesinger, Jr., recalled in *A Thousand Days* a comment Kennedy had made at the Kennedy home in Hyannisport, Massachusetts, in 1959 during a campaign strategy session. "I could understand if he played golf all the time with old Army friends," Kennedy said caustically, "but no man is less loyal to his old friends than Eisenhower. He is a terribly cold man. All his golfing pals are rich men he has met since 1945."

On the surface, all was fine. Eisenhower thanked Kennedy for the Camp David luncheon on May 2. "It was a delightful lunch" and an "intensely interesting and helpful conversation," Eisenhower wrote. He added: "You may be amused by some of the gossipy reports brought to me by one or two of the reporters who visited Camp David that day. They said that the officers and men were obviously pleased by the interest you took in the whole establishment and had great satisfaction in showing you through the plant."

Kennedy responded perfunctorily a week later.

"Dear Mr. President," he began, ignoring Clifton's insistence that Eisenhower preferred "General":

Many thanks for your kind note of last week following our luncheon at Camp David. I found our conversation rewarding and most helpful. It was good of you to come to Camp David, and I hope that from time-to-time in the future the opportunity for a further exchange of views will present itself.

I was delighted to learn that your Gettysburg office is satisfactory, and I hope that the work on your memoirs is going well.

With every best wish,
sincerely,
JF Kennedy

ABOVE THE BATTLE

Back at his office in Gettysburg, Eisenhower opened the door to television executives and magazine publishers who arrived to discuss future projects. In late spring he agreed to tape a series of interviews with Walter Cronkite of CBS about his years in the White House, highlighting his views on McCarthyism, right-wing extremism, and his role in the 1960 election. Eisenhower signed with the *Saturday Evening Post* to write a collection of articles on defense questions and foreign policy. In addition, representatives from all three major television networks attempted to persuade him to host documentary films about historical subjects. ABC proposed a program titled "The Eisenhower Years"; CBS asked Eisenhower to become a roving commentator; and NBC sought to have Eisenhower elaborate on the thoughts expressed in his farewell address.

Some of the television and magazine executives Eisenhower saw that spring were old friends; several he met for the first time. In any case, the Eisenhower these men got to know was an entertaining and absorbing conversationalist, passionately expressive about current events and the new administration. Each in turn attempted to persuade Eisenhower to speak out in front of the cameras, in CBS executive Fred Friendly's words "for the sake of history." Eisenhower proved to be a reluctant subject.

Eisenhower had many ideas he wanted to explore in articles and to communicate to the public. One afternoon late that spring, he told Ben Hibbs of the *Saturday Evening Post* that he was considering an article, or perhaps a television appearance, to expand on the subject of the "military industrial complex." He explained that he was looking for ways to lay out his views on the economic, military, and moral balance required of the nation under Cold War conditions, hoping to impress the public with the significance of the vast technological advances of recent decades. Digressing into history, he pointed out that the French and British weapons during the Hundred Years War were not much more advanced than the weapons used by the Ptolemies of ancient Egypt. As recently as World War I, a French general had actually been wounded by a lancer.

But little things seemed to get in the way. "I considered doing a piece with NBC to discuss the implications of these changes," Eisenhower told Friendly some months later; "however I learned that this was to involve two skunks [two TV journalists] who had distorted U-2 [the Soviet downing of a U.S. spy plane that derailed the 1960 summit meeting] to our disadvantage — and when the network came back with a Lincoln idea, I just got busy."

A persistent stumbling block was Eisenhower's time-honored "rule against discussing personalities." Retirement had not softened the rigor of this self-imposed rule, nor had the critical articles and books on Eisenhower that had appeared in recent years. Eisenhower had veered close to technical violation of his rule when he derisively labeled an unnamed Democratic candidate for president in 1960 as "this young genius." But except for that lapse, he had confined himself since to broad and often ambiguous pronouncements about the Democrats and Kennedy. Eisenhower also observed a "rule against answering criticism." "I don't answer criticism as such," Eisenhower evenly told Hibbs. "I just lay out the facts."

Eisenhower was wary of being drawn into criticism of Kennedy or of the Democrats except at the level of "principle." That June in Gettysburg, *Saturday Evening Post* editor Ben Hibbs almost persuaded Eisenhower to attack Kennedy's decision to downgrade the cabinet, an evident move by Kennedy to take personal credit for all the accomplishments of his administration. When Eisenhower expressed the suspicion that Kennedy was afraid of being overshadowed by independent voices on his staff and in the cabinet, his indignation rose to fever pitch. "The country has confidence in strong, able men around the President," Eisenhower thundered righteously. He recalled the example he had set in bringing self-made individualists into the cabinet, choosing, for the moment, not to remember how irritating these individualists had been when they departed from the official administration line.

Hibbs hopefully asked Eisenhower to commit his thoughts to writing. "But no personalities," Eisenhower replied. "Perhaps I will present the idea in the abstract. After all, there is nothing so cheap as columnists maligning people for money."

In a later meeting that year with Hibbs, Eisenhower discussed future projects for the *Post,* including governmental reorganization, the Republican Party, and the interdependence of government, business, and defense. Hibbs offered Eisenhower a chance to criticize administration policies on Berlin and Kennedy's decision to accept the neutralization of Laos. In an article for the *Post,* Eisenhower had sidestepped the question of the Berlin Wall erected that August by the Soviets and instead focused on the genesis of the Berlin situation, the question of Allied rights in the city, and his own role as general and president in Berlin's history. After three years of tension with the Soviets over Berlin, Eisenhower was taking the view that West Berlin's freedom was secure. As for Laos, despite his misgivings, Eisenhower would remain silent.

Lastly, there was the injunction of "knowing when to quit." Eisenhower had seen many wartime colleagues make vain attempts to stay in the middle of public affairs past their prime and he was mindful of ex-President Truman's unsuccessful forays into Democratic nomination politics. Eisenhower's sense of personal dignity compelled him to maintain a low profile.

But visitors learned that Eisenhower had a healthy regard for the job he had done as president, and that despite his ambivalence about politics, he had liked public service and missed it. In early January 1960, on the eve of the presidential campaign, Eisenhower at a press conference had dropped a casual suggestion that it might be legal for him to offer himself as a candidate for national office again, as vice president. A week later, under questioning, Eisenhower revealed he had consulted the Department of Justice several hours after the press conference, and it had tendered an opinion that it was indeed constitutional under the Twenty-second Amendment, which barred him from seeking a third term as president, for Eisenhower to be elected vice president. Now retired, he was beginning to think that the amendment had been a mistake, telling a visitor that he "had a dream recently that the amendment had been repealed . . . and it wasn't a nightmare."

Eisenhower had a well-deserved reputation for modesty but he also enjoyed flattery, even if he often failed to recognize it as such. My father recalls particularly the example of Eisenhower's business partner Pete Jones. Jones had been born impoverished, and in the pattern of Horatio Alger rose rapidly as a young man to the top of the corporate ladder of Cities Service Oil Company despite his lack of education. Jones carried ten thousand dollars cash in his wallet at all times as a reminder of what he had accomplished, and was famous for leaving hundred- and two-hundred-dollar tips at roadside restaurants on a whim. Jones also had difficulty restraining the praise and wonderment he felt about Dwight Eisenhower. "Who would ever have imagined," Jones was fond of saying in Eisenhower's presence, "that I would ever walk in the White House as a guest, and know the greatest man in the world?" Jones's reverence for the White House was something Eisenhower shared, and his frequent praise of the Eisenhower administration was, in Granddad's view, factual.

To defend the party and his legacy, Eisenhower met with Republican leaders in Gettysburg and kept in touch with his political associates and friends. Richard Nixon, while toiling away at his memoir in

California, called occasionally to keep Eisenhower abreast of political developments and planning for the 1962 off-year elections, while Bryce Harlow kept Eisenhower informed of developments in the Congress. By late April, in the wake of the Cuba news, Eisenhower gave serious thought to the idea of forming something like a "shadow government" built on maintaining close links to his former cabinet and GOP elective officials. Following a suggestion made by Wisconsin congressman John W. Byrnes, in early May Eisenhower hosted two meetings. On May 1, a congressional delegation led by Senator Dirksen arrived for a breakfast meeting and discussion of the current congressional session. On the 11th, Eisenhower hosted a larger group of former cabinet officials and advisors for lunch at his Gettysburg office. The group included former Secretary of Commerce Sinclair Weeks, Senator Thurston Morton, former budget director Maurice Stans, former UN ambassador James Wadsworth, former NSC secretary Gordon Gray, former attorney general William Rogers, and former secretary of agriculture Ezra Taft Benson.

The purpose of the meeting, recorded in formal minutes, was to entice Eisenhower into accepting the role of opposition to

Kennedy and using a speech he was scheduled to give at the National Armory on June 1 as a springboard. In the judgment of many present, the so-called honeymoon had gone on long enough and Republicans were justified in assuming the role of partisans. The party had underestimated Kennedy's political talent, and the receptiveness of pundits and popular opinion to the views of the young president. The idea of demurring to the Kennedy White House and simply waiting for events to bring Republicans back into the spotlight was too passive.

James Wadsworth raised the matter of Eisenhower's support of the President after the Cuban disaster. Eisenhower replied by describing his meeting with Kennedy at Camp David and his promise of bipartisan support for Kennedy's effort to counter communist penetration of the hemisphere. He indicated he sympathized with Kennedy's plight to some degree, and that he had warmed to the President's query, "Where do we go from here?"

Rogers countered this line of thinking. The Kennedys were doing everything they could to undermine the Eisenhower record, calling members of the press directly in order to appeal to their awe of the office and to line up reporters as political supporters. They were playing Cuba two ways, with Kennedy accepting blame for the Bay of Pigs fiasco in public, while Robert Kennedy and White House staffers intimated to others that the plan had been inherited and carried out merely at Eisenhower's wish. Rogers added that Kennedy's appointment of General Taylor to investigate the CIA sounded to him like an effort to scapegoat Allen Dulles, a holdover, for an "intelligence failure" when of course the Cuban operation had fallen apart because of command failures and Kennedy's lack of resolution.

Eisenhower shared their lament. He was mystified by the effort in the press to minimize the dimensions of the Cuban fiasco by comparing it with U-2, the secret 1959 overflights of Soviet territory — a comparison Eisenhower rejected. "The U-2 merely unmasked a highly successful operation from which we derived great benefit," he said, "while the 'Bay of Pigs' was a failure from the outset." Eisenhower felt that Republicans should applaud Kennedy's purpose to oust Castro but recognize that "once a resort to force is made, you must ensure its success."

He digressed into a discussion of the failed tactics: placing all communications aboard one ship; changing the landing beach to a remote corner of south Cuba, encircled by swampland, with few roads leading out of the landing area; no fire support; and the general lack of aggressiveness when opportunities to move ashore did present themselves. "There was one intelligence failure," Eisenhower added: "the Cubans had jets."

Eisenhower related to the group that the previous year he had authorized the CIA to assemble a group of refugees eager to return to Cuba. The group had lacked leadership or means, and so the CIA had provided extensive training for what had been anticipated to be a protracted paramilitary effort. The pro-Batista elements had been weeded out and an effective leadership cadre was being identified and organized. "But the 'Bay of Pigs,' " Eisenhower stated, "has all the earmarks of a new venture, based on the expectation of an uprising within Cuba itself, and yet the administration blames the CIA, but perhaps the CIA was not off all that much since over 200,000 Cubans in Cuba have been jailed since the failure." Eisenhower added his familiar criticisms of Kennedy's organization of the White House staff. The President had dispensed with cabinet meetings, holding only two before the Cuban adventure. And only after the fiasco had Kennedy consulted Eisenhower, Nixon, Hoover, and MacArthur in "an effort to diffuse responsibility." "I will not be held to blame for Cuba having been consulted after the fact," Eisenhower said.

Discussion moved on to another sore point, the media's downplaying of Secretary of Defense Robert McNamara's recent briefing in which he blandly discounted the existence of a "missile gap," laying bare as false one of the basic claims of the Kennedy campaign. Other complaints surfaced and temperatures around the room began to rise.

Morton urged Eisenhower to "let fly in his June 1 speech." "It's a keynote and the party is waiting for what you have to say, though you should probably remain bipartisan in foreign affairs."

"People still have faith in you," Benson added. "Take the gloves off. Opposing Kennedy is not the same thing as disloyalty to the United States."

Eisenhower appreciated the expressions of support and the implicit sense of pride being expressed in the Republican record, and his own. But Eisenhower was unsure. "As emeritus," he said, "I must be silent."

Stans disagreed. "I think you should hit hard at 'gapsmanship' — all the business about the education gap, the growth gap, the missile gap, all the gaps that the administration is busy creating." Morton seconded Stans by reminding the group of recent administration statements that blamed the balance-of-payments problem on Eisenhower.

Gordon Gray cast the question in more fundamental terms. "This is an increasingly conservative country," he observed. Gray reported that his three sons at Harvard were "considerably" to the right of himself. The party, in his opinion, should take cognizance of the growing appeal of conservative ideas that the Eisenhower presidency had advanced. It should appeal more to youth. The weekly "Ev and Charlie show," he intoned, referring to Republican congressional leaders Senator Everett Dirksen and Representative Charles Halleck, "is doing nothing." But, he added, "is it wise to yell 'failure' after one hundred days?"

Gray's question answered itself and his counsel carried the day. The first — and last — shadow cabinet meeting adjourned, recommending that Eisenhower "remain above the battle." Grievances and frustrations had been aired, but an opposition role for Eisenhower was inappropriate and the issues to be developed against Kennedy remained unclear.

And so in the spring of 1961, Eisenhower reached an informal resolution to retire from national politics. But the sense of incompleteness remained and his interest in Republican Party affairs would, if anything, increase in the coming months. The clearest indication was his ongoing correspondence with Nixon, who was weighing important decisions about his political future.

On his last full day in the presidency, Eisenhower had set the bar high for Nixon's future political service, writing him from the Oval Office: "The passage of years has taken me out, so far as active participation is concerned, but the future can still bring to you a real culmination in your service to the country." Eisenhower made it clear he was defiant about the 1960 outcome, writing, "As you know, I am not an individual that accepts defeat easily. When I have to recognize a major set-back, my sole reaction is to redouble effort in order to recover lost ground." Later that year, Eisenhower would strongly urge Nixon to accommodate the party and run for governor of California.

Nixon himself was conflicted. On July 13, he wrote "Dear General . . . I continue to lean strongly against the idea of entering the race if we can find another candidate who will have some reasonable chance of being successful." Shortly afterward, he traveled to Gettysburg to consult with Eisenhower in person. He had already discussed financial support with several of Eisenhower's sympathetic friends and was busy canvassing high-level Republican opinion around the country. In a follow-up note to Eisenhower on July 25, Nixon set forth the pros and cons. First, the pros:

1) that I can win . . . 2) there is a great risk that any of the other candidates might lose . . . 3) if I were to run and win, the office would provide me with a staff . . . and a respectable forum for any public statements I might want to make . . . 4) it would also provide an opportunity for building a team of young administrators . . . and the chance to develop a reputation for handling administrative problems.

The cons . . . 1) If I were to lose, I would be virtually finished as far as public influence goes . . . 2) a California governor is saddled with programs which are more liberal than the type of program a Republican presidential candidate would want to stand on . . . 3) I would have to devote my full attention almost exclusively to the problems of California.

He concluded:

This latter argument is the strongest one against running as far as I am concerned. My experience in government has been in national and international affairs. I think the problems which governors have to handle are immensely important but my interests are simply in other fields.

Nixon thus articulated a case against himself that his opponents later would eagerly exploit. He was less interested in being governor than in being president. He was less interested in state affairs than in national and foreign affairs. Finally, Nixon was seeking a platform from which to launch an eventual campaign for the White House. Political realities would force him to say otherwise and to pledge that he would serve a full term in California, but Nixon's heart would palpably not be in such a pledge.

Eisenhower, however, was adamantly in favor of the race. Through former GOP national chairman Leonard Hall, he exerted pressure on Nixon to consider whether, without the governorship, he would retain an ability to command national attention, assuming New York governor Nelson Rockefeller's reelection. Eisenhower wanted California to be in Republican hands, and Nixon offered the best chance of victory. Six days later, September 11, Eisenhower wrote a letter that proved decisive in Nixon's thinking:

In my own mind I can find no alternative to an affirmative decision. None of our other Republican "friends" would stand a chance, in my opinion, of defeating the incumbent. If Knight, for instance, should run and be defeated (assuming you backed him, as assuredly you would have to do), then in effect you have suffered a defeat. If you run and win, as I believe you can, you offset to a large extent the razor-thin margin by which you lost the Presidential race last November. Finally I see no reason why, if you are elected Governor, you cannot, if you wish, make the 1964 Presidential race — and I think you would be in a far more powerful position as Governor, controlling a large delegation, than otherwise.

So, for whatever it is worth, I have

added my two cent's worth.

SUMMER OF '61

As school let out, I began work on the farm, tending the vegetable gardens near the residence, repainting the fences, and caring for the horses, a chore I shared with my sisters. Granddad kept four horses on several acres. Granddad, however, no longer rode, because his activities were restricted. In 1955 he had suffered a major heart attack, in early 1956 he had undergone an operation for ileitis, and in late 1957 he had had a minor stroke. None of his illnesses had impaired him significantly as president, and officially he had left office in "robust" health. But he was under the care of physicians, making regular visits to Walter Reed Army Medical Center in Washington and observing a careful regimen at home in Gettysburg under the supervision of a local doctor, C. H. Johnson.

The horses were used by the grandchildren. I "owned" Sporty Miss, a hickory-brown quarter horse with a proud black mane. My sister Anne "owned" a chestnut-colored quarter horse named Doodle de Doo. Two Arabians, gifts from President Habib Bourguiba of Tunisia, "belonged" to my younger sisters Susan and Mary Jean.

Granddad cherished the hope that we all would become accomplished equestrians.

This meant a daily horseback ride, brushing down the horses before retiring them to pasture for the evening, cleaning the stables, and polishing the saddles, halters, and bits. In time Doodle de Doo became uncontrollably wild and we had to restrict her to foaling. Sporty Miss, on the other hand, remained a good-natured, well-mannered riding horse.

My middle sister, Susan, emerged as the accomplished rider in the family. She entered horse competitions in the Adams County area. My parents set aside a corner of the family recreation room to display her trophies. Whenever possible, Granddad took time away from the office to watch Susan compete. She became the model of deportment and finesse astride a horse, the example held up to the rest of us, a matter of some irritation to me. My faults on horseback were technical: no bearing, a preference for the uncouth western saddle over the more refined English saddle, a thirst for speed and excitement.

Granddad indulged the horses in a way he indulged no other animal. The Angus were raised for slaughter and show. Granddad had issued a "shoot on sight" order regarding the barnyard cats that wandered on and off the property. The bird dogs nicknamed Art (Arthur Nevins) and George (George Allen) were confined to a kennel and trained strictly for fetching pheasants and quail. Because the dogs chased butterflies and mice more aggressively than game, they were periodically shipped off for obedience training.

One evening, Susan lost control of the two Arabians while brushing them down at a hitching post next to the stalls. The Arabians, in full view of Granddad and a number of guests enjoying a cocktail on the sunporch, galloped away to romp over the pastures adjoining the backyard. After several laps, the Arabians darted toward Granddad's putting green and sand trap. Susan watched, mortified, as the horses rolled around in the sand, reared up in ecstasy over the green and scattered the sand and dirt. According to the guests, Granddad observed the destruction of his practice green with speechless equanimity. As the Arabians grew bored with sharpening their hoofs on the putting surface and trotted away, Granddad turned to his stunned guests and beamed, "Isn't that the loveliest sight you've ever seen?"

Granddad was also tolerant of one of my

major transgressions. As a thirteen-year-old farm employee I had two privileges that I cherished: I could invite friends over to play war games in the barn haylofts; and I had the right to drive the four-gear "Ike and Mamie" Crosley golf cart up and down the farm lane and on the gravel roads connecting the eastern pastureland to the farm. Unfortunately, on one of my maximum-speed jaunts, I stripped the gears. I explained what happened to Sergeant Leonard Dry, Granddad's driver, who maintained the automobiles. I got word that I would be retaining my driving privileges and could resume driving the Crosley as soon as it was repaired. It never was.

Meanwhile, Granddad decided to get his driver's license. He had not driven since 1941. Since the automobile was the key to his independence now that he was out of office, he approached the study of traffic safety brochures with the same grim determination he had used studying tactics thirty-five years earlier at Command and General Staff School at Leavenworth, Kansas.

The family did not know whether to be amused or concerned. We supposed that the state would pass him, regardless of his performance on any test. We knew that

Granddad's reflexes had deteriorated, and that from his trial runs around the farm after returning from Eldorado he drove from rote since his feeling for the technique of driving had vanished. At the same time we could barely suppress our amused anticipation of the ordeal some courageous member of the Pennsylvania State Police would undergo in the front seat of Granddad's Chrysler Imperial. The driver's exam would require Granddad to execute turns, parallel-park, and navigate the open drive from the Department of Motor Vehicles branch on Chambersburg Road past the Lutheran Theological Seminary and back.

In August 1961, the state of Pennsylvania licensed Dwight Eisenhower to drive a car. Predictably, the grader pronounced him an "excellent driver" before a battery of local reporters, and licensed the general "without hesitation." It was a moment of terror for the family, especially for Dad and me. Dad, who was helping Granddad write his presidential memoirs, would have to ride to work the two miles between the white gated entrance to the farm and our house on its corner, and the new offices now located on the campus of Gettysburg College. Occasionally, I would be on the hook for a five-mile trip between our home and the golf course for a late-afternoon round.

The drive to the course was a traumatic experience. Thankfully, the speed limits kept us at 25 miles per hour along Confederate Avenue because of the caravans of tourists who parked along the road to inspect the monuments. Granddad took corners sharply; the squeal of rubber against concrete and gravel roads never ceased to surprise him, or unsettle me. Each time we screeched, pitched, yawed, and lunged all the way out and back. Every bump and lurch elicited a faint "damnation," and every other driver on the road was evaluated by the literal standards Granddad had memorized from his driving brochures. Granddad drove with total concentration.

I remember approaching a carload of tourists drawn up one afternoon alongside a cluster of Confederate cannons near the Virginia monument and the statue of General Lee riding his famous horse Traveler. The rear end of their station wagon extended onto the road and the inattentive driver and his passengers dangled out the windows on the right side of the car snapping Brownie photos of the cannon. "No oncoming traffic" I noted anxiously as Granddad applied hard left rudder. "Damnation!" he roared, reflecting his irritation with the flouting of the rules.

Passing the station wagon, Granddad leaned on the horn, which blared like an air-raid alert. The driver appeared to collapse on top of the steering column, looking stunned. With another "damnation," the Imperial squealed to the right, back into our lane. As Granddad's eyes remained fixed on the road ahead, I peered back to see if anyone had died of fright. Slowly the driver struggled back to his upright position behind the wheel.

Granddad's hard expression had melted and a benign look came over his face.

"When you get your license," he said deliberately, "you must never impede access along a public thoroughfare."

"Yes, sir."

By now the family's move from Washington was complete and historic Gettysburg had become home. That summer it was a place of endless adventure and fun. We lived on the south end of town, and so most of my earliest friends — the Teeters, the Hills, the Deardorfs, and the Millers — were children of parents who ran the law firms and the proliferating tourist-oriented businesses south of town. But the first year of junior high school had brought the north and south ends of town together. I got to know more kids, some whose parents taught and worked at the college: the Richardsons, the Horners, the Codoris, the Raffensbergers, the Rosenbergers, and the Pickerings. Republicans and Democrats, Yankees and Pirates fans, ballplayers and musicians, I felt I had the best circle of friends I'd ever made.

There were countless games of pickup baseball and basketball. The weeknights centered around Little League and Big Little League baseball, which were huge social events involving everyone's parents, sisters, and brothers. Every home in town was accessible by bicycle. On Friday nights, a group of twenty of us would angle for permission to camp out at a tree house north of town near the Eternal Light Peace Memorial. This gave us license to explore the area by night, crashing Gettysburg College parties at various ends of the battlefield.

My parents and grandparents became concerned about our nights out after receiving complaints from the Park Service about pranks by "campers" near the peace memorial. Thus there were several discussions with my grandparents about park regulations, bicycle safety, and "staying out of trouble." My dad later explained that

Granddad and Mamie were protective on all matters of personal safety. It was because they had lost their first son, Doud Dwight, "Icky," the older brother my dad never knew. Because of Icky, Dad felt he had been overprotected by his parents. He did not want me to grow up feeling the same way, and so he did not object to the bicycles and Friday nights at the tree hut.

By August, a grand drama gripped the country and Gettysburg. In baseball, 1961 had become the year of the "M&M" boys, Mickey Mantle and Roger Maris of the New York Yankees, and their fabled pursuit of Babe Ruth's single-season record of sixty home runs. The Mantle-Maris drama fired ambition in me to play for the Yankees someday.

By August, everyone in the family became interested in the race. Dad was a Yankees fan. He had lived in dozens of places and had never developed attachments to a local team, but had instead followed the World Series every year, which in those years meant following the Yankees. I remembered Dad's remark once that Mickey Mantle was "the best" at his chosen profession, and worthy therefore of the high salary he was being paid. "Mantle will never have to worry about a job," he told me, which was one of the most impressive things I had ever heard said about anyone. Dad had less interest in Maris, questioning the legitimacy of it all since 1961 was an expansion year for the American League, which meant lower-quality pitching and eight extra games. Dad seemed satisfied with Commissioner Ford Frick's ruling that any homer total exceeding Ruth's 60 after regular season game number 154 would go into the books with an asterisk. Granddad thought home runs were overrated.

I liked both Mantle and Maris, and was pulling for the two of them to break Ruth's record, Mantle preferably, but Maris, too. In early September, Mantle succumbed to injury and attention shifted to Maris, who braved a mid-September slump to accumulate fifty-eight homers by game 154, needing two to satisfy Frick's edict.

There were privileges in being the "grandson of," and a memorable night was in store for me. My orthodontist, also a big baseball fan, was able to arrange tickets to the Yankees' game 154 in Baltimore. After a few arguments at home — Dad was expecting nothing to come of game 154 and was reluctant to allow me to go — I was allowed to leave school early in order to be in Baltimore by game time.

I vividly remember that September night: listening anxiously to radio reports about the rain and high winds in the Baltimore area, which threatened to postpone the game. Phil Rizzuto's pregame show kept breaking up because of bad weather. The news via radio was that Mantle would be sitting out with a leg abscess while Maris was set to play. We shared binoculars at the game so we watched Maris closely as he batted and took the field. He popped out his first time at bat. His fifty-ninth homer in the fourth inning brought the crowd and the television audience to the edge of their seats. Maris batted three more times, striking out, fouling deep down the right-field line before flying out to far right field, and then tapping back to the pitcher for his final out.

I got home late that night, and Dad, not having listened to the game, was waiting at the front door. "Did he do it?" I recounted the game in detail. When I described Maris's fifty-ninth, Dad shook his head, "amazing." I took it from Dad's reaction that Maris, like Mantle, would never have to worry about getting a job.

Soon it was football season. Playing junior high school football was required of anyone who wanted to play basketball that winter, since Don Bickel coached both sports. Afternoon practice was an ordeal since football brought us into contact with some tough farm kids, many of them a year or two older from having to repeat grades, and some weighing nearly two hundred pounds. In the 1960s, the rural areas of Adams County would be classified Appalachia as part of the Kennedy-Johnson War on Poverty. The Gettysburg school system was one of the few east of the Alleghenies to grant a day off to a pupil, upon request, to hunt deer. Occasionally, rumors would swirl in school about the latest welfare caseworker who ventured onto one of the backwoods farms only to be driven off by gunpoint.

Granddad was very interested in the football team, having played at West Point and coached at several Army posts early in his career. He felt that football, above all other sports, built character and was excellent conditioning. A superb athlete himself, he had been touted as a potential all-American until a knee injury ended his career. Apparently, Granddad had also been an excellent baseball player, though the facts were somewhat murky. At the time, it was rumored that Dwight Eisenhower had actually played professional baseball the summer of 1909 in the Kansas-Oklahoma-Missouri (KOM) League, but under the pseudonym "Wilson" to preserve his amateur status and eligibility for college sports.

Years later, I attended an Angels game with Arthur "Red" Patterson, once publicity director of the Brooklyn Dodgers. Patterson brought up the rumors. He told me that in 1948 he had accompanied General Eisenhower to a game at Ebbets Field. "General, we have heard you once played in the KOM under the alias Wilson. Our records show there were two Wilsons who played in the league in 1909. I am wondering," he asked, "which Wilson was Wilson and which was Eisenhower?" Eisenhower had grinned. "I was the Wilson who could hit," adding, "that's between you and me."

NAKED FACTS

By fall, Granddad had turned in earnest to the writing of his presidential memoir. In addition to my father, who was on extended leave from the Army, his chief assistant was William Ewald, a former White House speechwriter on loan from IBM. The two assistants were hard at work on drafts of chapters that Granddad would edit and shape to his satisfaction.

In 1947, working twelve-hour days with

thirty minutes off for lunch, Eisenhower had completed *Crusade in Europe,* a long, lucid account of his wartime service, in less than ten months. But he found writing a presidential memoir to be very different. Granddad devoted only several hours a day to his writing and relied heavily on Dad and Ewald. The comparative lack of zeal for his presidential memoir is understandable. The wartime experience had meant more to him. The story recounted in *Crusade* had been his introduction to the great personalities of the era — FDR, Winston Churchill, General George Marshall. Granddad's conduct had been bathed in acclaim and the war in Europe had been carried on without any significant questioning of the purposes of the Allied leadership. In *Crusade in Europe,* Granddad focused on explaining the operational and strategic considerations that had guided his decisions.

An account of the Eisenhower administration confronted him with more difficult problems. A discussion of the presidency required deeper explanations of actions for which he was solely responsible. In addition, he felt he had to be relatively circumspect due to his role as senior statesman. And he knew his presidency lacked the drama that permeated *Crusade.*

Eisenhower undertook the first volume of his presidential memoir, *Mandate for Change,* braced for mixed reviews and a relatively apathetic reading public. At the same time, he determined that he would not attempt to enhance his account of the presidency in any way to create drama for the sake of greater readership. His concept of his memoir was to provide a debriefing, an unemotional, practical, and careful explanation of his presidency. As he observed years later: "a record of personal experiences can have several useful purposes, none of which is basically to amuse or entrance. If the story is about conflict, the conscientious memoir writer does not seek to contrive such tense situations as are dreamed up by gifted historical novelists . . . [T]he drama, if any, should be in naked facts."

Eisenhower's approach to his memoirs concerned his editors at Doubleday, who hoped he would unwind and speak freely. He had dealt with many fascinating personalities in the White House. His presidency had, in fact, encompassed moments of high drama, and with a few embellishments, Eisenhower could write a suspenseful and colorful account. The editors wanted a livelier narrative; details about the Korean

War settlement, the showdown with Senator Joseph McCarthy, the election campaigns, Eisenhower's dealings with the Soviets and Khrushchev, his clash with the British and French at Suez; in other words, more insight into the emotions he experienced in making the big decisions of his presidency.

Sharp disagreements arose over Eisenhower's dry treatment of the McCarthy period. His editors could not comprehend Eisenhower's reluctance to dwell on the personal battle that had raged between the two men for almost eighteen months; Eisenhower could not grasp why his editors found the McCarthy story so interesting. He was not influenced, as Dad recalls, by "the intensity of feeling which existed among those groups that McCarthy had abused, which included the intellectual and publishing world." Eisenhower's policy had been one of refusing to argue with McCarthy, and whatever the damage to his image of leadership on this vital issue, in his view his policy of ignoring McCarthy had worked.

Eisenhower had realized McCarthyism was a massive distraction that imperiled everything he had fought for in the 1952 campaign. He had run in 1952 in order to bring the Republican Party back from oblivion and restore a two-party system after twenty years of one-party rule. As president, he had been determined to point a "modern" Republican Party forward and to induce Republicans to move beyond old arguments about the war in Europe, Social Security, and the principle of government intervention in economic affairs, all policies Eisenhower had regarded as vital and had supported under Roosevelt and Truman.

Eisenhower and his editors also discussed his relationship with John Foster Dulles, to whom he would devote an entire chapter of the second volume of his memoirs. Dulles intrigued the editors, yet despite their urging, Eisenhower did not feel compelled to set the record straight about a complex partnership that he now chose to insist had been wholly cooperative and mutually beneficial. His veneration of Dulles had begun at the secretary's funeral in May 1959, one of the grandest pageants of the Eisenhower years, but only one of the several monuments that Eisenhower erected to his secretary of state. In July 1959, Eisenhower had announced that Chantilly Airport, under construction west of Washington in the Virginia suburbs, would be named "Dulles International Airport." By 1961, Eisenhower likened his partnership with Dulles to that between Robert E. Lee and his trusted and indispensable lieutenant Stonewall Jackson.

Eisenhower's chapter on Dulles would be one of the few he would write without significant aid. He would devote long passages to evaluating Dulles's great abilities, portraying his secretary as an effective instrument of his will and presidency. In discussions with his editors, Eisenhower tossed aside suggestions that Dulles had manipulated him and that the two had not enjoyed a smooth or easy partnership. "Well," Eisenhower reflected, "if people want to make you stupid and say that other people are leading you around by the nose, there is nothing much you can do about it. History will tell the story anyway. . . ."

As he wrote in his memoirs, Eisenhower had marveled at Dulles's personal courage and his refusal to accept painkillers after cancer operations in 1956 and 1959, so his mind would remain clear and he would be available for consultation with his State Department.

Dulles and Eisenhower had not been social friends, but Eisenhower fondly recalled their many sessions in the Oval Office in which the two had discussed topics well removed from foreign affairs. Dulles had feared the effects of affluence and had often talked about the American quest for the soft and easy life. Philosophically, Eisenhower tended to agree with his secretary that "battle is the joy of life." He also agreed with Dulles that in mid-century America, the principle of representative government was "on trial." Occasionally they commiserated about the insatiable demands for federal outlays and spending by Washington pressure groups that would, in time, undermine the vitality of America's self-governing society. He recalled Dulles's favorite expression, "the brotherhood of man under the fatherhood of God," and his belief that the United States should take the offensive on moral and ethical questions.

"Small men made life very tough for Foster," Eisenhower recalled. And he himself had been guilty of a mistake: "I got so I disliked Truman's idea of keeping in his desk a liquor bar. Now with Foster, I have thought of it since. If I had only had the sense to give him a scotch and soda — he loved scotch and soda — he would have just sat and talked things over, loosened up more. . . ."

As the writing of the book proceeded, Doubleday again asked for more controversy, divided decisions, agony, regret, and mistakes. Dad recalled how he, Granddad, and Bill Ewald huddled for hours to discuss ways of accommodating the suggestions. As my father recalls, the three of them "couldn't think of anything." In reporting to the editors, the best Dad could do was to shrug contritely.

Dad later told me that ironically, as a staff officer in 1929, Eisenhower had been in the position of recommending to John J. Pershing that the latter enliven his long and tedious account of his experiences during World War I. Pershing's obsession with literal accuracy went to fantastic lengths. He wanted to include items like the reproduction of formal engraved invitations to state dinners, menus, calendars, appointment logs, and weather reports. Major Eisenhower, solicited for his advice, had strongly urged that Pershing do more highlighting and put less stress on literal descriptions in order to make the book more readable.

But Pershing had also consulted a young brigadier general in Washington named George C. Marshall. Marshall and Eisenhower met for the first time while conferring on the project. Marshall rather liked the details and disliked departing from literal accuracy into "the realm of speculation." Eisenhower, outranked, decided he was not the one to challenge Marshall's judgment or Pershing's and so he dropped his suggestions.

Thirty-three years later, Eisenhower found that tackling a presidential memoir opened an entirely new set of issues from those he had encountered when advising Pershing and Marshall. In a presidency spanning eight years, problems recurred and often defied resolution. By the fall of 1961, many of the issues Eisenhower thought he had disposed of as president were, in fact, unresolved. For example, one of the key events of Eisenhower's first term was the end of the French war in Indochina in 1954, which resulted in a settlement in Vietnam and partition of the country into a communist north and pro-Western south. For the rest of the Eisenhower presidency, the partition in Vietnam held, but the Laotian conflict had erupted in late 1960 and a year later, as Eisenhower began writing the Indochina section of his memoir, North Vietnam had resumed a war to unify north and south under communist rule.

Uncertain of the administration's likely course, in the winter of 1961–62, Eisenhower would feel compelled to slash by 50 percent his detailed draft on Indochina lest it constrain President Kennedy's freedom of action and that of the South Vietnamese government of President Ngo Dinh Diem. In the Preface to *Waging Peace,* as volume two of his memoirs would be titled, he also would carefully note: "This does not pretend to be, nor shall it be taken, as an index to the specific current or future policies of the United States."

That America was moving toward direct intervention in Vietnam had been made plain to Eisenhower by Bryce Harlow, his White House congressional liaison and now a lobbyist for Procter & Gamble in Washington. In March 1962, Harlow passed along a memo given to him by William Sprague, an unidentified Washington insider, about the merits of calling for a joint resolution in Congress to acknowledge the developing war in Vietnam.

In detail, the memorandum provided by Harlow described a "guerilla war of increasing ferocity" that had developed in 1961. In South Vietnam, Viet Cong insurgents were "running rampant," putting the Diem government in an increasingly "precarious position." Quietly, the U.S. troop presence had been built up from the Geneva Treaty limit of 685 to 4,000. U.S. "training mission leaders" were in fact leading Vietnamese army platoons in combat, "shooting first and often." A special command had been formed in anticipation of full-scale intervention, and a major Marine force was standing in readiness to enter the theatre on "a few hours notice."

The memorandum summed up the "beneficial effects" of a congressional resolution:

1. Testimony and debate would serve to inform the public of the true situation and develop popular support.
2. The Communists would be on notice.
3. Such a resolution would stiffen the spines of the Administration.
4. It would confirm bi-partisan support. . . .

There is no record of any move by Eisenhower to persuade GOP congressmen to back a joint resolution concerning the situation in Vietnam, but the memo was a vivid reminder of how difficult it was to get a handle on the facts of the growing crisis in Southeast Asia.

Concern about Vietnam did not escape even my attention as a thirteen- and fourteen-year-old. One of our closest family friends was Colonel Fred Ladd, lionized in

David Halberstam's *The Best and the Brightest* as one of the most effective Special Forces advisers in the 1961–62 period. Back from Vietnam and now stationed at the Army War College in Carlisle, Pennsylvania, Ladd — Dad's high school classmate at Fort Lewis, Washington — was an occasional visitor in our Gettysburg home. More than once I sat quietly in our playroom listening while Ladd described to Dad the Dantesque inferno developing in Vietnam. It was a war waged at night by peasants in black pajamas who were friends by day. "We just don't know who the enemy is in Vietnam," Ladd said. "I've never seen anything like it."

As autumn lengthened, the topic at dinner at the Gettysburg farm was war — not Vietnam, but the Civil War and the centennial observances that would unfold over the next three years. These dinners were formal occasions and children were to be "seen and not heard." But by now I was thirteen, an avid reader of military history, and I could enjoy the lively discussions between Dad and Granddad and any guests present.

Granddad spoke as a real expert. He had first visited Gettysburg in 1915 with his West Point class to study the terrain. During World War I, as commander of Camp Colt, Granddad had used Big and Little Round Top and the adjoining fields as a training ground for the fledgling U.S. Tank Corps. When he served on Pershing's staff, touring and studying battlefields had become a hobby, which he imparted to Dad, who subsequently took me to the Civil War battlefields Manassas, Fredericksburg, Petersburg, and Chancellorsville. More vivid than the military lessons learned was the experience of walking through the entrenchments and imagining the units mustering to the sound of bugles.

One of Granddad's most memorable dinner subjects was General George Meade. For almost a hundred years, historians had fixed in legend the idea that Meade, commander of the Union forces at Gettysburg, had forfeited an opportunity to end the Civil War in 1863 by failing to pursue Lee's defeated forces after Gettysburg. It was interesting to me that Granddad often offered facts about Meade that, to his way of thinking, explained, if not vindicated, the General's caution in the aftermath of the first decisive and significant victory for the Union.

In hindsight, in these evening seminars about the Civil War, Granddad was reviewing his wartime service. In the summer of 1944, Dwight Eisenhower, like Meade, had been accused of failing to exploit the victory in Normandy in ways that might have ended the war that year. The situations faced by Meade, Grant, Lee, Thomas, and other Civil War commanders were analogous to the situations Granddad had faced; but unlike the Second World War, the Civil War was a safe topic.

A theme of these dinner conversations was the importance of planning, and of the unexpected. Once Granddad told a story about his days at the Command and General Staff School in Leavenworth in 1926. Every officer who studied at Leavenworth knew about the "Young Turks," a group of students who in 1912 had convinced the faculty to modernize the curriculum by scrapping old battle problems based on the German-French campaigns in the Alsace-Lorraine and substituting the Gettysburg and Manassas campaigns. Their argument was that these were battles fought on American soil "where the American army might fight a battle" in the future.

"About a few years after that happened, World War I started," Granddad recalled. "We were fighting in the Alsace-Lorraine." The moral: "When you are planning for an emergency, you must start with this one thing — the very definition of an emergency is that it is unexpected." Meade had faced the unexpected at Gettysburg, and so had Eisenhower in 1944.

As the office records show, these family seminars carried over into office hours. In Dad's records is a memorandum of a conversation between Granddad and Civil War historian Bruce Catton, who visited Gettysburg to discuss the prospect of a joint appearance on an hour-long television special on the topic of Lincoln's attributes as a wartime "Commander-in-Chief." According to Dad's notes, in response to Catton, Eisenhower rated Lincoln as occupying a "separate category" as president (along with Washington), and rated Lincoln's capacities as a wartime C-in-C as outstanding.

"The principles of war," Eisenhower explained, "are neither exclusive nor specialized. They are the principles of life which are fulfilled whenever an individual has a task or an objective to perform. They are a matter of common sense. Human nature is constant, as are the elements of political power, military power, economic power and morale," adding, "an army is not licked until it admits it."

Eisenhower opined that Lincoln's one

weakness was his "propensity to appoint political generals," offset by his key appointment of Grant. The minutes continue:

In response to a question, General Eisenhower said Grant was particularly noteworthy for his common sense. He had the foresight to bring the war to the population . . . that it was impossible to rely on a mere defeat of military forces. Grant was also outstanding in the selection of his subordinates, picking such men as Sherman. He had to go way down . . . the list to pick Phil Sheridan. . . . McPherson was one of Grant's selections and might have had a political future had he not been killed at the battle of Atlanta. Grant had had no use for McClernand but selected Thomas personally, a man that nobody could scare. Grant had respected Meade . . . and had essentially refrained from running Meade's business.

By late 1961, there was one more topic of dinner conversation that had been quietly discussed by my parents and grandparents for over a year — my future. Twelve months before, Granddad had received a visit from General Milton Baker, superintendent of

Valley Forge Military Academy, a well-known boarding school, which incidentally provided part of the setting for J. D. Salinger's *Catcher in the Rye.* Baker offered to accept the President's only grandson on a complete all-expenses-paid four-year scholarship. This offer had ignited a yearlong debate within the family.

Granddad was intrigued by the Valley Forge Military Academy. First, he loved Valley Forge itself, in his view one of the "two or three really inspirational locations" in the United States. Second, Granddad had visited the campus and been impressed by the precision drills, the snappy discipline, and the academy band. Baker did not have to try hard to persuade Granddad that Valley Forge was the place for me. Granddad was convinced that I would "benefit by discipline," undoubtedly not reflecting upon how a young fourteen-year-old Dwight Eisenhower, fifty-five years earlier, would have taken to the restrictions of military school.

My parents countered that military school would be too abrupt a transition for me. In fact, Dad took the position that his son would go to the academy "over his dead body." His views prevailed. At Thanksgiving, we learned three items of news. First, I was slated to enter Phillips Exeter Academy in the fall. Second, the family would be spending part of Christmas in California, a state I had never visited. Third, my sister Anne and I would probably be accompanying our grandparents on a trip to Europe the following summer. My days as a farmhand were numbered.

2
NEW HORIZONS

RESTLESS ENERGY

With completion of their home at Eldorado expected in late 1961, the Eisenhowers decided to spend winters in California. It is interesting that they chose to live five months of the year thousands of miles away from the favored retreats of their old Augusta, Georgia, friends. Since the late 1940s, the Eisenhowers had spent as much time as possible in Augusta. They had a "cabin" on the tenth tee and looked forward each year to a week there at Thanksgiving and again in mid-April after the Masters Golf Tournament. Now, by relocating to Eldorado, the Eisenhowers were moving on again. They were relative strangers in the desert community. Eisenhower had not known the California crowd well when president. But in choosing to spend winters in Palm Desert, they were still surrounding themselves with the familiar trappings of wealthy homes and exclusive clubs in a remote but desirable area.

Eldorado is located between the towns of Palm Desert and Indian Wells in California's Coachella Valley. It is one of the last stops before the wastes that stretch for two hundred miles between Palm Desert and Phoenix. By 1961, Eldorado, site of the thirteenth Ryder Cup, had become the most exclusive residential and golfing club in the Palm Springs–Palm Desert area. Like Augusta, Eldorado provides its guests with complete protection from the curious.

Eldorado is a place of leisure where men accustomed to clockwork punctuality and the relentless pressures of high finance linger. Golf is taken seriously, but played in a courtly, deliberate manner. The villas weaving in and around the golf course are compact, one-story dwellings, functional in design. None of the homes has more than two or three bedrooms. Kitchens open onto dining rooms. Golf carts, lawn equipment, golf clubs, and children's toys are housed in small garages, which border a system of cart paths that link the neighboring homes with the clubhouse. The sentry on guard at the gate once chauffeured for George Humphrey, Eisenhower's former secretary of the Treasury, and greeted everyone passing through the gates with a pleasant and well-founded familiarity. Eldorado is a place where no one worries about locking the car, the front door, or the garage — and where everything can be charged instantly with a club member signature.

As the pinnacle of desert society, the club, according to legend, refused membership to Walter Annenberg on the grounds that he was Jewish. Annenberg, the man once described by Bob Hope as someone who "when he talks, E. F. Hutton listens," settled defiantly behind the twenty-foot hedge surrounding his desert property and constructed the finest golf course in Palm Springs–Palm Desert for his private use. Eisenhower became Annenberg's bridge between his estate — "Sunnylands" — and Eldorado, becoming a regular house guest and golfing partner.

At Eldorado, Eisenhower mingled with a new group of lawyers and businessmen eager to play host to a former president. There, on the desert, Eisenhower found shelter from the demands made upon him in Pennsylvania by politicians and the news media. He could socialize and never fear anyone violating the ironclad code against revealing to the press the General's candid statements.

Eisenhower loved the desolate beauty and serenity of the desert. The Coachella Valley is an accident carved out of a patch of uninhabitable land at the foot of the Santa Rosa Mountains. To the east of the desert communities, sand and sagebrush stretch beyond sight. To the west, mountains stand between the desert, Riverside, and the Los Angeles basin. Northwest, snow-covered Mount San Jacinto dominates the valley, lending the impression of immensity to what really are foothills of barren volcanic rock. The valley stands over an immense aquifer that nourishes the land and provides the margin between luxury and an arid void. In the desert, Eisenhower felt secure as one feels secure in a large ship during a storm. He believed that the dry air and the sea-level temperatures would extend his life. The evenness of the desert climate contrasted with the fickle weather patterns of Gettysburg, and even Augusta, which in the past thirty years had experienced unheard-of cold and storms due to a slight shift of the Gulf Stream.

A visitor to the Coachella Valley cannot help but marvel over the transformation of the desert into groves of palm trees, lush green fairways, rows of low-lying, single-story dwellings, and the beachside atmosphere of the honky-tonk strip running along Highway 111 connecting the desert towns. Transplanted natives confidently predicted that the valley's prosperity knew no bounds and that eventually the kind of desert comfort enjoyed by the few would be available to anyone with a modest income.

Yet in the idyllic desert setting, Eisenhower was restless. When alone, he prowled the Eldorado cottage like a caged lion. Mamie's difficulties were not unlike those of any military wife accustomed to a husband being gone for long stretches of time. Even in Gettysburg, Mamie had never really regained the ability to pacify and entertain her husband. The difficult hours were the inactive ones. Mamie attempted to fill them by persuading Eisenhower's small staff located at the nearby Cochran Ranch in Indio to work Saturdays. "Take him off my hands," she often begged secretary Rusty Brown; "alone here he just goes wild."

One morning shortly after moving into his Eldorado home, Eisenhower listened to a challenge he could not refuse. His guest, Charles Jones of Richfield Oil, boasted that with an air rifle he happened to have with him, he could shoot a silver dollar off the silver service coffee urn at twenty-five paces. The two men paced off twenty-five steps;

Jones turned, fired, and scored a direct hit.

"Let me do it," Eisenhower growled. Eisenhower missed, and the BB-size pellet ricocheted skyward, knocking a small hole in an eighteen-inch strip of glass above the door leading to Mamie's bedroom. Inside, Mamie lay bound up in towels while a local masseuse rubbed her shoulders and back.

Granddad and Jones hid the rifle. Moments later Mamie appeared at the door wrapped in a bathrobe as the masseuse slipped past and out the front door.

"Darndest thing, Ike," she declared suspiciously. "The masseuse told me she couldn't rub too hard — little pieces of glass all over my back — now what do you suppose?"

At Eldorado, the friendship between Eisenhower and Freeman Gosden blossomed into an intimate partnership based on affection and trust. Gosden became Eisenhower's companion, golf starter, and link to the communities of Palm Desert, Palm Springs, Indian Wells, Rancho Mirage, Cathedral City, and Indio.

Although Gosden had met Eisenhower through Augusta National, he was an atypical man in the Eisenhower circle. Like Eisenhower and his friends, Gosden was restless, driven, and impatient. But he also was sentimental, naturally and easily moved

130

to tears, a person motivated by loyalty and small favors. Another difference between Gosden and Eisenhower's staid Augusta set was that he had achieved his start in vaudeville. By the 1930s he created and acted in the phenomenally successful radio program *Amos 'n Andy,* a gentle satire of black life. The program later moved to television, but by the 1960s, with the rise of the civil rights movement, *Amos 'n Andy* had vanished from the airwaves, recalled only reluctantly by its producers and writers.

As an entertainer, Gosden clung to associations many of Eisenhower's old friends felt were odious, specifically Frank Sinatra. He had befriended the young matinee idol during the 1940s. Once, when Gosden's eldest daughter lay in a hospital awaiting a major operation, Sinatra had responded to Gosden's urgent request to surprise the girl with a bedside visit. Sinatra serenaded her in her hospital room, an act Gosden credited with saving his daughter's life. A bust of Sinatra stood in Gosden's study in his Beverly Hills home. For years Gosden attempted to persuade Eisenhower to meet Sinatra. But Eisenhower refused for a variety of reasons: Sinatra's business ties; his lack of service in World War II; Eisenhower's schedule.

Indeed, Eisenhower's routine in the desert

was anything but leisurely. He habitually arose shortly after daybreak. On weekdays, Eisenhower drove ten miles from Eldorado to his office at the Cochran Ranch. He spent mornings editing and dictating notes for his memoir, answering correspondence, and receiving visitors. At noon he would return home for lunch and a nap. When possible, he played a round of golf in the afternoons. In the evenings the Eisenhowers met friends for dinner and bridge.

Granddad enjoyed acting as chef, often donning a tall white chef's hat. Just as he had at the White House when two grills were set up on the roof, Granddad grilled steaks and a variety of fowl. The pièce de résistance was his barbeque sauce, which he concocted with Sergeant Moaney:

Eisenhower's Barbeque Sauce
1/4 cup butter
1 no. 2 can tomatoes, sieved (2 cups)
1/4 cup vinegar
1 tbs. sugar
3 tsp. paprika
1 small onion, finely chopped
2 tsp. salt
2 tsp. chili powder
1 1/2 tsp. Worcestershire sauce

1/4 tsp. Tabasco sauce or more according to
taste
1 tsp. black pepper

Mix ingredients and simmer for about 15
minutes.

Use for basting meat or chicken, and serve
as sauce for it as well.

Makes enough for 5 pounds of meat (or
chicken).

On weekends, or when friends from out
of town were visiting, socializing began in
the mornings with a big breakfast of wheat
cakes, sausage, scrapple, coffee, juice, and
toast prepared by Eisenhower and Moaney.
Following breakfast, the crowd, dressed in
sweaters due to the early morning coolness,
would set out for a morning round of golf.
After golf, Eisenhower would retire for a
nap, then rise in mid-afternoon for some
light work or painting at the easel placed
near a sliding door looking out on the barbeque pit, and the eleventh fairway nearby.

Dinnertime conversation bored Eisenhower. With the clearing of the dessert
plates, he immediately led the way to the
bridge table. Evenings broke up by 10 P.M.
and Eisenhower was promptly in bed, reading a western until falling asleep.

Old age had not mellowed Eisenhower's competitive edge around a bridge table. His friends in the desert, unlike the Augusta crowd, were not students of contract bridge and, consequently, they maneuvered among themselves to avoid winding up at Eisenhower's table.

His most terrifying habit was "running the hand," a postmortem conducted on the play of every single card, delivered with the precision of a mathematical genius. Eisenhower claimed to be able to look at two tricks and deduce an opponent's entire hand from ace to six. Gosden recalls a sensation akin to panic when dinner ended and the assignment of bridge tables began, a tightening in the throat, a shortness of breath. He and the other guests would slip away discreetly to draw lots to determine who would play at Eisenhower's table. One night after dinner at Thunderbird, Gosden and businessman Paul Helms argued unpleasantly after Gosden had drawn a queen to Helms's four.

"I'm out," Helms insisted, grabbing Gosden by the arm.

"Paul, you drew a four," Gosden retorted sharply. Helms claimed vainly that he had outdrawn Gosden for the privilege to be excused, but there were witnesses. Bested,

Helms pleaded, "He makes me nervous."

"Paul," Gosden replied, "he makes everyone nervous."

As during the White House years, Eisenhower's favorite partner was General Alfred Gruenther, who actually enjoyed Eisenhower's company at a bridge table. Gruenther had a reputation in army circles for bridge prowess, a reputation that grew through the years like tales of the fish that got away. During the 1930s, while instructing at West Point, Gruenther occasionally refereed matches in New York City. With the passage of years, myth and reality grew up around the rumor that Gruenther invented several bridge stratagems, coached the greats, and defeated the great bridge master Charles Goren himself. Whatever Gruenther's real talents, he is remembered best for his singular ability to stand up to Eisenhower's ill humor and intolerance of ineptitude at the bridge table.

Gosden recalled a heated game one night in which the Gruenther-Eisenhower team was set two tricks in a game contract. Eisenhower sat back in his chair, removed his glasses, and blearily, almost searchingly, studied Gruenther for clues about what he had overlooked. "What did I do wrong, Al?" he finally asked. Gruenther sat expressionless across the table and motioned to an opponent to start dealing the hand. Without returning Eisenhower's gaze, Gruenther replied evenly: "Everything."

Gruenther's hold on Eisenhower went beyond bridge. Desert friend Justin Dart, chairman of Dart Industries, recalled the afternoon he and Eisenhower shared a golf cart. On the eleventh hole, as they waited for a group in front of them to move away, Dart asked, "Mr. President, if you could put your finger on one man and name him president, who would it be?"

"Al Gruenther."

"That's pretty fast, sir," Dart observed.

"You asked me, didn't you?" Eisenhower replied.

The two men discussed Gruenther's forthcoming retirement as president of the American Red Cross. Gruenther had reached sixty-five, the maximum age, and was looking for something to do.

"He ought to do something productive," said Dart.

"He's the brightest man I know," Eisenhower replied.

"Well, that too is a pretty high compliment. Do you think he would fit on our board?"

"Go get him."

Dart got him.

Granddad's thirst for company and activity often drove Mamie to distraction. She was increasingly grateful to have Freeman Gosden in the vicinity, a man whose restless disposition matched her husband's. Everywhere the two went, legions of admirers, autograph seekers, and the curious followed. Eisenhower never minded the autograph requests and the hand shaking. The two men spent off hours touring neighborhood grocery stores, where Eisenhower loved to shop for beef. As a boy, he had been taught to be discerning when purchasing meat, to take the trouble to know the butcher, to insist on the proper cuts and treatment of beef. Now, running an Angus farm, Eisenhower had become an expert on cattle. Somewhat out of place in the modular efficiency of nearby supermarkets, his habit of lingering by the butcher's counter brought the brisk pace of shopping to a standstill. His single concession to the mass-marketing techniques of chain food stores occurred while paying the bill. With a twinkle, he always warned the checkout girl that if she forgot the trading stamps, "Mamie will make me come back!"

Freeman and Ike especially enjoyed visiting the Desert Art Museum located in nearby Palm Springs. As an amateur painter since his days as president of Columbia University, Eisenhower particularly enjoyed painting landscapes. Desert art, with its bright colors and luster, fascinated him.

A calming influence on Eisenhower was the ever-present George Allen, who arrived for a visit lasting several weeks. George soon felt exhausted. Mamie recalled Ike and Freeman's attempt to arouse Allen after a Moaney-Eisenhower breakfast for a trip downtown to process Freeman's photographs, and to see if strawberries were in stock. That morning, Allen was content to sit, nap, and let breakfast settle. Before he could reply to their invitation, Granddad and Freeman stood near the entrance awaiting the car to transport them away. George remained immobile. Mamie thought to herself, "Why that old man George will live forever."

Another calming influence on Ike was Mamie's uncle, Joel Carlson, who was a regular guest during their winter visits. Joel was born near Mamie's birthplace in Boone, Iowa, in 1880. He went to work at an early age for the local bank, where he began as a teller. In middle age, Joel took an interest in literature and became a self-taught scholar on the subject of Abraham Lincoln. At the age of fifty, during the height of the Depression, Joel decided to marry. Several years later, he retired from the bank as a vice president with a gold watch given to him as a token for his long years of service. During Eisenhower's presidency, Joel, now a widower, was a frequent guest at the White House.

Granddad was fond of Joel. Joel knew from thirty years of retirement how to entertain himself and was a most unobtrusive house guest. His straitlaced ideas befit his appearance, which remarkably resembled the male subject of the famous painting *American Gothic.* Joel enjoyed outings to the supermarket to shop for beef with Eisenhower and an occasional walk.

At the desert house he provided companionship for Mamie. He spent mornings and afternoons reading in the living room near Granddad's easel overlooking the eleventh fairway. Mamie habitually set up her solitaire game at the card table next to his easy chair. The noise of the cards was too faint to bother Joel, who was slightly deaf. Mamie regarded Joel as a link to her mother and Boone, and enjoyed having him nearby, though Joel rarely had much to say. Granddad always made a point of asking Joel to join in any activity he had going. Joel would matter-of-factly reply that he preferred reading. Whether eating alone or with Granddad and Mamie, at mealtime Joel always wore a coat and tie.

Joel was one of the few people able to impose his personal schedule on Eisenhower. He insisted on breakfast at 7:30. Joel then took a Coca-Cola at 10:45. Lunch was at 1:00 P.M. and another Coca-Cola at 3:00. At 6:00 P.M. sharp, Joel ate dinner, and at 9:00 P.M., without a minute's deviation, Joel retired to bed, regardless of whatever activity the Eisenhowers had going on. Joel lived by the tick of the clock, and for the days of his visits, Eisenhower's restless energy was tempered by Joel's emphasis on a steady and healthy routine.

I once asked Mamie if Granddad's compulsive restlessness, his habit of maintaining company around the clock, revealed a weakness, perhaps a fear of being alone, or a nonexistent inner life.

"Well, I don't know," she replied. "Wouldn't you guess? After the White House, I built him a perfectly wonderful studio for painting upstairs in the attic on the farm, and would he touch it?" she asked rhetorically. "Why no such thing — it just gathered dust. He had to sit downstairs where he could poke his nose into everything, just like at Marnes La Coquette [Eisenhower's residence during his years as NATO commander] when he used to hide behind that paintbrush and listen to what all the gals were saying in the next room."

My question unanswered, I asked her if she felt she had really known Dwight Eisenhower. She paused. "I'm not sure anyone did."

CORDIALITY

Despite strong differences, Eisenhower and Kennedy had managed to remain on polite terms throughout 1961. Kennedy wrote and thanked Eisenhower for his various statements condemning right-wing extremism. He also complimented Eisenhower's interview in *Life* magazine and his article in the *Saturday Evening Post* that had endorsed Kennedy's handling of the construction of the Berlin Wall by the Soviets. As the year drew to a close, the two enjoyed a burst of intimacy. Kennedy wrote Eisenhower on December 13, 1961, informing him that he had ordered John McCone to give him a thorough briefing on the international situation. McCone arrived in the desert several days after Christmas bearing a box of golf balls engraved with the presidential seal and a handwritten note from the President that read:

Dear General:
I received these golf balls for Christmas, but regrettably, because of my back, I cannot use them for many months. You are the only other golfer I know entitled to them — and I send them with my best wishes.

Cordially,
JF Kennedy

But the cordiality would soon be strained. Nineteen sixty-two was an election year. John Kennedy's confidence in his ability to handle the presidency was growing, as was Eisenhower's unease about Kennedy's policies and his skill in promoting them. Small incidents chipped away at Eisenhower's inclination to be silent.

Eisenhower, as owner of his presidential materials, reasoned that he was entitled to protection from a succeeding administration using his papers for partisan advantage. The Kennedy administration had no quarrel with this view, doubtlessly anxious to protect its own materials in the future. Consequently, Kennedy aides had to request permission to look at documents. On

January 18, 1962, a staff officer assigned to the office of International Security Affairs (ISA) under Robert McNamara called my father in Gettysburg wanting to inspect Eisenhower's file concerning Douglas Dillon's discussions with French officials at the time of the Suez affair, which had triggered a crisis in U.S.-French relations. Specifically the aide sought information about contemplated joint American-French action to counter Khrushchev's blustering threats to unleash atomic missiles against Britain and France, whose forces had invaded Egypt. Dillon had been the ambassador in Paris in 1956 and now served as Kennedy's secretary of the Treasury. Dillon's recollection of the American-French conversations differed sharply from the version given by Gaullist officials. The discrepancy, explained the aide, was causing "misapprehension." In essence, Dillon was seeking through ISA access to his own memoranda written while serving Eisenhower.

Dad immediately telephoned Granddad in Palm Desert about the request. Dad told him that since he knew the ISA official personally, he suspected the administration was trying to gain access informally rather than going through proper channels. Eisenhower was furious. The question, in his view, was one of principle. Dillon's memo belonged among Eisenhower's papers. Requests for access to Eisenhower's papers would not flow from junior staff member to junior staff member, but from McNamara to himself, or "there will be no possibility of cooperation." The request was dropped.

Several weeks later, Bill Ewald called Palm Desert from the Gettysburg offices with the news that a controversy had developed around allegations in Nixon's newly published memoir, *Six Crises*, being serialized in *Life*. Nixon had revealed the story of Kennedy's alleged "abuse" of the confidential information Kennedy had received during the 1960 campaign from a briefing by then-CIA director Allen Dulles about plans for an invasion of Cuba. Nixon claimed that Kennedy in the fourth debate advocated an invasion knowing one was planned — and that Nixon would have to remain silent on the matter before the television audience. Kennedy thus gained unfairly by the misimpression that Nixon was soft on Castro. Moments before Ewald's call, the White House, through Press Secretary Pierre Salinger, issued a statement denying that Kennedy had been briefed by Allen Dulles as alleged. But Nixon was standing by his version of the story.

Eisenhower, anxious to avoid embarrassing the Nixon campaign for governor of California, directed Ewald to comb the files for evidence Kennedy had been briefed. Dad called Gordon Gray to ask whether the NSC 5412 group had known of the content of the Kennedy brief. Gray replied no, and warned Dad that Dulles had just written an article for the *Washington Post* that day vindicating Kennedy's claim that he had not learned of the planning until after the election.

The files located by the office staff revealed nothing conclusive. There was, however, a postconvention telegram from Eisenhower to Kennedy offering the briefing, and a Dulles memorandum dated August 3, 1960, about his conversations with Kennedy and Johnson in which he noted: "Both Democratic candidates showed great interest in Cuba in their July 23, 28 briefings."

Eisenhower remembered ordering Allen Dulles to brief Kennedy on all matters Nixon was informed about as vice president, and specifically about Cuba. If Dulles's article was accurate, Dulles had not followed orders. By the same token, Eisenhower was irritated that his former vice president had not consulted Dulles before publication of *Six Crises* to confirm or deny the briefing. Eisenhower suspected Dulles of fabrications, but Dulles, recently fired by Kennedy, seemingly had no motive to distort the truth in favor of Kennedy.

Eisenhower called Dulles and the two men spoke at length. Dulles vigorously stood by his *Post* article. Moments later, Jerry Persons, Eisenhower's former chief of staff and a Nixon ally, called expressing "skepticism" about Dulles's version, and warned Eisenhower not to say anything damaging about Nixon. Former interior secretary Fred Seaton called next, claiming that he remembered Dulles saying he had briefed Kennedy on Cuba at the time of the fourth debate. Eisenhower received word that John McCone, Kennedy's director of the CIA, was saying that Dulles had "categorically" told him that Kennedy had been briefed. Finally, Eisenhower received a call from Dulles reporting that Salinger and the White House were "eager to drop the matter."

In the end, Eisenhower approved Nixon's release of a statement clarifying his claim in *Six Crises:* "President Eisenhower had given instructions that in regard to U.S. intelligence activity abroad, Senator Kennedy was to be as fully briefed on our foreign problems as I was." In response, Kennedy announced at a press conference that he would not comment on the allegation and considered the matter closed.

That winter, Eisenhower in Palm Desert and Nixon in Los Angeles found themselves neighbors. After New Year's, Pat and Dick Nixon, with their teenage daughters, Tricia and Julie, were weekend visitors. Mamie took the girls for ice cream and shopping while the men played golf and discussed politics. Months before, the former vice president had become a member of the exclusive hole-in-one club, which had prompted the General to write him:

Dear Dick,

You ought to know that I am taking all the credit allowable for your hole in one. I go around telling people that my game at Burning Tree the other day inspired you.

Incidentally, from the publicity in the Eastern papers (including editorials) I would venture that a hole in one is roughly equivalent, publicity-wise, to a dozen articles on the Berlin situation. It occurs to me that for eight years we went about our politicking entirely the wrong way.

With warm regard — and congratulations!

As ever,
D.E.

On the afternoon of February 20, 1962, John Glenn became the first American to orbit the earth. Dwight Eisenhower, Freeman Gosden, "Slats" Slater, and several friends decided to play golf at Eldorado. Excited about Glenn's bold undertaking aboard *Friendship 7,* before leaving his cottage Eisenhower had fastened a small transistor radio to a metal bar supporting the canopy over his golf cart to enable the foursome to listen to the voice of mission control during the takeoff and splashdown. Glenn's capsule reentered the earth's atmosphere as the Eisenhower foursome hit second shots on Eldorado's tenth hole.

As Eisenhower hovered around the radio, he noted sadly that nothing had been said about his administration. The coverage implicitly treated this latest bold demonstration of American technological might as an accomplishment of the Kennedy administration. Eisenhower was visibly disappointed.

The oversight was understandable since

space had become a Kennedy issue, and not without justification. Earlier than most politicians, John Kennedy had grasped the sheer artistry and adventure of space exploration. He had eloquently pledged before Congress to put a man on the moon by the end of the decade. He also had identified his administration with the daringness that characterized Glenn's mission. In contrast, in an effort to stem panic after Sputnik, Eisenhower had given less emphasis to space. He had approved the production of Atlas missiles and other rockets that made space exploration possible, and had approved the Mercury manned-flight program and selection of the first team of astronauts. But privately, he had disparaged the "space-race" mentality and authorized White House chief of staff Sherman Adams's famous crack at the "outer space basketball" mind-set among congressional panic mongers who clamored for immediate action after Sputnik. While reviewing the administration request for NASA funds in his final budget, Eisenhower had quipped wistfully to his budget director, Maurice Stans, that had he been a dictator, there "would have been no manned space program, period."

Eisenhower's disappointment that afternoon was passing, more apparent than real.

He could be excused for momentary regret about being overlooked in one of the most stirring events of the decade, and by the politics practiced by the Kennedy administration in not acknowledging the space progress achieved during Eisenhower's term. But Kennedy, envisioning himself a champion of space, was not eager to share the laurels.

The Glenn mission triggered a more somber mood at dinner and the bridge tables that night. For the first time since leaving office, Eisenhower opened the topic of his farewell remarks. Slater's diary reports:

He is still terribly unhappy about what he considered careless spending and the complete lack of interest in the soundness of the dollar and the disregard for what inflation will do to the savers. He has added concern of the continuing build-up of the military, the space scientists and armament industries. This combination can be so powerful and the military machine so big that it just has to be used.

Eisenhower talked about the defense industry advertisements he had seen in several magazines promoting missiles, aircraft, tanks, and small weapons, most manufactured under government contracts. "It all leads people to a mistaken view that missiles are what this country is all about," he continued. Eisenhower's comments provoked an argument among his friends, some of whom had silently questioned the motive and wisdom of his farewell address.

By now, there were many critics of Eisenhower's farewell address and its warnings against the "military industrial complex." Some saw it as a case of sour grapes for having been bested in 1960 on the Kennedy claim of a "missile gap" with the Soviet Union, which had pervaded the election year. Some assumed that Eisenhower's warning had been inserted conspiratorially by quick-witted advisers trying to use him. But until now, none of the criticism had been discussed within his earshot. Suddenly the suppressed misgivings emerged.

Slater, an ambulance driver on the western front in World War I, argued that war is cyclical, occurring at intervals of twenty to thirty years. "I can't believe that I am fortunate enough to have seen the last great conflict, that war stopped for all time in 1945." He added that if history proved true to its pattern, "the United States had better be prepared."

Eisenhower would not accept Slater's premise that wars were a natural and recurring feature of history, and replied that he hoped Slater was wrong. The discussion lasted into the evening. No one at dinner had the temerity to point out the contradiction in Eisenhower's visible sense of disappointment that afternoon on the golf course, and his lecture at dinner about the budget-busting demands of the military and the space race with the Soviets.

The discussion did make an impression. Eisenhower later developed a kind of split personality about the most controversial speech of his life. Among business friends and military colleagues, Eisenhower became defensive and even self-critical about his speech. To Lucius Clay, Eisenhower conceded that his ideas were "best expressed by someone without a military background," perhaps a Churchill or Adlai Stevenson, "someone more eloquent, more cogent who would not lend the dark connotation of experience." His own background had "given the speech a more ominous tone than intended." Yet with others, Eisenhower was assured and precise about his meaning, and confident that the idea required forceful expression.

Committing his view on the farewell address to history in the second volume of White House memoirs, *Waging Peace,* Eisenhower once again cited the dangers posed by the need to maintain large military forces in peacetime, and the possibility that public policy could become "captive of a scientific-technological elite." Cloaked in the mantle of national security, special interests could override "the convictions of responsible officials who were determined to have a defense structure of adequate size but are equally determined that it shall not grow beyond that level." He continued: "I could think of no better way to emphasize this than to include a sobering message in what might otherwise have been a farewell of pleasantries."

Eisenhower would devote significant attention in his second memoir to his views on space. He did not oppose space exploration, just the emphasis on a space race. In 1965, Eisenhower would be quizzed by astronaut-in-training Major Frank Borman about his criticism of manned space projects. In reply, Eisenhower explained:

What I have criticized about the current space program is the concept under which it was drastically revised and expanded after the Bay of Pigs fiasco. . . . It immediately took one single project or experiment out of a thoughtfully planned and continuing program involving communications, meteorology, reconnaissance and future military and scientific benefits and gave the highest priority — unprofitable in my opinion — to a race, in other words, a stunt.

Several weeks later, Eisenhower and Kennedy met at Palm Desert. The President, in California for a series of political appearances on behalf of Pat Brown, Richard Nixon's gubernatorial opponent, was spending the weekend at the nearby Palm Springs home of his brother-in-law actor Peter Lawford. Their meeting was pleasant. Eisenhower made several requests of Kennedy, including a promotion for Colonel Schulz, his trusted and efficient chief of staff. They avoided discussing the space race, the Nixon-Dulles incident, or Kennedy's appearance in California against Nixon. Following their Palm Desert meeting, the two men went through the motions of denying their mutual wariness, which was now clear to both men. In his letter of thanks to Kennedy for swift compliance with his personnel requests, Eisenhower added:

One other thing: while it is of course well known that in the domestic field there are governmental proposals and programs concerning which you and I do not agree, I assure you that my political views, though strongly held and sometime vigorously expressed, contain nothing of personal animus on my part. Any allegation to the contrary that may come to your ears — and I have heard that such a one has — is either untrue or highly exaggerated and would I hope be wholly ignored. I am confident that anyone in your position finds — certainly this is my own experience — that some individuals will never hesitate to distort or falsify in striving for a feeling of self-importance in the limelight that plays about the Presidency.

With best wishes,
Respectfully
Dwight D. Eisenhower

Kennedy replied on May 17:

Dear General:
  As you perhaps know, I have been a great admirer of yours since our first meeting in Frankfurt, in 1945, when I accompanied Secretary Forrestal on a trip to Europe. I agree with your view concerning

the differences that could easily arise between us, and will certainly do everything in my power to prevent any misunderstandings of thought, actions or motive from eroding our association. I fully understand that there will be differences on some matters, especially on domestic issues, and at the same time, feel that in matters of national concern, especially in foreign affairs, we will see eye to eye. . . . With best wishes and warm regards — and those of long standing.

Sincerely,
JF Kennedy

VAN BUREN?

By now, as the Eisenhowers moved back to Gettysburg, it was becoming plain to all that the Kennedy administration, having passed through a year of trials, was hitting stride, and that the Republicans would be facing a real challenge in the fall elections.

In the summer of 1961, Bennett Cerf, Random House publisher, had visited Eisenhower in Gettysburg to win his endorsement of a book about Eisenhower's life. The former president had erupted with a sermon. Pronouncing the virtue of avoiding hysteria in governmental matters, citing Sputnik as an instance when political immaturity had bred demands for crippling waste in federal spending, and provoked by the crisis rhetoric of the Kennedy administration, Eisenhower declared: "We should plan our security, defend our rights, and live with the situation in the world — no Napoleonic brooding, or impulse. Panicky policies condemn people to live in apprehension, not serenity which is their traditional birthright."

From time to time, Eisenhower met with his former press secretary James Hagerty, now vice president of ABC News. In one meeting, they discussed their refusal to use television to exploit the theatrics surrounding presidential decisions. Eisenhower said he had been informed by Bryce Harlow, his former chief of congressional relations, that the Kennedy people had "no scruples about television at all — they are even willing to go on television appearances that have commercials!" he exclaimed.

Eisenhower and Hagerty discussed a number of complaints circulating about the Kennedy administration's use of the media. Hagerty told Eisenhower that the Knight papers, Garnett Horner of the *Washington Star,* and others were being denied access because they were "unfriendly papers."

Eisenhower was amazed. "Then why

haven't they attacked Kennedy personally?"

Hagerty cited the growing influence of television, Kennedy's understanding of the medium, and his belief he could use it effectively. And, Hagerty added, just as the importance of remaining on good terms with television journalists grew, the importance of good relations with the print media journalists had diminished.

Hagerty related that he had just spent an entire day in the Oval Office, taping the President going about his job.

"What about equal time?" Eisenhower asked.

"It hasn't been requested yet," Hagerty replied. "Anyway, all the Republicans have are Dirksen and Halleck." He added, "Kennedy is good at selling himself."

"Perhaps we were unimaginative," Eisenhower replied ruefully.

"No," Hagerty replied reassuringly, "there is a great danger that Kennedy will lick himself by trading so heavily on the presidency and corrupting the office."

Eisenhower lit up. "Yes, like that statement that he'd be his own secretary of state and do everything himself — shows his complete unawareness of the job."

But Kennedy was gaining ground, and as he did, assessments of the Eisenhower presidency suffered accordingly. In the company of his book staff, Eisenhower revealed disappointment about the contemporary verdict among historians that his presidency would not rank high in history. Later that summer, an article would appear in the *New York Times Magazine* reporting the results of a poll taken by Harvard professor Arthur Schlesinger, Sr., that ranked presidents in order of greatness. Eisenhower stood twenty-eighth on the list out of thirty-three.

The poll was hardly objective. It was conducted by the father of Kennedy's assistant and official historian, Arthur Schlesinger, Jr., and at a time when the strong leadership qualities so vaunted about Kennedy dominated assessments of presidents. Eisenhower was more a target of this poll than a subject. Indeed, the wide publicity that attended the story was laden with partisan overtones. Revealingly, John Kennedy's first reaction to the poll, as described by Arthur Schlesinger, Jr., in *A Thousand Days,* centered on its implications about Eisenhower. "He was greatly pleased that Truman made the near great class," Schlesinger wrote. "He was also interested that Eisenhower rated only twenty-eighth, near the bottom of the 'average' category.

He said, 'At first I thought it was too bad that Ike was in Europe and would miss the article, but then I decided that some conscientious friend would send him a copy.' "

Later Kennedy, jokingly or half jokingly, blamed Eisenhower's vigorous entry into the 1962 congressional campaign on the historians' ratings. "Eisenhower has been going along for years basking in the glow of the applause he has always had. Then he saw the poll and realized how he stood before the cold eye of history — way below Truman; even below Hoover. Now he's mad to save his reputation."

Eisenhower might have simply discounted the poll as partisan. But instead he would take it to heart and, in my father's words, "The old man was wounded by the thing." Eisenhower's sober self-appraisal was that owing to the lack of war during his tenure and his refusal to be stampeded into sweeping social reform amid the first rumblings of the civil rights revolution, he would not be ranked high by historians. In 1955, while recuperating from his heart attack at Fitzsimmons Army Hospital in Colorado, he wistfully had contemplated the odds against a second term. "I suppose this means I'll be Martin Van Buren — one term, no war, no greatness." Eisenhower had gone on to serve two terms, but his self-assessment stood. He had understood his responsibility in the White House to be, in addition to making correct decisions and administering the government, one of defusing the atmosphere of crisis that had pervaded national politics since 1932. He felt strongly that he had been successful.

RETURN TO EUROPE

The family spent May and June in preparation for our trip to Europe. In late July of 1962, Granddad would address the World Confederation of Organizations of the Teaching Profession in Stockholm. He decided to extend his trip to Denmark, Germany, France, England, Scotland, and Ireland, places he had been eager to revisit as a private citizen. My parents, assured this trip would be relaxed, unlike the proposed Soviet state visit in 1960, had given permission for my sister Anne and me to accompany our grandparents.

I had little desire to go. I was scheduled to enter boarding school that fall and wanted to spend the remaining days I had before school with friends in Gettysburg. The decision to go to Europe involved complications for my grandparents, too. They wanted to invite a couple to travel along to fill the free time not taken up by Eisenhower's semi-official appearances and press conferences. The choice boiled down to inviting Freeman Gosden, his engaging wife, Jane, and their twelve-year-old son, Craig, or his old friends George and Mary Allen. Granddad chose the Gosdens, primarily because their son would be a companion for Anne and me. Joyce Hall, founder of Hallmark Cards and affiliated with People to People International, would also be along for part of the trip with his granddaughter Libby, a companion for Anne. I vaguely remember an awkward encounter between Granddad and George Allen near the barbeque pit that spring in Gettysburg. Granddad, wearing his tall white chef's hat while flipping steaks over the coals, spoke apologetically in low tones. He seemed uncharacteristically evasive and tentative. George seemed downcast.

Their relationship had changed. Allen had lost much heart and good cheer since his onetime friend Truman, in response to the republication of George's book *Presidents Who Have Known Me* with an added glowing chapter about Ike, had cracked Allen "would do anything to suck in." Allen had health problems and was ending his involvement with the Eisenhower farms. Meanwhile, Freeman Gosden had become a close friend and important to Eisenhower in his new life on the desert. Freeman had the energy for a trip that would involve dozens of diplomatic receptions and public events.

Our trip to Europe would entail all of those things, and in a sense it would take us back to the splendor of the White House days, which Anne and I assumed were behind us forever. Our thirty-eight days in Europe would be reminiscent of times when my sisters and I had roamed the state rooms of the executive mansion and been on call to greet de Gaulle, Churchill, Montgomery, Khrushchev, Nehru, and Queen Elizabeth, among many other world leaders. In fact, the sights and sounds of our tour in 1962 would be at times even more impressive than the White House as Granddad's itinerary took us on a journey through the European capitals and countryside where his armies had achieved victory in World War II. To ensure we would remember the trip, Anne and I were given journals that we were to update nightly with summaries of our day.

It all began on July 18 at 11:30 with an exciting sea voyage. Because Mamie would not fly, we traveled to Europe aboard *Queen Elizabeth II* with plans to return aboard the SS *United States.* The voyage to Europe was elegant and exciting. Accompanied by personal staff including the Moaneys, we traveled in first-class suites. The ship's five-day course was along a well-traveled shipping lane and almost hourly we hailed a passing vessel on the high Atlantic. Nearing France, we encountered summer storms of the kind that had plagued the Normandy landings eighteen years earlier.

The children spent mornings and afternoons together playing Ping-Pong, roaming over the broad decks, or playing hardball under the ship's stacks topside. The *Queen Elizabeth* stocked first-run movies like *West Side Story* and *Rear Window*. We saw previews of Darryl Zanuck's *The Longest Day*, based on Cornelius Ryan's account of the Normandy invasion. The blockbuster film would tell the story of D-Day at all levels, command and troop, and focus on the human-interest aspect of the great invasion. Zanuck had offered Granddad a feature role in the film playing himself, but Granddad had declined, even finding it impossible to sit through the film after it was released that fall. When he went to see the movie with Mamie, minutes into the show, Granddad leaned over and whispered that he wanted to leave.

"Ike, you can't do that," Mamie scolded.

"The hell I can't," he whispered in reply. After a pause, Granddad drew himself up and walked out.

Years later, I asked Mamie what it was that Granddad could have possibly disliked about *The Longest Day*.

"Oh you know," she replied, "literary license."

Each night, the Eisenhower and Gosden families gathered for dinner in the mezzanine dining room. We ate under chandeliers, serenaded by a band and entertained by the ship's captain with sea stories about his years with the Cunard line. After dinner we roamed the ship again, wandering out onto the deck for fresh air in search of people our age while the older folks retired to a sitting room that linked the suite Granddad and I occupied to the one Mamie and Anne shared. The grandparents retired early, and at bedtime I had to undress in the dark while Granddad slept several feet away.

Arriving in Cherbourg on July 23, we boarded a special train car for a slow rail tour of the Normandy area en route to Copenhagen by way of Paris, Namur, Liège, Aachen, Bremen, and Flensburg, for the first round of embassy dinners and receptions. Usually the most vivid glimpses the children caught of the ceremonial and official aspects of the trip were from aboard the train, where our departures and arrivals were met by huge crowds.

Every detail of the semi-official trip was painstakingly planned. Typed schedules were distributed to members of the traveling party daily. For instance, forty-eight hours before our arrival in Stockholm, we were given the following memorandum:

The train from Copenhagen will be stopped at Central Station, Stockholm, so that the exit from the General's private car is directly opposite the Royal Entrance. . . .

Press photographers will cover the arrival on the platform, but it is not anticipated that the General will make a Statement or reply to newsmen's queries on the platform where formalities will be limited to brief introductions.

It is suggested that the General and his party together with the welcoming officials move directly through the corridor of the Royal Entrance to a furnished reception room at the further end of the corridor. Here the General will sit and meet the press briefly with an informal statement and replies to questions.

Seats will be provided near General Eisenhower for Mrs. Eisenhower and the two Eisenhower grandchildren. It is anticipated that radio and TV will be there and will expect to cover this brief meeting with the press. . . .

At the Grand Hotel the General will proceed through a revolving door, up a few steps and across the lobby obliquely to the left to a waiting elevator.

At the first floor the General will leave the elevator, proceeding directly across the hall to his suite.

Room Assignments — Grand Hotel

Enter thru 118 for
116 — General Eisenhower and David
119 — Mrs. Eisenhower and Anne
122 — Sergeant Moaney and Mrs. Moaney
125 — General and Mrs. Schulz [newly promoted Brigadier General Schulz was in charge of all arrangements]
218 — Mr. and Mrs. Gosden . . .

The thirty-eight days abroad made me understand in a new way that Granddad was a world figure. Of course, I had known Granddad was important ever since the 1952 presidential campaign, when I was four years old. At that time I called my grandparents "Ike" and "Mimi." All of a sudden, my parents explained to me that I could no longer call my grandfather "Ike" since it was not fitting for a man about to be elected president of the United States. From then on, I was to address him as "Granddad." In grade school, being the grandson of the President made me special in every class. But most of my classmates had fathers who had served in the war, and so Granddad's military background seemed less unusual. Granddad did not discuss his war experiences around his grandchildren. I learned what I knew from books in his library and documentaries I had seen on television. On the voyage over, Joyce Hall told Anne, Libby, Craig Gosden, and me that Granddad was a hero in Europe because of the war and had an important role to play in strengthening international exchanges. In fact, he added, Granddad held "the key to international peace."

Thoughts of the war proved inescapable. Normandy, Paris, Cologne, and London all bore visible marks of the conflict. Seeing serene, prosperous Copenhagen and marveling at Hans Christian Andersen's Little Mermaid statue at the mouth of the harbor reminded me of the summer of 1958 working at the farm and of Chief West's elderly Danish mother-in-law and her story of how much her country had suffered during the war. One night she had come up to my room to talk. She knew I had undertaken the project of reading the Old and New Testament in the family Bible given to me at Christmas. Deeply religious, she talked to me of the scriptures, and about her native Denmark and a time so horrifying that youngsters born since the war would never fully understand the pain of her homeland under Nazi occupation.

On the day the Nazis occupied Copenhagen, she told me, without warning the citizens of the city had awakened to the noise of the Luftwaffe. By mid-morning, the skies were dark with German planes, like an approaching cloud of locusts. The radio announced that the king of Denmark was permitting German occupation without a fight in order to save the country from needless destruction. She saw the terrible sight of the Nazi flag being hoisted at the entrance of several buildings in the city, signaling five long years of torment by the German secret police. People my age, she said, could never really appreciate what it was to cheer the arrival of the liberating Allied armies. All this would be forgotten, she told me, including what Supreme Commander Dwight Eisenhower had meant to the people of Europe.

From Copenhagen, we traveled by train to Stockholm so that Granddad could fulfill the main purpose of the trip, his address before the World Confederation of teachers. Before arriving in Sweden, he issued a statement qualifying a well-publicized remark that he had made two years earlier at a political fund-raiser in Chicago. Having lambasted Sweden's social welfare system as an example of decadence spawned by dependence on a centralized bureaucracy, Eisenhower now regretted any implication that he had criticized the "social security condition in Sweden."

Granddad's topic at the conference was not the war but its aftermath, the Cold War and how it could be ended. In his speech, he proposed "a school of global understanding" to provide a forum for testing communism versus Western ideas. The school would gather two to three thousand international students under the sponsorship of the United Nations to study world problems "with total objectivity." As president, he had advanced similar ideas, which reflected his unbounded faith in the manifest superiority of the American system and the vital importance of the free exchange of information in resolving the Cold War. Granddad's idea was that the free flow of information would induce the communists to change from within. He told the delegates:

I am before you solely as a witness to and a participant in the affairs of the world during a half century.

That period has been marked by tempest and turmoil, ravaging wars, revolutionary change and violent reaction; and by instances of appalling corruption of national purposes and inhuman abuse of human beings. At times respect for moral law has seemed to disappear from vast areas of the earth.

There is, therefore, excuse for those who label this period the most shocking, the most brutal in modern history.

In the same years, however, great tidal waves of new knowledge have washed away forever plagues and evils that had scourged mankind through many centuries. New machines and devices of science and technology have erased physical barriers and reduced the vast distances that once separated men and nations.

One of the greatest advances made

during this era has been the world's recognition that education is the birthright of every individual; independence, of every nation; peace, of mankind. . . .

There is, then, ample justification for those, not enshrouded in pessimism, who would term these recent decades the prelude to a golden age. I am one of them.

The delegates stood and gave him a warm ovation at the conclusion of his remarks.

Following Granddad's address in Stockholm, the train pushed on to Sofiero, the Swedish royal summer palace located at the southern tip of Sweden near the town of Helsingborg. After lunch, Queen Louise and King Gustav VI led us on a tour of the grounds. At 3 P.M., under a particularly tight schedule, the Eisenhower party formed up in a rapid motorcade to drive to the ferry that would transport us to Copenhagen for an embassy reception at six and another round of dinners.

In the car Mamie nearly fainted upon discovering that one of her earrings was missing, presumably dropped somewhere on the vast acreage of lawn and gardens surrounding the palace. Granddad dispatched General Schulz back to inform the palace of the missing earring, with instructions to hurry.

Schulz apparently interpreted the order to mean "find the earring." For forty-five minutes, he stained his brigadier general uniform searching the palace grounds. Meanwhile, for an hour we sat aimlessly on the train car mounted aboard the ferry waiting for Schulz to return. As Granddad paced the dining car, he grew angrier by the minute. Next to a lack of punctuality, he fumed, what he disliked most was wasting time, and Schulz, usually the perfect aide, was "wasting time" looking for the earring. From a corner of the car came a relieved "my goodness." Mamie had just found the earring in her purse.

Schulz missed the ferry and caught up with the car on the Danish side of the border sometime later. Breathless and harried, he arrived aboard, upset by his failure to locate the earring. His expression soon froze into consternation at the "good news" that the earring had been located. Granddad calmly asked us to leave the dining compartment so he could have a "prayer meeting" with Schulz. We left as Schulz passed by us, breathing heavily. Several minutes later, he emerged ashen, hands trembling, face motionless.

"Come on in," Granddad waved cheerfully to all of us clustered outside the door. With the day's frustration vented, Granddad settled back in an easy chair to listen to one of Freeman's many funny stories as the train rolled on toward Copenhagen.

Germany was the most interesting stop on the trip and again, memories of the war predominated. From 1942 to 1945, Allied bombers had pounded German cities and industry. Eisenhower had commanded the conquering armies that had crushed the German army in the west, and for six months had governed the American zone in Germany with the powers of a dictator, ruthlessly weeding out Nazi elements from positions of influence in government, business, and finance.

In the years since, Eisenhower's relations with the German government had become friendlier. As NATO commander, he had repeatedly visited West Germany — the country had been divided in two following the war — readying the nation for entrance into the NATO alliance. He also had visited the West German capital Bonn as president in the fall of 1959 and had received a tumultuous popular reception from hundreds of thousands flooding the streets.

But as we made our way to the border

crossing the night of August 1, there was tension aboard the train. I wondered what to expect in Germany in the morning. At dawn on the 2nd, tens of thousands of cheering well-wishers greeted the Eisenhower train near Cologne station. Our motorcade passed through immense crowds lining the route to the Excelsior Hotel Ernst, near Cologne's famed cathedral, one of the few structures in the city that had survived the massive bombing.

By mid-morning we were installed in the hotel. In the square below, thousands had gathered under the hotel balcony chanting "We like Ike" with a distinctly German accent. As I noted in my diary, the cheering, studded by the pealing of the cathedral bells, created a thunderous and exhilarating sound. At nightfall, after we returned from a private dinner with West German chancellor Konrad Adenauer, the crowds and chants grew louder.

In the penthouse suite, Granddad was reluctant to greet the crowd. "Can't start this," he said. Then, around eleven o'clock, he asked Mamie to cover her shoulders with a shawl to protect herself from the coolness of the evening, and the two stepped out on the balcony to acknowledge the gesture of reconciliation by the people of Cologne below. The crowd grew delirious. From our bedroom, I peered through the shades and watched Granddad bow in thanks and raise both hands in an expansive gesture of welcome. Mamie waved modestly, one arm around Granddad's waist. The noise grew; the crowd threatened to become unruly. Granddad waved goodbye and stepped back inside the hotel apartment. For a time the noise continued unabated, distracting our feeble attempts at conversation.

Shortly after, Granddad went to bed and soon he was reading a western that had been placed at his bedside by Sergeant Moaney. I told him I thought the crowd had been touching and wonderful. He shrugged, placed his book aside, and changed the subject. He discussed his health. Opening his pajama top he revealed an abdominal scar, and lifting his leg demonstrated the muscle damage caused by surgery. "This is from eating too rapidly," he explained. "The doctors tell me that had I taken my time eating while growing up, something I didn't start to do until I was twenty-eight years old, that I wouldn't have had this problem. I have been watching you — you eat too quickly." As always, I listened dutifully to yet another of Granddad's "tips" on good living.

Soon the lights were out, Granddad was asleep, and the remnants of the street demonstration had dispersed.

Paris was beautiful. On August 5, I wrote in my journal:

We arose at 9:00 and went to church in the American chapel in Paris. After a sermon on "Being Kind" we went to a luncheon given by Ambassador and Mrs. [James] Gavin [which included President de Gaulle]. It was an enjoyable affair.

We went to the C'quo Hardy [Coq Hardi] for dinner. Afterwards, we went to the fireworks display which was magnificent. Granddad remarked on the way out that this was the first time in 28 years he had flowed with a crowd. . . .

But Anne and I missed home. Letter writing was absorbing most of my energy and had become such an obsession that my grandparents became alarmed. They had some misgivings that my sister and I were too young for the trip. Every day around noon, Anne and I attached ourselves to the American Express representative who traveled with the party, and we waited for the delivery of mail.

To ease my homesickness for Gettysburg,

Granddad frequently returned from official functions with little gifts he had been given or had bought earlier during the day — gifts for my friends at home, "things" as he put it, "to impress the gals." After a sentimental visit to Rocquencourt and NATO headquarters, Granddad arrived with an asymmetrical silver five-star pin presented to him that day. "See," he said, as he revealed an engraving on the back of the middle star, "it says DDE" (I was DDE II). He added proudly, "Your girl would never be able to deny who gave it to her," and then he handed me the pin.

Several times he came back with ties to "wow" the girls, invariably in loud colors with touristy patterns. One was a brownish pink silk tie with maple leaves that appeared three-dimensional and glowed in the dark. "I'd wear this myself, but you can put it to better use," he said, beaming with a touch of innuendo. Carelessly, I lost the five-star cluster pin, but I still cherish the maple leaf tie.

We spent nearly a week in London. With the Gosdens, my sister and I toured the Tower of London, Parliament, St. Paul's Cathedral, Madame Tussaud's Wax Museum, and Piccadilly, and spent several afternoons in Hyde Park watching orators on nearby street corners. Meanwhile my grandparents attended a series of luncheons, and meetings with wartime comrades and government officials. On August 10, Granddad visited Winston Churchill briefly at Middlesex Hospital, where Churchill was recovering from a broken hip sustained in a fall. On the 14th, my grandparents attended a luncheon given at the Pilgrim's Club. Along with Eisenhower, the honored guests included Lord Ismay, Lord Portal, and Sir James Gault. Notably absent was Sir Bernard Law Montgomery whose war memoir critical of Eisenhower still rankled and whose presence might have been newsworthy and awkward.

Our trip to Europe coincided with a bold Soviet space initiative. During the final week in July, the Soviets had launched two astronauts simultaneously into orbit to test linkup procedures, establishing a new "first" in space exploration. During the orbital mission, the two cosmonauts spoke to each other by radio while their movements were flashed back to the Soviet Union by television. Once again, space commanded headlines, and the Soviets trumpeted another propaganda victory.

Eisenhower met frequently with the press during his trip. Inevitably, the question of

American prestige and Soviet space achievements arose. While in Paris, an article by Eisenhower appeared in the *Saturday Evening Post* in which he blasted the Kennedy administration's space program:

> I frankly do not see the need for continuing this effort as such a fantastically expensive crash program — why the great hurry to get to the moon and the planets? We have already demonstrated in everything except the power of our booster rockets we are leading the world in scientific exploration. From here on, I think we should proceed in an orderly, scientific way, building one accomplishment on another rather than engaging in a mad effort to win a stunt race.

Later in London, Eisenhower debunked the continuing press and editorial comment on the two-man orbital space accomplishment by the Soviet Union. Referring to articles claiming the Soviets had created another "gap," Eisenhower sniffed: "In fact, I don't like the word 'gap,' and don't believe in it."

Everywhere, Eisenhower met newsmen who were eager to explore the dimensions of the personal and political disagreement between himself and President Kennedy. An article had appeared in the *Washington Post* in early June that quoted Republican congresswoman Catherine May of Washington state as saying Eisenhower had announced to a group of congressmen at the farm that spring he would "go to jail in a test case" in defiance of the Kennedy administration's farm bill. He had characterized the bill as a "naked threat" because of administration hints of plans to dump surpluses on the open market if farmers failed to approve controls.

But Eisenhower refused to criticize the President on foreign soil. When asked to state the major difference between himself and Kennedy, Eisenhower replied that any such discussion would be "profitless." He did wade into California's politics on behalf of Nixon, however, describing Nixon's defeat for the presidency in 1960 as the "greatest disappointment" of his eight years in the White House.

The longest stop was a week at Culzean Castle, owned by the National Trust for Scotland which had given Granddad a lifelong tenancy in a suite of rooms. Culzean is a sandstone fortification standing high on bluffs overlooking the Firth of Clyde near Ayershire, the home of the Scottish poet

Robert Burns. The castle is guarded by a moat and surrounded by thick walls erected 150 years earlier in anticipation of Napoleon's invasion of England. Its original twelve-pound cannons are still in place. Ironically, Culzean was the traditional seat of the Scottish clan Kennedy. Naturally on this trip, a number of stories appeared attempting to link the Scottish branch of the Kennedy family with the Irish branch.

The Eisenhower apartment, reached by a spectacular circular staircase, is situated at the top of the three-story residence. The lower floors are open to the public and contain knights in armor and other historical artifacts. The apartment is decorated in rich, comfortable Chippendale furniture. Because the Gulf Stream produces warm water in the vicinity of the Firth of Clyde, the air is mild and drizzly and much of the vegetation is tropical, the gardens full of luxuriant roses and palms.

By now the Eisenhower party had been living in close quarters for nearly a month. Nerves were taut. The children caused a minor incident sleeping through a tour of Robert Burns's birthplace arranged by the local government. Craig Gosden and I had also missed a tour of Scotland Yard. Granddad exhibited increasing irritation over a small record player Anne carried and played nonstop in her room. Her favorite 45 was Del Shannon's "Runaway." Granddad was shocked to learn that "O Sole Mio" and "Army Blue," two of his favorite songs, had been "adapted" by Elvis Presley as "It's Now or Never" and "Love Me Tender." He weighed banishing the music from his range of hearing.

The last stop on the trip was Dublin. The Gosdens, my sister, and I huddled conspiratorially one night to plot ways of convincing Mamie to make the transatlantic flight home, thus shortening our trip by five days. Freeman volunteered me to broach the subject with Granddad before bed and to couch it in terms of my wanting to get home to see friends before going to Exeter.

Granddad was angered by my suggestion. When the children came back from a walk in a nearby park the next day, we returned to bedlam. Granddad had ordered Schulz to make plane reservations for me on the afternoon flight leaving Dublin and I had missed the plane. It was my turn for a "prayer session." I pleaded with Granddad to understand that my suggestion had been a "whim."

A hurricane chased the SS *United States* across the Atlantic, catching us seven hundred miles off the coast of New York. Craig and I spent twenty-four hours wandering through the vast, deserted rooms of the ship looking for signs of life. Everyone in our party was seasick except for us, because we were able to keep eating. On August 28, we at last returned. Our thrilling but arduous journey was over.

Granddad, however, had a final task to complete. Throughout the trip, he had been traveling in a semi-official capacity. Two weeks after our return, President Kennedy invited Granddad to the White House to report on his conversations with de Gaulle, British Prime Minister Harold Macmillan, and Adenauer, as well as on Berlin, NATO command issues, and the looming problem of British membership in the European Community.

Eisenhower began by describing a positive development, a growing French-German entente. The relationship between France and Germany was "improving markedly," he said. Adenauer and de Gaulle were now committed to a "complete rapprochement," open borders, and integrated economies. There was a feeling in the capitals he had visited that the Berlin crisis had passed and the overall picture was bright.

That brought Eisenhower to anxieties

voiced about any changes in U.S. and NATO strategy, which had successfully held the line in Berlin. Specifically, Adenauer had raised questions about General Maxwell Taylor, soon to be appointed JCS chairman. "I must tell you," Adenauer informed Eisenhower, holding up a copy of Taylor's *The Uncertain Trumpet,* "that if this book is to be adopted as NATO policy, there will be disastrous consequences. If a conventional forces strategy is adopted in Europe it will mean that the United States is ready to see Europe overrun by the Russians." Though he had reassured Adenauer about Taylor, Eisenhower told Kennedy frankly that he shared Germany's misgivings about any step taken toward a policy of "flexible response" in Europe.

At length, Kennedy and Eisenhower discussed lingering questions about Berlin and whether rigid NATO doctrines of "massive retaliation," in place since 1958, exposed Western Europe to piecemeal Soviet challenges. Eisenhower believed not, citing no lesser authority than Nikita Khrushchev. Eisenhower described his conversation with Khrushchev at Camp David in 1959, recalling the premier's boast that Warsaw Pact forces could overwhelm any conventional NATO forces defending Berlin, and his acceptance of Eisenhower's point that if war erupted over Berlin, "there will be nothing conventional about it." Eisenhower's message was clear: that after four years of Berlin tensions, the Soviets were checked and would stay checked unless U.S. and NATO decisions unwittingly reopened the issue.

Kennedy appreciated Eisenhower's report on the settled scene in Europe and their conversation was cordial, even friendly. Tossed aside in all the cordiality were the looming and tougher questions of future import: Vietnam and Asia, rumors of Soviet moves in Cuba, the budget, and the fall elections.

GRIN AND FIGHT

Two weeks later I left Gettysburg for Exeter. I did not want to leave Gettysburg, where I felt established in athletics and activities, but at least I was not going to Valley Forge Military Academy. In the family tradition, I tried not to complain and instead tried to look at Exeter in the way my father and Grandfather had regarded the many moves in their lives, as necessary, enriching, and a duty to oneself and family.

My parents decided to drive me the entire distance to school. At 7 A.M. on the foggy and cold morning of my departure, we left our house on the corner of the farm and had breakfast with my grandparents at their residence. George Champion, chairman of the board of Chase Manhattan, was a weekend guest. For thirty minutes all of us chatted about the fine school atmosphere at Exeter, the importance of doing well, and the opportunities open to Exeter graduates. At the doorstep, Granddad attempted to draw attention away from the tears welling up in everyone's eyes. "David, this is like going to West Point," he said. "Just think, now you are six years ahead of me. I left home at twenty, and you're fourteen."

"Master David," said Sergeant Moaney stoically, "you come home soon, hear?"

By late afternoon the fog had turned to rain. Our trip was slow and dreary. Reaching Exeter late at night, we had trouble finding our hotel. The rains broke by daylight the next day, enabling us to move trunks and suitcases into Peabody Hall. Suddenly I was sitting at a desk by a window looking out toward the Squamscott River and a row of unfamiliar New England Federal period houses and ivy-covered dorms. It would take a while to adjust to the sophisticated world of British-accented professors, Ivy League aspirations, the absence of Gettysburg friends, and the New England weather.

Compensating for much was my roommate, Fred Grandy, already an accomplished young actor and the son and brother of Exeter graduates. Fred knew the ropes. I turned to the challenge of academics and of staying in the top quarter of my class, and I lived for vacations and, come spring, the Exeter baseball season.

My parents, grandparents, and I wrote frequently. They reported on my sisters and friends and what little news they heard around town about the high school and college. Life went on.

Back from a political trip in late September, Granddad found himself at loose ends at the farm. Reacting to the depressed quality of my early letters, he penned a handwritten letter. Formally he began:

26th of September 1962 (1918)

Dear David,

I doubt that the date written above would have significance for you, since you were not born until after World War II was over and the 26th of September 1918 marked the beginning of the Argonne battle of World War I. For me it brings back much of America's efforts in that conflict — and the mere reference to it does call attention to the difference in our respective ages as I was almost twenty-eight when that battle began.

He wanted to know how much history I was taking and how I was adjusting to methods of teaching at Exeter different from the ones that I had grown accustomed to in Gettysburg. He reminded me that my golf shoes remained in his locker and would be there when I came home. He suggested that I get a pair for use at school and keep shoe trees in my golf shoes from now on, "for only with trees can you keep your shoes looking decently and feeling properly on your feet." My father, he informed me, was in New York for ten days working with the editors of Doubleday. Mamie was at Walter Reed for dental work. My mother and three sisters had just left the farm following dinner, in order to go to a movie playing at the Majestic, Gettysburg's one theater. At the end of his note, Granddad sat back and began to dream:

Well if you are learning to box, keep your left eye almost out in front so that your jab would have the power of the shoulder behind it; the right fist close, the glove close to your chin and your weight so evenly distributed you can move rapidly in any direction. Keep alert and watch the other fellow's gloves, particularly his right. The right carries the real punch. And of course you'll learn about hooks, jabs, crosses, short punches, etc. Well — that's a funny thing to write about, isn't it? Take care of yourself and send me a card sometime, when you are not too busy. I miss you very much, and Mamie and all the others do too!

Devotedly,
Granddad

Boxing was one of Granddad's favorite metaphors for politics. His flight into boxing was a sign that politics was heating up. As I was to learn later, on the stump Granddad often drew on sports to rally supporters and answer critics.

One of his most famous political speeches had come on October 14, 1958, at a birthday breakfast at the Washington Statler Hilton hosted by the Republican National Committee. In it he had vigorously defended his administration's accomplishments: the reversal of the trend toward centralization of power in Washington; restoration of confidence in the economy; the end of wage and price controls; six consecutive balanced budgets and a policy of long-term economic growth without inflation; building air, sea, and ground defenses that had never been so strong; the end of the war in Korea; containment of communism in Asia without involving American troops; an Iran prevented from falling into the Soviet orbit; and a West Germany restored to sovereignty and respectability within the NATO alliance. He had challenged his Republican audience to consider why that record should not command broad support in the nation. Then he told a story:

As a young staff officer years ago, I had a very wise, understanding and skillful boss. One day I said to him — because he knew, I guess, that I was a slightly ambitious young officer — I said to him, "What would you consider the most important qualification of a staff officer?"

Well, he looked at me and he said, "Why that's easy: a ready grin . . ."

This "grin business" reminds me of a little incident that goes much further back when I was at West Point. I used to like to box. I boxed a man who had been a champion heavy-weight wrestler who was also a very strong, fine boxer. With his some forty- or fifty-pound advantage, he used to handle me rather roughly.

One day, hit with a very fast left, I went into the corner very rapidly, more rapidly than I intended to of course. But as I got up from this blow, he looked at me and said, "You smiled." I again shut my eyes and wondered what he meant.

But from that time on, I erred just once. I got knocked down again. I got up looking rather rueful. He just took his gloves off and threw them in the basket in the corner and said, "Well, I'm done boxing with you now." I said, "What's the matter?" He said, "If you can't smile when you get up from a knockdown, you're never going to lick an opponent."

The delighted crowd roared approval in learning the secret of the Eisenhower grin — that it was a gesture of determination, a reflex to being outwitted or overpowered. "If you see someone irritating you, just grin," Eisenhower said. "You haven't smiled when you've gotten up because once in a while they throw a haymaker at you. So what! You don't win a campaign in one battle. You win a campaign by sticking ever lastingly at it, with the kind of attitude that is the attitude of a victor."

IN THE THICK OF IT

Granddad had not planned to campaign extensively in 1962 but the titular leader of the party, Richard Nixon, was tied down in a bitter campaign for governor in California and another prominent Republican, Governor Nelson Rockefeller, was running for reelection in New York. Eisenhower was the only national Republican leader who could make a difference in a dozen or so races that year. In mid-September, he took to the hustings, criticizing the Kennedy administration's "grab for power." Seamlessly picking up where he had left off moments before Election Day in 1960, Eisenhower castigated the Kennedy administration for its heavy-handed threats during the recent steel negotiations, and attacked governmental centralization, the welfare state, and runaway spending.

On September 20, Kennedy, in retaliation, flew into Harrisburg, Pennsylvania, and delivered the most blistering direct attack on the Eisenhower administration since taking office. "At my Inauguration," Kennedy declared at the airport, "around the world the picture was dreary." Kennedy recalled that eighteen months earlier "people had been out of work, businesses closing, cities decaying, crime increasing, minorities and migrants mistreated . . . and the Congress and the President of the United States had for six years been locked in divided and divisive do-nothing government. The decline in our position has at least been reversed. And this country is moving forward again." Later that evening, at a rally, Kennedy went on to charge that Eisenhower had hamstrung defense for budgetary reasons and that he had debunked the space program. Kennedy claimed that the previous administration had been "determined to maintain a secondary position."

Harrisburg is only thirty-five miles from Gettysburg, and so Kennedy had ventured into Eisenhower's backyard to deliver the attack. Eisenhower regarded Kennedy's speech as freeing him from his "rule against discussing personalities." Eisenhower threw himself into the rest of the campaign with all the energy he could muster.

October 1962 was one of the busiest political months of Eisenhower's career. He spoke in Baltimore and Denver. Then on the 6th, he continued on to California for a series of appearances on behalf of Nixon's campaign, dubbed a "rescue operation" by the White House. On the 10th, Eisenhower flew to Boise and on the 11th toured Omaha, Minneapolis, and Cheyenne.

While campaigning, Eisenhower drew crowds of equal size or larger than the crowds attracted by Kennedy. *Newsweek* described him as "fighting mad," tired of "being characterized as a simple-minded has-been." Eisenhower drew ovations attacking the "callow youth" in the Kennedy administration, charging Kennedy with an "unconscionable power grab." What the President needs, Eisenhower roared in Minneapolis, is a "darn good influx of Republicans!"

Eisenhower poured extra fervor into his California appearance for Nixon. He felt a special responsibility because he had urged his former vice president, against Nixon's better judgment, to make what had suddenly become an uphill race.

Nixon's campaign had proven luckless from the start. He coupled his announcement for the governorship with the pledge that he would not run for president in 1964. His opponent Pat Brown immediately charged Nixon with a lack of candor, an issue that dogged the Nixon campaign until Election Day. In March, W. Alton Jones, Granddad's friend and one of Nixon's principal financial backers, died in an airplane crash, which cast a pall over the early phases of Nixon's campaign. The polls, which had been so promising in July 1961, turned sour. Ominously, a poll asking California voters how they voted in 1960 between Kennedy and Nixon revealed that the voters had a very short memory. As many as sixty-one percent recalled voting for Kennedy although Nixon had carried the state. By midsummer 1962, Nixon was campaigning as a clear underdog.

Nixon's biggest disadvantage was his bitter primary fight with rightwing state Republican chairman Joe Shell. Nixon was forced into a strong denunciation of the John Birch Society and "right wing extremism" to win the primary. Many of Shell's supporters in the primary sat home in November.

Campaigning for Nixon in October, Eisenhower pulled out all the stops. The two participated in a joint motorcade through downtown San Francisco. Over statewide television, Eisenhower delivered an endorsement that heaped all the praise on Nixon that some alleged Eisenhower had withheld while president:

Richard Nixon is one man, so intimately

and thoroughly known to me, that without any hesitation I can personally vouch for his ability, his sense of duty, his sharpness of mind, and his wealth of wisdom. Through eight years, in the Cabinet Room of the White House, and in weekly sessions of the cabinet and the National Security Council, he sat directly across the table from me — a mere few feet away. There, I came to know him as a man who can never be known from headlines about him or speeches by him. My knowledge of him — first hand, immediate, the product of my own close scrutiny — grew in times of crisis and of progress towards their solution; in times of decisive action and of an increase in America's leadership of free nations . . . [I]n every discussion our single guide was the welfare and security of the United States . . . [T]hroughout all these meetings, I could watch Dick Nixon; absorbed in the thoughtful and sober weighing of every word and idea.

Eisenhower's tribute went on for pages as he applauded Nixon's efficiency in handling presidential assignments, his role in "breaking down the walls of discrimination" as head of the President's Committee on

Government Contracts, his unmatched experience. He concluded, "No man of Dick Nixon's intellectual capacity, conscientious stewardship, and superb leadership should be permitted to stand on the sidelines." But Eisenhower aggravated one of Nixon's problems by inadvertently emphasizing how much the state of California had prospered and grown during the administration of Pat Brown. In his attempt to establish rapport with the viewers, Eisenhower described California as "the fastest moving state in the Union." He continued pointing out that "in the numbers of students enrolled in its schools . . . the numbers of men and women working in modern technology . . . California towers over most of the sovereign nations of the world."

In mid-October, Granddad traveled to New England to campaign. He took time away from his trip to visit me at Exeter. I still had not adjusted to boarding school and spent several hours every night writing home. I had yet to unpack the trunk that sat by my bed. But I was proud of Exeter and eager for Granddad to be as impressed by it as he had been by Valley Forge.

On the 16th, Granddad's helicopter landed on a soccer field near the Thompson Gymnasium. From there he was taken by station wagon to the headmaster's residence, where I joined him. After a brief reunion, we went on a tour of the campus, including a stop at my dorm. When we climbed out of our car to inspect several buildings on foot, throngs of students gathered. But they maintained a distance, observing him rather than greeting him. This was Greater Boston, Kennedy country.

I thought the reaction seemed typical of Exeter, too sophisticated to demonstrate emotion for a political figure, but too curious to resist a glimpse. For nearly twenty minutes, students and faculty members simply trailed along with us, hiking through the October sunshine and the mounds of dead leaves that announce autumn. Occasionally a student would interrupt the headmaster, who conducted the tour for us, to ask an earnest question about the Kennedy administration or the fall elections. Granddad would pause and answer the question courteously, sending a ripple of intelligent laughter or knowing applause through the group.

Shortly before he left, Granddad and I visited alone for several minutes back at the headmaster's house. Granddad seemed distracted and businesslike, diverted by the schoolwide attention he had attracted, but,

I noted, impressed by Exeter and by my roommate, Fred. For five minutes, I had a link to home. I reported to him about my life. I felt too homesick to enthuse, but too proud to beg a ride home. After the obligatory privacy, Headmaster William G. Saltonstall returned with elaborate details of how Granddad's transfer to the soccer field and the waiting helicopter would be accomplished. We drove to the field, Granddad boarded the helicopter, and he was gone.

When I wandered back to Peabody Hall to collect books for a class, I found a good friend who had been missing that morning. While Granddad had entertained the crowd, I had been busy scanning faces so that I could introduce the two.

He was two years older, a three-year veteran of Exeter, a member of a Yale family based in a bayside mansion near Boston. He lived under unbearable pressure to continue a family tradition at Yale. "Where were you?" I asked. "I wanted him to meet you."

"Well, I didn't want to meet him," he replied.

"Why?"

"I figured that man lives with intrusions like that every day of his life — I wasn't going to add to it."

On this trip, Granddad spoke in Boston, Kennedy's backyard, to reply directly to the foreign policy attack the President had leveled from Harrisburg three weeks earlier. In his speech, he denounced Kennedy's "dreary record" in foreign policy, alluding to the failure in Cuba and the unopposed communist construction of the Berlin Wall, which he contrasted with the "direct and courageous foreign policy" of the 1950s and the "defeat of Communist efforts in crisis after crisis." Following the speech, Eisenhower contacted a "mutual friend" of his and Kennedy's to convey a warning: "This is the beginning and not the end of it," he said. "One more attack like the one in Harrisburg and my position of bipartisan support in foreign policy will draw to a permanent end."

That winter, in a meeting with Friendly, Eisenhower noted with satisfaction that Kennedy's Harrisburg speech had been his last public criticism of the Eisenhower foreign policy. And his Boston Armory speech was Eisenhower's one and only public criticism of the Kennedy foreign policy.

CRISIS IN CUBA

In mid-October, Kennedy suddenly disappeared from public view. As the red, gold, and orange of fall spread over Exeter and much of the nation, the administration pondered the placement of Soviet offensive strategic missiles in Cuba.

Then, on October 22, in a nationwide address, President Kennedy informed the country about the missiles. The nation was on the brink of a nuclear catastrophe, he warned; no community was unthreatened. Even Exeter, sandwiched between a remote New England seaside resort and the White Mountains, was close to Portsmouth Naval Shipyard.

Our British-born dorm master, following government directives, assembled the students of Peabody Hall in the Commons to set out the procedures to protect against fallout and nuclear blast in the event of war. His white hair, aristocratic bearing, and impeccable Oxford English contrasted luridly with his clinical descriptions of "base zero" and "kill radius." Somberly he talked about our chances of survival in the turn-of-the-century brick dormitory. Similar scenes were enacted throughout the country.

Eisenhower's natural reaction was to question why Kennedy, who had had evidence of missile construction in Cuba for months, delayed informing the American public until late October, two weeks before the elections. He initially suspected Kennedy of timing the crisis to help the Democratic candidates at the eleventh hour.

Since late August, Republican senator Kenneth Keating of New York had been sounding public alarm over reports he had received from government sources about a buildup of Soviet arms in Cuba. Keating charged that the buildup included facilities for emplacement of offensive missiles capable of striking the continental United States. Publicly, administration spokesmen confirmed that Soviet supplies of arms and munitions flowed to Cuba but ridiculed Keating's charges that the Soviets were contemplating the use of the island as a forward base for strategic missiles. But the New York senator persisted, convinced that behind the scenes the administration was locked in bitter argument over Soviet intentions.

Within the administration, CIA Director John A. McCone, Eisenhower's onetime Atomic Energy Commission Chairman, had raised alarms about stepped-up Soviet military activity and base construction in

Cuba. In his view, the pattern of missile site construction implied a Soviet intention to deploy intermediate range strategic missiles (IRBMs) in Cuba — in addition to purely defensive anti-aircraft missiles (SAMs) — for the evident purpose of upsetting a global nuclear balance, which still greatly favored America and NATO. According to Elie Abel's account of the Cuban Missile Crisis, in late September, McCone hurried back from a honeymoon in Europe to plead the case for additional surveillance and action. When U-2 photographs taken on October 14 provided confirmation of McCone's suspicions, President Kennedy and his advisers acted promptly.

Kennedy decided to inform Eisenhower formally of the situation on October 18, two days after Eisenhower's foreign policy blast in Boston. Anticipating the General's negative reaction to the news, Kennedy asked for a cabinet member to make the initial call. McCone volunteered.

In their phone conversation, Eisenhower told McCone that he was frankly skeptical about the timing of the "discovery" just days before the 1962 election. He refused to commit himself, in advance, to offering public support of Kennedy's actions, if any, against the Soviet Union on the eve of the election.

Eisenhower would soon change his mind. On the night of the 20th, McCone telephoned Eisenhower again and asked him to meet with him in Washington. The next morning at CIA headquarters, McCone and a group of intelligence officers brought Eisenhower up to date on all developments in Cuba. The missile buildup had been under way for weeks, they confirmed, but the President and the intelligence community had been persuaded that the sites were being built for defensive weapons. The latest photos confirmed that the sites were being expanded and equipped for long-range missiles with a range of two thousand miles. McCone informed Eisenhower that three plans were under consideration; first, destruction of the sites by bombing; second, a bombing campaign carried out with a simultaneous invasion of Cuba; third, a blockade with measures to ensure the evacuation of thousands of Russians involved in the buildup.

Eisenhower told McCone that he saw no profit in the first course, but that he saw merit in options two and three, and he assured McCone that he would support the President in either course. He was not, he added, in possession of the background information necessary to judge between them.

Actions came on the 22nd, as Kennedy prepared to speak to the nation. Kennedy personally phoned Eisenhower, reaching him in Gettysburg. White House transcripts of their conversation reveal the President told Eisenhower he would be announcing a blockade of Cuba that night, the first step to force the Soviets to withdraw their missiles. Kennedy voiced his concerns. First, that the Soviets would respond to the blockade by declaring a U.S. attack on Cuba to be an attack on the U.S.S.R. Second and most important, that the Soviets would link the American move in Cuba to Berlin.

"They might," Eisenhower replied, "but personally I doubt it." The Soviets were opportunists, Eisenhower continued, and they stirred up trouble wherever possible, but did not link one situation to another. Eisenhower was confident that the Soviets realized that if they moved on Berlin, they would encounter "all of it." "I could be wrong, but I believe you will not find a relationship." Inevitably, Eisenhower offered Kennedy his full personal support for the decision not to tolerate Soviet missiles in the Western Hemisphere. On the 25th in Pittsburgh, Eisenhower told a Republican rally, "We are, one and all, deeply concerned with recent events occurring off our southeastern coast. . . . Until this urgent problem is solved to the satisfaction of our nation, every loyal American will without hesitation carry out and conform to any instruction pertaining to it proclaimed by the Commander-in-Chief."

Important news came on the 28th. Kennedy called Eisenhower to inform him that Khrushchev had consented to withdraw the missiles from Cuba in exchange for a pledge by the United States not to invade Cuba. Kennedy told him that he had indicated his willingness to abide by such a pledge. He was concerned about Soviet compliance, and also concerned that the Soviets, checked in Cuba, would simply turn their energies on Berlin.

Eisenhower recommended that the United States insist on a land inspection of Cuba in order to guarantee Soviet compliance. "What you say you will do, whether it is an inspection by us, and in whatever concessions we are prepared to make, do this very specifically: make sure it is written down. And then by all means do everything you say you are going to do — because if you don't, pretty soon you will find that you possibly can't do it."

Kennedy demurred, explaining the Soviets had agreed to the provision early in their negotiations, but balked on inspections when Castro began insisting, "No . . . this is my country."

Eisenhower hinted at the line of partisan criticism that would emerge if Kennedy conceded too much to the Russians and Cubans. He urged Kennedy not to agree to any "blank check" guaranteeing that the United States would not intervene against Cuba in the future. And he pointedly suggested to Kennedy that he had lost a chance to dispense with Castro when the Cuban dictator declared in December 1961 that he was a "Marxist-Leninist." "Then you might have taken action against him," Eisenhower said, "and your actions would have been approved by the United States."

Kennedy tartly replied, "We didn't even think about it."

They again discussed Berlin. "Mr. President, again I could be wrong but I do not think you will see a connection. I hope not!"

Kennedy laughed. "Thank you, General."

Throughout the Cuban Missile Crisis, Eisenhower maintained public support. Kennedy had once again sprung a surprise on Republicans and informed them after the fact, as he had with the Bay of Pigs, but this time the United States had gained a clear victory over the Soviets. Khrushchev, though granted concessions, was obliged to withdraw the missiles in the glare of international publicity.

On October 30, in a letter to me, Granddad wrote acidly:

> There is no telling what the final result will be of the elections. After a long series of provocations, the government finally acted with some decision in the Cuban affair and this fact may make a great difference. No one can tell exactly what will happen although our polls show that we were doing very well up until the Cuban Crisis started.

On Election Day, Republicans won several key victories, notably Romney in Michigan and Rockefeller in New York. But off-year congressional gains, normally in the neighborhood of twenty to thirty seats for the party out of power, were held to four and the Democrats gained seats in the Senate. Along with the Democratic Senate victory, the big political news was Richard Nixon's defeat in California by a margin of 250,000 votes. In a press conference the day following the election, Nixon announced his withdrawal from politics.

Eisenhower and Nixon both blamed Nixon's defeat largely on the Cuban Missile Crisis. The timing had all but drowned out Nixon's ability to extend the momentum his campaign had gathered in mid-October, reducing him to issuing statements praising the courage and statesmanship of the Kennedy administration.

Arthur Schlesinger, Jr., in *A Thousand Days,* recalled that the news of Nixon's defeat in California was received with "amusement" by the Kennedy White House. Some in the press reacted with undisguised glee. ABC News anchorman Howard K. Smith hosted a television special twenty-four hours after the fact titled *The Political Obituary of Richard Nixon.* Smith's panel included convicted perjurer Alger Hiss, whose spying for the Soviets had been brought to light by Congressman Nixon and the House Un-American Activities Committee in 1948.

Eisenhower was furious with ABC's lack of taste in gloating over Nixon's defeat and in giving Hiss a forum to heap abuse on the man who had helped build a perjury case against him. He contacted his former press secretary James Hagerty at ABC and demanded Smith be fired. When Hagerty attempted to defend Smith's freedom of speech as a reporter, Eisenhower threatened to urge advertising sponsors of ABC to withdraw their support. Hagerty also received angry phone calls from other Republicans. Several weeks later, Smith left the anchor job to become a roving reporter on permanent special assignment. He would return to anchor *ABC Evening News* a few years afterward.

By Christmastime, the first volume of presidential memoirs was approaching completion and Granddad, in Eldorado, had time on his hands. The rest of the family had remained behind in Gettysburg over Christmas. Back at Exeter, I received a long letter that Granddad typed out on a typewriter he kept in his bedroom:

> I've been wanting to write you a letter for a long time, but I have been busy and bit out of action as well. Nothing serious. . . . But I have had a bad shoulder and have missed about ten days of golf and on top of that I couldn't raise my arm up to the keyboard of this machine and it is getting quite impossible for me to use a pen. . . . As soon as we reached this place Mimi fell ill with the flu and did not get out of the

house for something like three weeks. I am most thankful that she seems quite well.

Your dad was here about four days ago and we got a lot of work done — but though I was anxious for him to stay long enough to play a couple of rounds of golf he felt that he had to hurry back. He was looking well and fit.

Some months ago I taped a television conversation with the historian Bruce Catton. The subject we talked about was Lincoln and his relations with his generals. The picture will be shown on NBC on the evening of February 11th. If you have time to view it I think you will find it at least mildly amusing.

I do not need to tell you that Mimi and I miss you all tje [sic] time. We constantly talk of you and your sisters; wondering how you and they are getting along in school and with your friends and associates. I do not mean that we worry — we have too much confidence in you for that, but we are deeply interested. Your dad has taught you to take your own part but never to be arrogant; to be polite and courteous but never servile; to value true friends above material things, and to be honest and loyal to all those people and those teachings that command your respect. No, we don't want to advise, preach or argue — we just xxxx want to see you and possibly have a good "burnt" steak with you so we could talk of all the things that interested the Walrus in Alice's Wonderland.

I have a feeling that this typing is just (xxx) about as bad as my writing — I'd better stop.

See you — devotedly
Granddad
Dwight David Eisenhower II, Exeter

3
CHANGING TIMES

EQUAL JUSTICE

The Cuban crisis marked a turning point in Kennedy's relationship with Eisenhower. Imbued with confidence in the aftermath of Cuba, Kennedy began to point U.S.-Soviet relations in a different and less confrontational direction. At the same time he felt less need to consult with Eisenhower on foreign policy. In hindsight, the Cuban crisis marks a demarcation between the Eisenhower and Kennedy eras, which Kennedy himself suggested in his well-known American University speech of June 10, 1963, in which he announced a U.S.-British-Soviet agreement to end atmospheric nuclear weapons testing and, in effect, proclaimed a détente in Europe.

European questions lingered, however. Because Kennedy had been obliged to act unilaterally at the height of the Cuban crisis, de Gaulle had been alienated in a way that probably preordained his decision to withdraw France from permanent NATO commands. Likewise, U.S.-British relations would be strained by differences on atomic cooperation. But the Soviet Union's five-year-running "policy of crisis" had apparently run its course. And, in the United States, the focus of national politics quickly turned inward to civil rights and domestic issues. Nineteen sixty-three was to be the time of the "great awakening" on the issue of civil rights for all Americans.

For two years, the Kennedy Justice Department had encouraged legal challenges to Jim Crow and civil disobedience in the South by extending protection to "Freedom Riders," who sought to integrate interstate transportation. In September 1962, Kennedy had intervened at the University of Mississippi on behalf of a qualified black applicant, James Meredith, who had been admitted by the university, then turned back and barred from admission.

By the fall of 1962, the Little Rock school integration crisis was five years old and the *Brown v. Board of Education* Supreme Court decision declaring "separate but equal" education invalid had been in place for eight years. As yet, however, desegregation was barely taking hold in the border states, and it was becoming apparent that school segregation in the South might persist throughout the decade. It was also becoming apparent that after solving de jure school segregation and Jim Crow in the South, federal authorities would have to shift their attention to northern public schools and job and social discrimination in the desolate ghetto districts of New York, Philadelphia, Detroit, Cleveland, Los Angeles, and elsewhere.

Early in 1963, the Kennedy White House had prepared a major legislative push for civil rights, indicated in Kennedy's State of the Union address and a special message on civil rights in early February, invoking the hundredth anniversary of Lincoln's Emancipation Proclamation. The trigger for civil rights legislation came that spring in Alabama. In Birmingham, Martin Luther King's Southern Christian Leadership Conference led a campaign of civil disobedience against the city's Jim Crow institutions. In early May, Birmingham police had brutally suppressed a demonstration, prompting federal intervention and Kennedy's ultimate decision to submit a civil rights bill to Congress. By the summer of 1963, the struggle for civil rights was reaching what Ralph Bunche called its "climactic phase." Roy Wilkins of the NAACP called 1963 the "due date for freedom," the start of a new day which would come about as a co-operative effort between black and white.

As the Kennedy White House formulated its proposals, however, there were signs of trouble ahead. A civil rights bill would encounter the die-hard opposition of southern Democrats and Goldwater Republicans. Although racial violence and disturbances were still confined to the South, where the cause of equal justice seemed clearest, thoughtful observers, including writer James Baldwin and sociologist Gunnar Myrdal, predicted widespread violence and a white "backlash" because of the rapid evolution of civil rights from the "Negro problem," in James Reston's words, to a "revolution."

Eisenhower took pride in his administration's role promoting "real" progress on civil rights. At the time, Eisenhower and his staff were finalizing the first volume of his memoirs. Because this volume did not go beyond Eisenhower's decision to seek a second term in 1956, it did not cover the 1957 Little Rock events when the President, amid criticism, had mobilized the military to execute the court's decision in *Brown*. During the Little Rock crisis, Eisenhower had stressed compliance with the laws and had laid the foundation for steady but certain progress, without loss of life. By contrast, when James Meredith attempted to desegregate the University of Mississippi in 1962, Eisenhower noted in his diary on October 1: "I have just received the news that in a clash between federal troops and mobs attempting to prevent a Negro entering Mississippi University last night, two people were killed and scores hospitalized. I wonder what these same 'authorities' will now have to say about their administration. . . ."

Civil rights had been the most important domestic issue of Eisenhower's second term. "This is a matter of justice," he had declared in 1956, "not of anything else." Eisenhower's presidential documents in Abilene demonstrate that he was a steady advocate of equality before the law and that his White House, his attorney general, Herbert Brownell, and the Warren Court worked more or less in tandem. During the course of argument of *Brown,* Eisenhower privately held out hope for a decision that would reconcile the existing doctrine of "separate but equal" with the policy imperative of ending dual school systems in the South. But Eisenhower's views, communicated to Brownell and others, primarily focused on his practical concerns about implementation and southern acceptance, over time, of unitary school systems and the end of Jim Crow. When the *Brown* decision came down, Eisenhower questioned the court's reliance on sociological data as the basis for its findings that "separate but equal" public schools were inherently inferior. Enforcement of *Brown* entailed problems: since the decision could not be justified by judicial precedent, the court in *Brown* had in fact assumed a political role, which compelled a kind of role reversal. Eisenhower and the executive branch assumed what amounted to a judicial role, converting a political decision by the court into a judicial decree that would be accepted by all as the "law of the land."

Behind the scenes, Eisenhower had worked long hours on civil rights, fashioning legal history along the way. During the arguments in the cases dealing with implementation of *Brown,* Eisenhower had authorized the Justice Department to take the side of the plaintiffs. According to Brownell, he had carefully scrutinized the briefs and arguments with the skills of a lawyer, writing comments in the margins, quizzing William Rogers and other Justice officials about the implications of the various court outcomes for the Justice Department and state authorities. Years later, Brownell told me that one of Eisenhower's penciled notations found its way into the text of the court's ruling: the implementation of *Brown* should, in Eisenhower's words, proceed "with all deliberate speed." This phrase became the basis of decades of additional litigation.

Years later, I had a long conversation with General Lucius Clay, who served as a military adviser to Eisenhower during the war in Europe, military governor of Germany, and a key presidential backer in 1952 and 1956. Clay had special insights into the successes and failures of the Eisenhower presidency, but none more interesting than his views on Eisenhower and civil rights, including the relationship between the President and his chief justice, Earl Warren. Clay observed that when Eisenhower was president he may have been too impressed by the possibility of white resistance to integration and too inhibited in seeking gains that were within his grasp.

In hindsight, Clay looked back on the summer and fall of 1957 as an important beginning in dealing with a problem that was still very much a part of America. Whatever the relationship between Eisenhower and Warren, he noted, the two men had functioned as partners. Warren had set the agenda and guided the court. Eisenhower, by stressing compliance with *Brown,* had lent stature to what had been essentially a political decree, effectively countering segregationists who opposed civil rights measures on "states' rights" grounds. Eisenhower had enforced a ruling of the Supreme Court with military force, rendering talk of nullification or defiance futile. Clay viewed Eisenhower in hindsight as the "indispensable man" with regard to civil rights. Earl Warren, the leader of the judicial revolution that galvanized the changes, "simply needed Eisenhower."

Clay was candid about Eisenhower's regret in appointing Warren. Eisenhower suspected that the chief justice, who once had harbored presidential ambitions, had compensated for his frustrated political hopes by expanding the power of the court well beyond its traditional and appropriate limits. The issue between Eisenhower and Warren, Clay said, had little to do with politics or even the appropriate role of the courts on civil rights matters. Indeed, Eisenhower's appointments to the court had by and large been "liberal." His real misgivings centered on Warren's habit of issuing broad judicial pronouncements with profound political consequences that lacked the essential legal and constitutional foundations sufficient for them to be accepted by the political branches as final. This complicated Eisenhower's task of enforcing the law and making it work.

"In his most private thoughts," Clay added, "Eisenhower's esteem for Warren was certainly higher than Richard Russell's [who led the southern critics in the Senate] esteem for Warren, but perhaps less than Kennedy's. . . ." According to Clay, Eisenhower regarded the *Brown* decision as a burden, not a blunder. The decision had taken him somewhat by surprise. A ruling on the scale of *Brown* should have been issued as the logical culmination of precedents, developed in lower courts, perhaps disposing of *Plessy v. Ferguson,* the governing precedent. It was the "perceived departure" of *Brown* that made defending and implementing the decision difficult, but Eisenhower had implemented it.

Eisenhower had seen the necessity of the court's action in *Brown* and would take care to endorse it in the second volume of his memoirs when he covered civil rights in depth. But he dissented from Warren Court jurisprudence in principle, insofar as the court proceeded to discover new "inherent" rights not enumerated in the Constitution, amounting, in *New York Times* columnist Arthur Krock's words, to the boldest assertion of judicial supremacy since Chief Justice John Marshall's dicta in *Marbury v. Madison.* Eisenhower in particular deplored the Warren Court's holdings in the 1962 school prayer decision; in *Baker v. Carr,* in which the court struck down all legislative districting laws that violated "one man one vote"; and in *Abington v. Schempp,* where the court ruled that school-sponsored Bible reading in public schools was unconstitutional. This last decision prompted Eisenhower to make his feelings about the Warren Court known to his neighbors in Gettysburg.

By 1963, the Eisenhowers were established members of the Gettysburg community. Granddad was regularly seen going to and from his office, where he reviewed drafts of his memoir to be published in the fall, received visitors, and prepared for a trip he planned to take to Normandy later that year for a CBS filming of *D-Day Plus 20 Years* with Walter Cronkite, which would air in 1964. Routinely, Eisenhower stepped out for a round of golf at the nearby Gettysburg Country Club before retiring to his home for a quiet dinner and evening on the sunporch with Mamie.

The townspeople saw the Eisenhowers every Sunday when they attended services at the local Presbyterian Church. Granddad was especially fond of its minister, Reverend James MacAskill, who had attracted the Eisenhowers to the congregation. Granddad admired the young clergyman's sermons, his command of the English language, his sincerity and low-key manner. MacAskill was an eloquent speaker, and under the spotlight of having a former president in his audience, his reputation began to grow. Offers from other churches came in, and at one time toward the end of Eisenhower's second term, MacAskill was tempted to move to a larger congregation that offered him financial security and better educational opportunities for his children. With the advice and help of his Washington pastor Dr. Edward L. R. Elson, Granddad arranged for a raise, which kept MacAskill permanently in Gettysburg.

As a teenager, I was spellbound by Mac-Askill's sermons. He was diminutive in stature and his face pocked, but he had a photographic memory and was a brilliant storyteller. MacAskill wrote his sermons on Thursday, awoke before dawn on Sunday to rehearse his delivery, and then strode out to deliver a letter-perfect twenty-minute sermon complete with appropriate pauses for emphasis.

MacAskill and Eisenhower met frequently for lunch and discussion. Eisenhower's Carlisle Street office was across the street from the Lamp Post Tea Room, MacAskill's favorite place. MacAskill's attitude was typical of the community. Gettysburgians respected Eisenhower's privacy. There had been no stampede to fill Granddad's time with requests to attend parties or functions, or to participate in events at the local schools or at Gettysburg College. MacAskill did not try to get personal with Granddad or elicit his innermost feelings. He scrupulously observed the well-developed rules of Granddad's relationships with most people: tend to business. MacAskill's business was his church. He was available when Granddad desired to discuss sermons and current events. He was also unavailable from time to time, which doubtlessly contributed to Granddad's respect for him.

Eisenhower was, in MacAskill's words, "dynamically" interested in discussing ways of involving the church in improving national and global problems. He listened intently to MacAskill's practical suggestions on how this might be done. Eisenhower was also interested in church liturgy. Nor was he shy about expressing preferences for certain sermon topics and hymns. The psalms impressed him, MacAskill recalled, "as speaking to the dignity of man and the majesty of creation."

In turn, MacAskill appreciated the quality of Eisenhower's religious convictions: practical, world-wise, and deep without being doctrinaire. In their early talks after Granddad's return to Gettysburg, MacAskill observed how gracefully Granddad had adapted to the withdrawal of his authority. Here was a man who did not dread retirement, MacAskill recalled. Another quality that impressed him was Granddad's resistance to fads and passing ideas common in church life. He valued steadiness and disliked dramatic and cathartic conversions as much as he disliked "people dwelling within themselves." In Eisenhower, MacAskill saw a man who knew himself, a man of action, an extrovert about life and religion who saw all things in balance. He regarded his religious affiliation and faith as a mystery and a reality, an aspect of life that he channeled outwards toward the concerns he had developed and formulated in his wide travels and experience.

"The church is the conscience of the nation," he told MacAskill, and he for one respected the right of religious groups to express themselves on politics, stressing the "free exercise" aspect of religious freedom. Eisenhower approved of church involvement in politics because he had lived through the 1930s, when the churches in Europe had accommodated fascism with such terrible consequences. Based on his own experience, he questioned whether religious, moral, and political questions could be divorced from one another without sacrificing all morality in politics. Democracy, he believed, had grown out of religious commands to respect and regard the rights of others and the acceptance of restraints on one's personal behavior. Indeed, the drive for civil rights was being fueled by churchmen, which Eisenhower believed to be wholly proper. To overcome segregationist resistance in the South, President Eisenhower had repeatedly enlisted the clergy, most notably the Reverend Billy Graham, to preach respect for the law and tolerance on race. In his view, the Warren Court's bias against the church undermined its promotion of equal rights because sociology was no substitute for moral teaching.

That June, MacAskill imposed on the friendship slightly just as the *Schempp* decision was announced. He asked Eisenhower to give a talk on the involvement of the church in contemporary affairs on the occasion of the dedication of the new church building. Eisenhower agreed.

A tape of Granddad's talk, delivered in the church sanctuary, survives and was one of MacAskill's prized possessions. As MacAskill described it, on that day in late June, 1963, the thick stone walls of the church fended off the sweltering heat. Faintly audible in the background of the tape is the sound of the cooling system and people coughing from summer colds. MacAskill introduced Granddad as a parishioner and someone the community of Gettysburg was proud to call a neighbor. He yielded the floor and the crowd applauded.

Eisenhower's voice came through as strong, though subdued. He spoke in a matter-of-fact tone, and without notes, beginning with a short, informal discourse on the history of the Gettysburg area, which he had first gotten to know at Camp Colt, just south of town. He told the parishioners that he considered the ground to be nearly sacred. Exactly a hundred years before, the Army of the Potomac, led by the oft-misunderstood General George Gordon Meade, had turned the tide of the Civil War and thus the tide of American history. Here the principles for which Union soldiers fought and won their first great victory would be immortalized four months later by Lincoln's Gettysburg address.

"It is proper and fitting that even a layman can ask a number of questions in the field of theology — some bother me," Eisenhower stated. "First, the question of giving children education of a religious nature in the public school." Referring to the language of the court's decision, he continued: "Is it not possible to give our children the basic kind of religious instruction without bringing religion into the curriculum?" The American system of self-government and citizenship required the kinds of teachings that religion imparted.

We don't object to the reading of the Declaration of Independence, yet it involves God's sanction in the words "man is endowed of his natural rights by his creator," which is the fundamental theory of the constitution. . . .

There is no direct reference to the Deity Himself in the constitution. Our founders, though, as in all other great civilizations, recognized that the life of one man marked the beginning of an era. . . .

Our form of government is the political expression of a deeply felt religious faith.

He spoke on in this vein, slowly and deliberately, with a trace of wonder that he felt compelled to spell out ideas of such manifest logic and application:

You could spend a whole semester on the preamble, but suppose we drop the thought of a Deity and study the secular man, and secular developments resulting from his life. . . .

The theory of the equality of man is religious in origin. . . .

To raise our children in a moral atmosphere is to recognize the existence of a Supreme Overlord. . . .

I do not see how any Supreme Court in the world can declare teachings in this vein illegal. There is no reason for Americans to raise their children in a communist type school that denies the existence of a God. . . .

To listen to the talk, one is struck by his use of the term "Supreme Overlord." OVERLORD was the code name for the cross-Channel invasion of Europe. Granddad's use of it in this context implied a clear connection between the mission of his forces and America's moral leadership in the world. His command of the Allied Expeditionary Force had taken on a distinctly religious tone, a "crusade," to end the demonic Nazi rule in Europe.

Eisenhower's talk revealed a good deal about his philosophy of life. Religious beliefs provide individuals with the ability to accomplish the necessary and good, he believed. Only by accepting one's subordination in a transcendent order can a person work toward something truly good. Like all those he respected, Eisenhower saw himself as a subordinate in a larger scheme, and had believed so all his life.

Sometime after his talk at the church, Eisenhower had several thoughtful conversations with MacAskill on civil rights. MacAskill found Eisenhower receptive and positive toward the Kennedy initiatives. As MacAskill put it, Eisenhower, who in 1957 had signed the first Civil Rights law since Reconstruction, strongly supported the Kennedy civil rights bill as it was developed, but he disapproved of "dramatic pronouncements" and demagogic appeals emanating from the right or the left. His voice, as always, was one of moderation and restraint.

Time had not dimmed Eisenhower's frustrations with Governor Orval Faubus of Arkansas and others of his ilk who, knowing better, had stimulated resistance to integration for political and personal gain. As for his management of Little Rock, Eisenhower told MacAskill that while he regretted the severe criticism he had encountered from both sides, he was confident he had handled the situation correctly. "I believe in a restrained use of force," he told MacAskill, "but I believe in its use when it can be demonstrated that employing it would produce results and where necessary to ensure the proper administration of just and impartial treatment."

OVERLORD

On June 10, 1963, Kennedy had phoned Eisenhower and informed him of plans to use the recent obstructions of Governor George Wallace at the University of Alabama as the springboard for a national address on civil rights. Although the legislative proposals were not entirely formed, the administration had resolved to go forward with an omnibus bill that included provisions to desegregate hotels, restaurants, and commercial establishments of all kinds engaged in interstate commerce. Eisenhower cautioned Kennedy against the omnibus approach, favoring curing the 1957 and 1960 laws on voting rights. "Define the steps," Eisenhower advised: "take them one at a time, concentrate on the vote and all the rest will follow." But when Kennedy asked for Eisenhower's help in lining up Republican support for an omnibus package, Eisenhower readily agreed.

That afternoon, Kennedy gave the commencement address at American University that historians say marked the beginning of a thaw in U.S.-Soviet relations and allowed the President to focus on pressing issues at home. Twenty-four hours later, Kennedy delivered his landmark civil rights speech. "This is not a legal or legislative issue alone," Kennedy declared on June 11.

It is better to settle these matters in the courts than on the streets, and new laws are needed at every level, but law alone cannot make men see right. . . . We are confronted primarily with a moral issue . . . as old as the scriptures and as clear as the constitution . . . [T]he heart of the question is whether all Americans are to be afforded equal rights and opportunities . . . and this nation for all its hopes and all its boasts, will not be fully free until all its citizens are free. . . .

On June 14, Eisenhower pledged his help, agreeing to support the President's "Omnibus" bill. He wrote to Kennedy, replying to a June 10 letter from the President:

Dear Mr. President,
   Your letter of June tenth was, of course, written before I called at your office, on which occasion you and the Vice President discussed this matter with me.
   As I then told you, I think this matter has become one that involves the conscience of the individual and the nation, and indeed, our moral standards.
   As to the details of the legislation that might be needed I am not able to give a definitive opinion . . . but I do believe that we must strive in every useful way to assure equality of economic and political rights for all citizens. Since leaving office I have always refused to try to influence the decisions and voting of Republicans in the Congress. Nevertheless, I do not hesitate to let them know of my personal convictions on any issue. In this case, I shall make a point of letting them know . . . the seriousness with which I view the entire problem. . . .

Granddad wrote me often at Exeter with

news from home and to discuss my spring semester. I had emerged as a freshman pitching sensation, despite a freak accident the year before when I was hit in the face by a baseball at close range by a teammate hitting fungos. With word of my broken nose, and of a complete game I pitched shortly after coming back, Granddad had dashed off a handwritten note:

I did not quite understand how you were hit by a line drive while you were pitching! The ball that hit you was, apparently, not the one you were using. Where did it come from? It was fine that you could win a game so soon after being so seriously hurt — the only thing you did not tell me was your batting average. Some pitchers, you know, are good hitters, others have little interest in batting. . . .

In the same letter consoling me about my black eye, Granddad unveiled what was to become a standing offer:

Maybe you and I could rig up a deal that might be good for both of us. I've been anxious to learn some simple Spanish (the kind I might use on a shooting trip to Mexico) and you might find some interest in trying to teach me. If you could hold me down to work to the extent of about two hours of instruction a week, it seems to me I could pay you for your work. Of course you'd have to keep a tight disciplining hand on me — I'm very lazy!

Take care of yourself, and think over the "teaching" job . . . Devotedly

Change was in the air that summer, even in Gettysburg, where the townsfolk prepared for the enactments and celebrations marking the hundredth anniversary of the fateful battle and the commemorations in November of Lincoln's immortal Gettysburg Address. In May, Vice President Lyndon Johnson visited the town to launch months of ceremonies, including those at which Alabama, represented by its segregationist governor Wallace, and other southern states would dedicate monuments to units that had fought in the battle. For the first time since serving as the Summer White House in August 1959, Gettysburg was the center of national attention. At our church, the men were involved in a beard-growing contest. Throughout town, volunteers stepped forward to participate in various battle reenactments scheduled for early July. Evident also in newspapers was a major changing of the guard in national and international politics. In late June, Kennedy embarked for Europe and what was to become a storied trip through Ireland, Italy, and Germany, retracing large parts of the itinerary of our trip in 1962. The highlight, and most dramatic harbinger of change, came at the Berlin Wall, where the President affirmed freedom, extolled the courage and steadfastness of the West Berliners, and in so many words acknowledged the end of the postwar crisis that had gripped Europe since 1945.

You live in a defended island of freedom, but your life is part of the main. So let me ask you, as I close, to lift your eyes beyond the dangers of today, to the hopes of tomorrow, beyond the freedom of this city of Berlin, or your country of Germany, to the advance of freedom everywhere. . . .

Freedom is indivisible, and when one man is enslaved, all are not free. When all are free, then we can look forward to that day when this country will be joined as one and this country and this great continent of Europe in a peaceful and hopeful globe. When that day finally comes, as it will, the people of West

Berlin can take sober satisfaction in the fact that they were in the frontlines for almost two decades . . . [A]ll free men, wherever they may live, are citizens of Berlin, and therefore as a free man, I take pride in the words *"Ich Bin Ein Berliner."*

The news stories and magazine pictures of Kennedy's trip and the events in Europe early that summer accentuated the new faces coming to power. Adenauer, who accompanied Kennedy to Berlin, was aging and was upstaged by West Berlin mayor Willy Brandt, whom Kennedy was promoting as next chancellor of Germany. Macmillan's government tottered in the wake of a sex scandal and fell in a vote of no confidence that July. Kennedy's itinerary had skipped France, where the aging de Gaulle carried on his battles against British admission to the Common Market, U.S. leadership of NATO, and the growing American intervention in Vietnam.

Six weeks after Kennedy's trip, Granddad made what was to be his final visit to Normandy, this time in his role as a "part-time" correspondent for CBS news to film the special entitled *D-Day Plus 20 Years.* This brief journey to southern England and

France, as later described by executive producer of *CBS Reports* Fred Friendly in his memoirs, "meant something more than just another television program to all of us who were part of the small army of cameramen, producers, jeep drivers and distinguished camp followers which the General referred to as 'Friendly's irregulars.' " Milton and my father were also along for the week of exploration and television shooting. The nostalgic mood on the trip and its informality contrasted sharply with the 1962 European tour and underscored the sense of changing times.

Eisenhower and Walter Cronkite started at Eisenhower's forward headquarters at the Portsmouth Naval Shipyard. They were preserved just as they had been left by the OVERLORD command in the week after D-Day. There, in the rooms where Eisenhower had unleashed the cross-Channel invasion in early June 1944, he and Cronkite painstakingly re-created the mood and the tense deliberations that had preceded the decision to go ahead, based ultimately on Allied weather forecasts. In a plane borrowed from NATO, the group, including CBS President Bill Paley, flew across the Channel for several days of filming in the Caen-Bayeux area. Weather permitting, each day Eisenhower and Cronkite set out in a jeep to capture Eisenhower's recollections of the Normandy landings.

Toward the end of the week, Paley hosted a dinner party for the Eisenhowers and the television staff. The final interview was to occur the next morning at the American cemetery on the cliffs overlooking Omaha Beach. With a 7 A.M. call the following day to get ready for the shoot, the party broke up early. As he left, Eisenhower asked Friendly to drop by his suite for a brief talk about the next day's events.

Eisenhower had much more on his mind than technical arrangements or deciding who would be driving the jeep across the beaches and when. He was worried about what he would say on camera and wanted Friendly to give him advice. "Fred, this thing tomorrow at the cemetery is something I've got to do right. It's no time to talk about landing craft, or air power or high strategy. This program is going to be seen by thousands of families who lost sons and husbands and fathers at Normandy. . . . Tomorrow, I am going out there to speak to these families, I who came out of the war with enough glory to carry me on to other things. . . . What about their parents, what do they have to show that it was all worthwhile, that something decent and lasting came out of it?" He had been spending hours on his remarks, refining his thoughts.

Amid intermittent showers, the filming went forward successfully the next day. Taking turns at the wheel, Eisenhower and Cronkite drove a jeep along Omaha Beach and up the bluffs, touring the surrounding bunkers and the hedgerows, where for weeks the defending Germans had blocked the American drive inland. They visited St. Lô, where on July 25, American forces penetrated the German lines and began the battle of encirclement that ultimately secured victory. The final scenes were shot in the cemetery, and Eisenhower was prepared with words that eloquently summed up his reflections on the Normandy campaign:

Walter, this D-Day has a very special meaning for me. . . . On D-Day my own son graduated from West Point. After his training, he came over with the 71st division, some time after the landings. On the very day he was graduating, these men came here, British and our other allies, and Americans for one purpose only, not to gain anything for ourselves, not to fulfill any ambitions that America had for conquest, but to preserve freedom — systems of self-government in the world. Many thousands of men have died for ideals such as these, and here again, in the twentieth century for the second time, Americans along with the rest of the free world came across the oceans to defend these ideals. . . .

Now my own son has been very fortunate. He has had a very full life since then. He is the father of four lovely children that are very precious to my wife and me. But these young boys, so many of them, were cut off in their prime. They had families that grieved for them, but they never knew the great experiences of going through life that my son can enjoy.

I devoutly hope that we will never again have to see such scenes as these. I think and hope, pray that humanity will learn more than we . . . learned up to that time. But these people gave us a chance, and they bought time for us, so that we can do better than we have done before. So every time I come back to these beaches, or any day when I think about that day, twenty years ago now, I say once more we must find some way to work . . . to gain an eternal peace for this world.

DEVOTEDLY, GRANDDAD

Late summer 1963 marked the zenith of the Eisenhowers' involvement in Gettysburg, and of the farm operation. By now, the Scharfs had become fast friends and regulars for dinner, and the Gettysburg Hotel, as it had during the presidency, continued to cater political events at the downtown office and the farm. Like Granddad, Mamie became a familiar figure in town, a shopper who enjoyed an hour combing G. C. Murphy's for costume jewelry, nail polish, and knickknacks. Mamie joined the Gettysburg Women's Club and Granddad joined the Rotary and served on the board of the *Gettysburg Times*. The Eisenhowers became known for their support of local charities, including the American Red Cross and Annie M. Warner Hospital. Much of Granddad's philanthropy, however, was private. He had helped his White House chauffeur finance a home. He had provided much of the college tuition for a typist in his Gettysburg office whose parents did not see the value in higher education. He helped his longtime Gettysburg caddy, Roy Fairman, finance a set of golf clubs and set aside money for college.

Meanwhile, Granddad had become the sole proprietor of his purebred Angus herd and landholdings. Pete Jones's death had terminated the Eisenhower Farms partnership, and the Jones farm passed into the Jones Foundation, which in turn offered the 310-acre property to the national military park with the proviso that Eisenhower, paying for upkeep and repairs, retain use of the property. With Jones's death, Granddad purchased Jones's Angus herd, which brought his holdings close to one hundred Angus cattle in all, plus shares in several herd sires, including the prizewinning Ankonian 3551, a champion bull. The Eisenhower Farms brand was gaining notice. Two young bulls had been prizewinners within their class at the 1961 International Livestock Show in Chicago. The Eisenhower Farms would sell upwards of sixty thousand dollars' worth of young Angus cattle at various auctions. On July 27, 1963, *Pennsylvania Farmer* magazine conferred an "Honorary Farmer Master Award" on Granddad, signaling recognition of the Eisenhower Farms brand name and the importance of his operation.

Granddad, as usual, took the Angus business very seriously. He had become knowledgeable about all aspects of the Angus breed, including pedigrees and show features. Dinnertime at the farm and the social hour beforehand often included farm manager Art Nevins and his wife, Anne, and conversation centered on the farm.

I held two jobs in Gettysburg that summer. Two days a week I worked on the farm painting fences as well as my usual responsibilities in the vegetable garden and helping care for the horses. My second job, which kept me in touch with my Gettysburg friends, was part-time, two days per week at Gettysburg College collating text books and handouts. I was far more interested in the college job. In fact, I had several lapses of concentration at the farm. Over one lunch hour, my friend and I kept playing honeymoon bridge in Granddad's small den at the farm where we had eaten lunch, under the impression he had gone back to the office downtown. Twelve forty-five became 1, 1 became 1:15; 1:15 became 1:30. All of a sudden, the den door opened. Granddad's legendary temper was in full force. His lips were moving but I was paralyzed by fear and could not process what he was saying, except for three words: "You are fired."

As the storm passed, I walked away from the farmhouse, across the cornfield to our home, and went quietly to my room. About three hours later, at 4:15, the Chrysler Imperial pulled up at our front door. Granddad was at the wheel. We had a golf date.

We drove in silence to the Gettysburg Country Club. We played the first hole without a word, then the second. Then a par five over water. Near the green, Granddad broke the silence.

"I allow all of my associates one mistake a year. You've had yours."

I was rehired that afternoon, illustrating Alexander Pope's maxim, "To err is human, to forgive divine."

On August 28, 1963, Granddad, Dad, and Bill Ewald traveled to Berryville, Virginia, where the printers had begun to produce copies of *Mandate for Change*. By now, Dad had taken up flying as a hobby and offered to pilot Granddad and Ewald aboard a Cherokee he rented in York. To ease everyone's nerves, Dad stocked the plane with Scotch-and-water, magazines and a portable radio. Not surprisingly, Granddad, who held a private pilot's license he had earned in the Philippines, took the copilot's seat, from which he closely supervised the takeoff, navigation, and landing. As Dad recalled, the flight was somewhat of an ordeal, but the results were worth it. The Eisenhower party examined the first copies of *Mandate* with "delight," knowing that after two and a half years of research, writing, and painstaking editing, *Mandate for Change* was finished. It would spend a short time on the best-seller lists. The reviews in Dad's words were "generally good, considering the temper of the times."

Mandate for Change was also destined to become a much consulted book over the next several years because of its account of the first Indochina war. By fall, political and military crises enveloped President Ngo Dinh Diem of Vietnam, bringing to the fore the question of formal U.S. intervention. Many Americans perceived Eisenhower's refusal to intervene in 1954 as a meaningful precedent against intervention in 1963.

Because Kennedy was grappling with the Vietnam problem, Eisenhower's account of the Indochina crisis was carefully crafted to describe the precise circumstances his administration faced in 1953–54. In *Mandate,* Granddad explained his refusal to intervene with ground and air forces in support of the French during the closing days of the French war there. He related how his government had studied all possible means of assisting the French during the Dien Bien Phu battle and crisis: air strikes against exposed communist North Vietnamese regulars surrounding Dien Bien Phu; naval bombardment in support of the French forces; ground intervention.

Eisenhower made it plain that, in principle, he did not oppose land intervention in Asia as did so many military leaders of the era. But, he explained, U.S. forces, if committed in 1954, would have been fighting for French colonialism alongside French forces that had proven themselves unable to pacify the region in five years of war. Nor had France promised to grant independence to Vietnam once the fighting was over. If the United States intervened, Eisenhower wanted a broad coalition of forces, including the British, in order to limit the demands on American forces — but the British refused to pledge help. Finally, absent Chinese intervention, Eisenhower regarded Vietnam as an "internal situation" that did not fit with his overall concept of America's limited conventional military capacities. In *Mandate,* he re-created a discussion with his advisers: "If we, without allies, should ever find ourselves fighting at various places all over the region, and if Red Chinese aggressive participation were clearly identified, then we could scarcely avoid, I said, striking directly at the head instead of the tail of the snake, Red China itself."

Because Vietnam was heating up, Eisenhower's account tends to obscure the reasons he did not intervene while amplifying the reasons he might have, namely the threat of communism. He also stressed the successful containment of communism achieved in the outcome of the 1954 war: the creation of two Vietnams, an independent noncommunist South Vietnam backed by the United States, not the French, and a communist Vietnam in the north. Meaningfully, Eisenhower ended his Indochina account by emphasizing the importance of holding the line drawn in 1954: "The dilemma of finding a moral, legal, and practical basis for helping our friends of the region need not face us again."

In the book files for *Mandate,* there is further evidence that Eisenhower apparently changed his views about the feasibility of American ground intervention in Vietnam sometime between 1954 and *Mandate*'s publication in 1963. In *Mandate,* Eisenhower quoted a long letter he wrote to NATO Commander Alfred Gruenther in 1954 about the problems he was having arranging concerted action in Vietnam among the Americans, French, and British. Praising the heroism of the garrison at Dien Bien Phu, he urged Gruenther to preach "united action" whenever he met with the French and British. The key paragraph he deleted from the letter reads: "While I had some second hand reports of your feeling that the French leaders had practically abdicated, I had not known of your personal views with respect to the astonishing proposal for unilateral American intervention in Vietnam. Your adverse opinion exactly parallels mine."

By 1963, unilateral ground action was precisely the question Kennedy faced, and Eisenhower's deletion implies he did not want to foreclose it. Dad told me once that he had quarreled with Granddad's idea of tinkering with correspondence that he planned to reproduce in his memoirs. One afternoon, Dad interrupted Granddad, who sat busily at his desk redrafting a document that was five years old. When Dad objected, Granddad replied, "What's the matter, can't I misquote myself?"

Back at Exeter that fall for my second year, I read letters from home that were full of news. The farm operation was in fine shape. Anne was following in my footsteps and had become a boarder at Holton Arms in Washington. Susie was riding horses and Mary Jean was doing well in third grade. There was also unwelcome news from home that with publication of *Mandate,* Dad was considering job offers and that we might be moving from Gettysburg.

Letters from friends described the final round of centennial celebrations to mark Lincoln's Gettysburg Address, and the grand finale on November 19, when Granddad led the commemorative ceremonies. The *New York Times* chronicled the convergence of the Pennsylvania General Assembly, the state Supreme Court, and other dignitaries in Gettysburg for the luncheon and the retracing of Lincoln's journey from the town square down Baltimore Street to the cemetery. According to the *Times,* in brilliant fall sunshine, a massive throng was on hand at the National Cemetery. Marian Anderson, the gifted soprano who was famously barred from performing at Constitution Hall in segregated Washington, D.C., sang "He's Got the Whole World in His Hands," bringing tears to many. Speeches followed. E. Washington Rhodes, publisher of the black *Philadelphia Tribune,* emphasized the unfulfilled promise of emancipation and the imperative to move forward against all forms of segregation. "Were he to address this gathering," Holmes said, "Lincoln would declare that all second class citizenship, with all its attendant evils, must end." Governor William Scranton followed with brief remarks in which he acknowledged the "fierce battles ahead" in civil rights, adding that "the tyranny of prejudice is doomed because the American people in their common sense realize it is wrong." Granddad's short speech was covered in full. "Lincoln's faith that the Gettysburg battle would one day result in a peaceful union has been justified," he declared, "but the unfinished work of which he spoke in 1863 is still unfinished."

> True to democracy's basic principle that all men are created equal and endowed by the Creator with priceless human rights, the good citizen, as always before, is called upon to defend the basic rights of all others as he does his own; to subordinate self to country's good; to refuse to take the easy way today that may invite national disaster tomorrow; to accept the truth that the work still to be done awaits his doing.

At Thanksgiving time, my family decided to come to New England to join me, since I was less homesick for my friends in Gettysburg. On November 18, Granddad wrote,

Next week, the whole family is starting to Exeter to pay you a visit. If there is anything you would like me to bring along, (that is aside from a $10.00 bill) would you let me know by return mail? This possibility was brought up to me by your friend, Sergeant Moaney. He came to me at breakfast saying he thought you might like in your room either that picture I painted of you with folded hands — I think you were about 7 or 8 years old — or the much larger one which I painted of you dribbling a basketball. I am quite sure you don't want any picture of yourself — especially one by an amateur painter — in your room but because Moaney was so enthusiastic about the project I told him I would abide by your judgment. I am sure you won't want anything to do with them, at least while you are in school. I assure you that the last thing I would have done when I was at school was to have a picture of myself hanging on the wall, regardless of the individual that painted it. . . .

Granddad went on to describe pheasant hunting at the farm, Mamie's recent birthday celebration and the plans after Christmas to start for California, where he would serve as grand marshal of the Tournament of Roses Parade.

He ended his letter:

The last time I heard from you directly was by telephone when you told me about the disastrous test when you were too nervous to do your stuff. But I hear you almost made the "top" honor roll so I guess you are not doing too badly.

Take care of yourself and let me know if there is anything in athletic equipment like golf shoes that you might like me to bring.

Devotedly,
Granddad

DESPICABLE ACT

Four days later, on November 22, Eisenhower was at New York's Waldorf-Astoria Hotel for a Columbia University dinner and meetings with UN officials and with General Clay; Bill Robinson, formerly of the *Herald Tribune;* Augusta chairman Cliff Roberts; and Slats Slater, all major backers of Eisenhower in 1952 who were concerned about the bandwagon developing for conservative Republican senator Barry Goldwater. They were anxious to discuss moderate alternatives, including Pennsylvania's recently elected governor Scranton; the current ambassador in Vietnam and Nixon's running mate in 1960, Henry Cabot Lodge; and Michigan governor George Romney.

Shortly after 1:30, Eisenhower was called out of a meeting by General Schulz, who told him he had just heard the President had been shot in Dallas at 12:30 local time. Eisenhower returned to his hotel room and within the hour learned that John F. Kennedy had died in a Dallas hospital. By late evening, the Eisenhowers were in seclusion at their residence as Pennsylvania State Police and a small detail of Secret Service agents ordered by President Johnson took up positions around the farm.

The news from Dallas reached Exeter shortly after lunch, just before football and soccer practice. I was walking toward Thompson Gym when suddenly a friend rushed up and told me about television reports that someone had shot the President. He had no word of how badly the President had been injured, and so my first thoughts were of Granddad's illnesses in office and his ability to survive them. My further thought was that the miracles of modern medicine would be able to save the President.

The next hour was a blur. I remember arriving at the Thompson Gym, changing into soccer gear, and jogging outside just as whistles sounded, bringing all afternoon practices to an end. Returning to my locker, I passed dozens of classmates slumped on benches, many silently weeping. A coach stepped into the locker room to announce all school activities for the weekend were canceled. I slowly walked back to Peabody, alone with my thoughts about the impossible news of John Kennedy's death. I thought of the Secret Service agents who had been assigned to Eisenhower details. How many, I wondered, had been with the President in Dallas?

That night, I watched the dark aftermath of Dallas unfold on television: the arrival of the presidential plane at Andrews Air Force Base bearing the body of the slain president; Lyndon Johnson's brief remarks; the non-stop commentary and analysis throughout the evening, including interviews with leaders. I was startled when the television cameras showed Granddad emerging from the Waldorf. He read a brief statement in which he voiced his and Mamie's prayerful thoughts and condolences to the Kennedy family, and his "sense of shock and dismay that the entire nation must feel at the despicable act that took the life of the nation's President." In response to reporters' questions, Granddad voiced confidence that the "entire citizenry of the nation will join as one man in expressing not only their grief but indignation at this act and will stand faithfully behind the government."

November 23, 24, and 25 were days that would fix the Kennedy legend in collective memory. Upon his return from Dallas, President Lyndon Baines Johnson placed a call to Eisenhower and asked him to fly to Washington for consultations. During the two days Eisenhower spent in Washington, he conferred three times privately with the new president on the raft of problems he had suddenly inherited: the faltering American position in Vietnam; strained relations with President de Gaulle and NATO; and the civil rights bill languishing in Congress. Eisenhower had urgent, specific advice for the President. He should, as soon as possible, address a joint session of Congress that would eulogize Kennedy and allow him to grasp the reins of power.

The long and mournful state funeral brought Eisenhower and Truman together for their first real discourse in ten years. According to protocol, as former presidents the two men were scheduled to ride in the same limousine from Blair House to Arlington National Cemetery. Since leaving office, Eisenhower had seen Truman briefly when passing through Kansas City. They had encountered each other at the funeral of long-serving Speaker of the House Sam Rayburn in the fall of 1961. But, as always, they had maintained their distance.

With no possibility of hiding from each other, Eisenhower, Mamie, Truman, and his daughter, Margaret, who stood in for Bess Truman, decided to share a bourbon at Blair House before the procession to Arlington. Suddenly the two former presidents approached each other as friends, trading stories and observations as onetime comrades. On one thing they agreed, as Mamie recalled later, that as presidents their actions often had a rationale that could never be fully understood by historians or the outside world. It was best left that way. "We know what we did," Truman said. "We surely do," replied Eisenhower.

Under the immense shadow of the Kennedy tragedy, the two men seemed to understand each other. It no longer mattered that much who was more popular, Ike or Harry, or whether Ike had chosen to be a Republican rather than a Democrat. But these matters had been very important once. As Eisenhower had recorded in his long diary entry on New Year's Day in 1948:

> I've tried to make it crystal clear to him [Truman] that I'm determined to stay out of the political arena — that I always stand ready to do such little things as I could to help the govt — that I had felt an honor to serve, even in this office [Army chief of staff] so long as he felt I should! It seems to me that some of the 22 caliber people that get his ear must be doing some tampering. Why, I don't know unless it was that unfortunate "poll" that attempted to show I had a greater personal popularity than the President. . . .

But Eisenhower had entered politics and the relationship had changed. The Eisenhower-Truman reconciliation at Kennedy's funeral would be short-lived. The two men never communicated again.

As the nation mourned, our Thanksgiving plans went forward with the family gathering at my classmate Mel Ellis's home in Marblehead, Massachusetts. The Ellises were wonderful hosts, but the atmosphere was very subdued. All thoughts were on the tragedy in Dallas and on the sentiments eloquently expressed by Lyndon Johnson in his joint session address the day before Thanksgiving:

> I humbly hope that the tragedy and torment of these terrible days will bind us together in new fellowship, making us one people in our hour of sorrow. So let us here solemnly resolve that John Fitzgerald Kennedy did not live — or die — in vain. On this Thanksgiving, as we gather together to ask the Lord's blessing, and give Him our thanks, let us unite in those familiar and cherished words,

> "America, America, God shed his light on
>   thee
> And Crown thy good with brotherhood
> From sea to shining sea."

IDEAL CANDIDATE

Nineteen sixty-four was the year of Barry Goldwater's rise in the Republican Party; of Lyndon Johnson's obtaining passage of the Kennedy omnibus civil rights bill; of race riots in New York City, among other places; and of the beginning of major hostilities in Vietnam. Because of Nixon's defeat in California in 1962, Granddad again found himself in the role of titular leader of the party. That winter, a stream of politicians visited Eldorado to plot ways of using Eisenhower's influence to stop Goldwater.

But by 1964, Eisenhower was not well equipped to be the power broker in blunting Goldwater's drive for the nomination. He no longer had full-time political advisers, and was preoccupied with his second volume of memoirs and the management of the farm. Eisenhower also forbade the staff he did have from participating in his political discussions, confining them to work on his book and running his office.

There can be no question that Eisenhower opposed Goldwater. Among his desert friends, he recalled trenchantly in dinner conversations Goldwater's penchant for the memorable and salty phrase that had, as often as not, been aimed at Eisenhower. Goldwater had once called the administration a "dime store New Deal," and stated sarcastically "one Eisenhower in a generation is enough." Goldwater also cultivated right-wing Republican opponents of Eisenhower's moderate policies. During his primary campaign in New Hampshire, Goldwater promised a crowd he would see to it that "the right people," meaning the supporters of Robert Taft in 1952, would not be "kicked around this time."

Eisenhower had sympathy for Goldwater in one respect. The Arizona senator was attracting a press all too eager to convert his unstudied statements into major campaign embarrassments. By now, increasingly Granddad was consigning the press to the lower rungs of humanity inhabited by unnamed politicians. In a memorandum to himself on the topic of the press he wrote, "On the whole, the press group violates the old adage 'always take your job seriously, never yourself' — this old saw they largely apply in reverse. As a result, they have little sense of humor and, because of this, they deal in negative criticism rather than in any attempt towards constructive helpfulness. . . ." He continued:

I once heard that human minds are divided into three great classes, depending upon the kind of subject in which the greatest intellectual interest is taken. The essayist contended that the highest type of mind was concerned with philosophies and ideas and their application to the problems of life. He thought the second class of mind was concerned with the physical things about us, the products of our industry, the natural resources of the country, the machines we use, the food we eat, and so on. The third class he thought was concerned primarily with personalities. This kind of mind is the one, he said, that enjoys gossip.

If this kind of thing has any semblance of truth in it, I would say that it does not speak well for the average writer of the press. They love to deal in personalities; in their minds, personalities make stories.

Some years later, in December 1973, Goldwater would confirm to me in a backhanded way the tension between himself and Granddad. President Nixon invited Goldwater to dinner at the White House along with several of Nixon's advisers in an effort to induce the Arizona senator to be less outspokenly quotable during the debate on Nixon's possible impeachment because of the Watergate cover-up. I sat next to Goldwater during cocktails and he mentioned the coincidence that a nephew of Dwight Eisenhower had married Goldwater's longtime personal secretary and had named their son after the senator. "Barry Goldwater Eisenhower," the senator mused. "Why your granddaddy would roll over in his grave if he knew it."

Eisenhower had a dozen alternatives to Goldwater. He encouraged friends like Lucius Clay, Alfred Gruenther, and Herbert Hoover, Jr., to consider campaigning for the presidency. In 1963, Eisenhower's initial favorite had been his brother Milton, the man Eisenhower had often characterized as the "best qualified man" to succeed himself.

The notion of a Milton Eisenhower candidacy was not completely farfetched. His name had figured in backstage presidential politics ever since Dwight's heart attack in 1955, when party leaders first discussed Milton's running as a surrogate on the Republican ticket. Milton was a man of great distinction. During the 1930s, he had worked as assistant to Henry Wallace at the Department of Agriculture. In World War II, Milton served FDR in a variety of capacities: briefly as head of the War Relocation Authority and longer as deputy director of war information. Following the war, Milton participated in the establishment of UNESCO, the United Nations–sponsored organization designed to foster "better understanding among nations and peoples" through cultural exchanges. Interspersed with governmental assignments, Milton had served as president of Kansas State, Penn State, and Johns Hopkins universities.

During the White House years, though Milton had observed an unofficial sanction against nepotism, he exerted a strong influence behind the scenes. Dwight commonly lamented that the happenstance of Milton's birth had denied the cabinet one of its best minds. Milton was his brother's leading adviser on Latin America, his speech consultant, and a diplomatic troubleshooter. Republican leaders, including Richard Nixon, took Milton's prospects seriously if for no other reason than Dwight Eisenhower's enthusiasm.

Milton's liabilities, however, were considerable. The public's perception of him was murky. Friends and critics alike observed that he lacked the killer instinct necessary to survive in high-level politics. His main problem was his ambiguous political allegiance. Milton had served the New Deal enthusiastically. He was a person of outspoken liberal views and for a short period following the Kennedy assassination, Milton eagerly served as an unofficial consultant to the Johnson administration. Right-wing critics of Dwight Eisenhower passionately attacked Milton's influence in the Eisenhower administration, accusing him of weaving a

Rasputin-like spell over his brother. Milton could hardly command the partisan attachments and loyalties of the kind necessary to be the Republican nominee.

During the fall of 1963, Eisenhower had taken steps to promote Milton. He secured Milton's appointment to the Critical Issues Council, a forum with strong progressive leanings designed to develop position papers for incorporation into the 1964 Republican platform. At a testimonial in Harrisburg honoring his seventy-third birthday, Eisenhower shared the platform exclusively with his brother in hopes that Milton would gain stature in the eyes of the Republican leadership gathering.

It had not worked. Herbert Brownell, Thomas Dewey, publisher John Hay "Jock" Whitney, and Lucius Clay scheduled a meeting with Dwight Eisenhower in New York on November 23, 1963, for the purpose of discouraging Eisenhower from any further efforts on his brother's behalf. The assassination of John Kennedy forced postponement of the meeting, but the group ultimately met and convinced Eisenhower that promoting Milton was hopeless. Thereafter, Eisenhower adopted an unbending neutrality toward the presidential nomination, but there is no question that, as always, he was pulling for the moderate wing of the party in defiance of the conservative trend.

Eisenhower strongly believed in the concept of a "dynamic center" in national politics. Reflecting on conservative criticism that his "dynamic center" was too vague, Eisenhower had conceded to *Saturday Evening Post* editor Ben Hibbs that precise labels for his brand of Republicanism had always been elusive. He himself used labels like "middle of the roader," "dynamic conservative," "moderate conservative," and, lastly, "progressive conservative." When Hibbs commented that Eisenhower's basically moderate positions had been "sensible," Eisenhower replied, "Well, 'middle of the road' was a poor term, but moderation should govern human affairs."

"You made the middle of the road acceptable," Hibbs responded.

"Yes, well," Eisenhower answered, "except for moral issues and exact sciences, extreme positions are always wrong."

By early 1964, as the Goldwater forces moved efficiently through state conventions garnering delegates, a scramble ensued among moderate Republicans for an alternative candidate. Though locked into neutrality, Eisenhower lent support to the moderates by encouraging an "open convention."

Governor Nelson Rockefeller, the man John Kennedy had expected to be his opponent, appeared to offer a viable alternative. But his divorce and remarriage to a younger woman cut deeply with conservative voters in New Hampshire and with Republicans nationwide, who were being exhorted by Barry Goldwater to join in a crusade against the deteriorating social and moral fabric of the country. Rockefeller also encountered opposition because of his Wall Streeter's contempt for "Main Street" Republicans.

When Goldwater exploited these prejudices against Rockefeller in New Hampshire, Rockefeller retaliated by portraying Goldwater as an extremist and as a reckless politician out of the "mainstream." Both men lost the primary to a last minute write-in campaign waged by a handful of amateurs on behalf of U.S. ambassador to Vietnam Henry Cabot Lodge. Although Goldwater remained leader of the conservative forces, the leadership of the moderates was up for grabs.

Eight thousand miles away, in Saigon, and immersed in the urgent task of developing political stability in the aftermath of the assassination of South Vietnam's President Diem, Lodge hesitated about returning to commit himself to full-time campaigning. Governor George Romney, with his reputation as a "doer" owing to his service as board chairman of American Motors, was interested, but preoccupied with his own reelection campaign. Scranton of Pennsylvania remained undecided, telling backers, including my father, by letter that the demands a campaign would make on his family seemed too great. Nixon excited some speculation after receiving significant write-in votes in Nebraska and Oregon and consistently high ratings in Republican preference polls, but he realized he had no serious prospect of nomination, and, like Eisenhower, adopted a position of neutrality.

The moderate wing of the party seemed paralyzed — not persuaded that Goldwater had the power to win the nomination, but listless about rising in unison to do anything to prevent it. Thus, while moderates slept, Goldwater went about winning the nomination. He preached the unconstitutionality of federal antidiscrimination activism in an era of awakening sympathy for the black cause. He opposed government management of the economy despite the proven success of

New Deal measures that had lifted the country out of the Depression. He advocated confrontation with the Soviet Union in the wake of Kennedy's deft handling of the Cuban Missile Crisis. In New Hampshire, Goldwater called for placing Social Security on a voluntary basis, ensuring the desertion of older voters who otherwise might have been drawn to his self-reliant philosophy. He talked about delegating command and control of nuclear weapons to NATO commanders.

Goldwater was a series of contradictions: a self-proclaimed libertarian leading a revolt against nonconformity and a philosopher in love with America's pastoral origins, yet a man who was an advocate of technology, fascinated by the grim science of war. But typically, Eisenhower's principal objection to Goldwater rested on an obscure and technical point. In New Hampshire, Goldwater had been asked about reports he planned to break relations with the Soviet Union. Erroneously, Goldwater implied that as president he would not have the power to do so, overlooking Article II of the Constitution, which grants the president powers to receive and appoint ambassadors. Goldwater's remarks had been designed to reassure the voters of New Hampshire that he was not hell-bent on preventing peaceful coexistence with the Soviets. But Eisenhower fastened on Goldwater's inaccurate depiction of presidential authority. In his view, Goldwater's response had been well nigh disqualifying on its face. No person, Eisenhower reasoned, who lacked a fundamental understanding of the authority vested in the office deserved to be president.

At Exeter, I followed the campaign with interest, attending several campus debates. But the big news that winter was that my father had decided to leave Gettysburg and the Eisenhower staff. Granddad's second volume of presidential memoirs was well under way and, having resigned the Army, Dad was eager to embark on a new career independent of Dwight Eisenhower and the White House. As much as Dad admired his father, he had not always found him the easiest man to work for, especially in times of high stress. Dad illustrated the point with a story. During the tense days of the Berlin crisis in late 1958, Granddad had been particularly on edge. As staff assistant, Dad's job first thing each morning was to cull CIA and Defense cables and brief his father on the contents. The President seemed perpetually grumpy, greeting Dad each morning by thumping the desk: "What the hell do you want!" Dad took it all in stride, including coming home one night to be greeted by Mom, who reported she had received a phone call from Granddad earlier that afternoon. "He says you have been in a bad mood lately, Johnnie. What's wrong?"

Dad chose a position as executive vice president of the Freedoms Foundation, a patriotic organization based near the Valley Forge National Historical Park. He and Mom purchased a home in Phoenixville, several miles from the foundation and near Philadelphia's "Main Line" suburban belt. Phoenixville is a steel town, the home of novelist John O'Hara and the subject of many of his books. Because of its size and industrial base, Phoenixville would have lots of attractions, but I knew I would miss historic Gettysburg and the people I knew there.

With little energy to try to find new friends in Phoenixville during summer recess from Exeter, I wanted to work in Gettysburg. I considered Granddad's offer of a job at the farm, but my firing the summer before had diminished my zest for returning to painting fences, weeding the kitchen garden, tending the stables, and lofting hay. Granddad decided the matter by inviting me to live at the farm while working elsewhere in town. In a letter, adding icing to the cake, Granddad confided:

I hope I am not revealing another secret when I tell you that Mimi [the grandchildren's name for Mamie] expects to lend you the Valiant to drive back and forth to work (assuming that you then have your license) but she will probably exact from you several promises about not speeding, observing all traffic laws and keeping out of other automobiles driven by reckless people. However, I don't think this will be hard to take and the car is a little beauty as you may remember. So far I think it has been driven about 15 miles. . . .

By May, as the California primary heated up and as Lodge's prospects faded, Rockefeller represented the moderates' last best hope. He waged a vigorous campaign in California, running neck and neck with Goldwater according to the polls. Critics of Eisenhower's neutrality grew frantic. If only Eisenhower would intervene on behalf of Rockefeller, moderates could deny Goldwater a primary victory, win the huge California delegation, and bolster Rockefeller's leadership in the movement to stop

Goldwater.

In the final weeks before the California voting, Eisenhower appeared to be on the verge of supporting Rockefeller. He wrote a carefully phrased article for the *New York Herald Tribune* defining his "Ideal Candidate." As reporter Earl Mazo wrote in the *New York Times,* Eisenhower's definition would fit "all the potential candidates except for Barry Goldwater of Arizona." In particular, Eisenhower's "Ideal Candidate" stood for:

1. Loyal adherence to the United Nations, which Goldwater opposed.
2. Support for the 1960 platform, which Goldwater had labeled a "Munich"-style sellout to the Rockefeller wing of the party.
3. Vigorous action on civil rights, which Goldwater was opposing on the floor of the Senate.

Reporting from California on May 27, the *New York Times*' James Reston wrote that Eisenhower's article had "transformed the California primary election." In a public statement issued by his headquarters, Rockefeller seized on the apparent similarity between himself and Eisenhower's "Ideal

Candidate" and declared he fell "within the framework of that description." He repeatedly alluded to his service in the Eisenhower administration, and praised the former president for having "met the nation's needs responsively and responsibly."

Goldwater moved adroitly. Officially in a statement issued in Phoenix, Arizona, he praised the document as "most timely and relevant," adding, "I endorse General Eisenhower's forthright restatement of Republican principles." But on the day following publication, Goldwater delighted supporters at a rally in Redding, California, by crumpling a program under his arm and turning his profile toward the audience, simulating an arrow in his back. Goldwater's supporters besieged newspapers with angry letters claiming that the eastern press had distorted the meaning of Eisenhower's article.

Pushed along by Eisenhower's "endorsement," Rockefeller led in the polls by fair margins over the weekend before the voting. Goldwater backers began minimizing the significance of California's winner-take-all primary. But Rockefeller's luck suddenly turned for the worse. On Saturday, his new wife gave birth to a son, rekindling the issue of his divorce and remarriage. And on

Monday, Eisenhower inexplicably blunted the impact of his calculated rebuff of Goldwater. Cornered by newsmen on a New York City sidewalk emerging from a board meeting of Joyce Hall's People to People Foundation, Eisenhower called the anti-Goldwater reading of his article "a complete misinterpretation," and added, "You people [meaning the newsmen assembled] read Goldwater out of the party, I didn't."

Eisenhower's Monday comments might have been accidental. Or perhaps Eisenhower had developed second thoughts about any preconvention favoritism, mindful of Harry Truman's humiliating rebuffs at the Democratic conventions in 1956 and 1960 when he backed Averell Harriman against Stevenson, and Stuart Symington against Kennedy.

Laboring under these twin blows, on June 2, Rockefeller lost the California primary and any serious hope for nomination by a slim sixty-eight thousand votes out of several million cast. The narrow defeat left him spiritless and beaten, and he withdrew from active pursuit of the nomination.

The California primary also probably ended any chance of derailing Goldwater's campaign. On June 6, reacting to the California results, state and district Republican conventions and caucuses in Alabama, Colorado, Washington, Hawaii, and Virginia awarded sixty-four delegates to Goldwater, bringing his delegate strength to 532, within 150 votes of the nomination.

A REAL CHOICE

Having unwittingly contributed to Rockefeller's demise, Eisenhower now turned to Scranton. On June 5, Milton called Dwight and suggested that he encourage the Pennsylvania governor to become an active candidate. Eisenhower quickly placed a call to Scranton and invited him to a meeting in Gettysburg to discuss what Scranton had meant over the past few months about being available for a "genuine draft."

That evening, the television set on Granddad's porch failed, and my grandparents drove to our home at the corner of the farm to view the acclaimed and widely watched *D-Day Plus 20 Years.* Our viewing of the special was interrupted beginning around seven o'clock by worried phone calls from members of Granddad's staff: there were press inquiries about stories circulating in Harrisburg that Eisenhower was now prepared to back Scranton. Watching Granddad's reaction that night, I doubt that he had arranged the meeting with Scranton in order to offer his firm personal support. He grew visibly angry, complaining that "someone is running with the ball." As press inquiries mushroomed into an avalanche of requests for a statement saying yes or no, Granddad began pacing angrily about the room near the television set, his face crimson, his eyes dancing wildly with frustration. "Tell them nuts," Eisenhower snapped. Dad picked up the phone in the next room to order the office to refuse comment on all inquiries.

Promptly at 10:15 the following morning, Scranton arrived at Eisenhower's office for the hurriedly arranged meeting. For more than eighty-five minutes, Scranton and Eisenhower discussed Scranton's availability in terms that remain unknown and controversial to this day. Scranton's friends and staff have insisted that he emerged that noon with a promise of support from Eisenhower should the governor decide to launch a campaign to stop Goldwater, and that Eisenhower suggested that the campaign begin the next day in Cleveland, where Scranton would be attending the Republican Governors' Conference. Allegedly, Eisenhower even suggested that the essentials of their conversation be leaked to the press that afternoon to create interest in

Scranton's scheduled appearance Sunday morning on *Face the Nation* from studios in Cleveland. According to the Eisenhower version, he had simply encouraged Scranton to clarify "ambiguities" surrounding his stated willingness to accept a draft and reiterated his long-standing personal desire for an "open convention" in San Francisco. According to Dad, Scranton arrived in Gettysburg eager to run and had possibly "heard what he wanted to hear."

Scranton had promised supporters and friends that his remarks on *Face the Nation* would contain "interesting developments." Newspapers dispatched correspondents to Cleveland to gather information for editorials greeting Scranton's announcement of an active campaign for the White House. At noon Sunday, a nationwide audience tuned in expecting to hear Scranton declare his candidacy with Eisenhower's support.

Scranton shocked viewers and reporters with a wavering, tentative performance studded with pauses and circumlocutions. The anticipated announcement did not materialize. Something had gone wrong. Watching Scranton on the television at our house while repairmen worked on his own set on the porch, Granddad might have been one of the only viewers to express satisfaction with Scranton's performance. As the show ended, he remarked to Dad that Scranton had said "about what I had expected."

Two days later, a feature story appeared in the *New York Times* purporting to explain the "inside story" of how Eisenhower had "deflated Scranton's trial balloon." According to reporter Joseph Loftus, former secretary of the Treasury George Humphrey had reached Eisenhower by phone moments before Scranton's television appearance. A Goldwater supporter, Humphrey voiced displeasure with reports that Eisenhower intended to break his neutrality to back Scranton. Humphrey urged his former boss not to become involved in a "cabal" to deny Goldwater the nomination.

Eisenhower then allegedly phoned Cleveland to locate Scranton. Assuming Eisenhower was calling with encouragement, a staff member interrupted Scranton in the studio waiting room with news that the General was on the phone. But instead, Eisenhower reportedly told Scranton that he had reconsidered the matter, and now felt he should not "be part of a cabal to stop Goldwater," nor should Scranton. Stunned and abandoned, Scranton went on the program with nothing to say.

Eisenhower confirmed to reporters that he had spoken with Humphrey on Sunday morning but denied that he had discussed politics. My father states merely that he cannot "confirm or deny" Loftus's version of the Humphrey call and Eisenhower's subsequent conversation with Scranton.

Loftus's story exposed Eisenhower as indecisive and floundering. *Washington Post* cartoonist Herblock bitterly caricatured Eisenhower as a feeble old man, contrasting Eisenhower's fumbling in 1964 with the capacity for judgment he had demonstrated twenty years earlier on D-Day.

For six days, Scranton's campaign lay stillborn. Meanwhile, Romney made a bid to lead the moderate cause. In Cleveland, attending the Governors' Conference, Romney broke his Mormon observance of the Sabbath's injunction against politics on Sunday and rose to declare before his colleagues that Goldwater's nomination would be "suicidal self-destruction" for the Republican Party. One day later, Richard Nixon flew into Cleveland to sound out Romney's intentions and to urge coordinated action to oblige Goldwater to adhere to a set of principles including "the TVA, Social Security, the United Nations, diplomatic relations with the Soviet Union, and foreswearing a legislative ban on compulsory union membership."

Goldwater ignored Romney and labeled Nixon "another Harold Stassen," known as the perpetual candidate for president. On June 10, William Miller, chairman of the National Republican Party, stated "the battle is over." He declared that the party now had an obligation to unite behind the candidacy of Barry Goldwater. But the very afternoon Miller declared him the winner, Goldwater was in Washington casting his vote against a cloture motion, along with a bloc of Southern Democratic senators, in an effort to kill the civil rights bill.

Immediately the next morning, Eisenhower called a meeting with his brother Milton and former White House assistants Malcolm Moos and Robert Merriam at his Gettysburg office to discuss the implications of Goldwater's vote and Eisenhower's position of neutrality. Eisenhower blessed Milton's decision to become a Scranton delegate from Maryland and agreed to place a call to the Pennsylvania governor to assure him privately of his desire that Scranton run.

Eisenhower then spoke with reporters and stated that he found it "incomprehensible" that anyone could believe that "civil rights was an area in which the Federal Government has no responsibility." He added that he was "no longer sure" he could support a candidate "who viewed these rights as falling under the exclusive protection of states." He worked in an elliptical endorsement of Scranton's expected announcement in Maryland the following day, then reiterated his support of an open convention, and his confidence that one could yet be obtained. He added, "And Bill Scranton knows this better than most."

Scranton launched his brief campaign on June 12, before a Maryland Republican convention. Determined to save the party of Lincoln from falling into the hands of racists, Scranton announced he was in the race, with a play on the famous statement by Barry Goldwater that he offered a "choice not an echo." Scranton declared, "I reject the echoes so far we have been handed. . . . I come here to offer the party a real choice."

Scranton's courageous and impossible fight for the nomination was a stirring chapter in Republican politics. He attracted few endorsements since most Republicans were convinced of Goldwater's inevitability and eager to come to terms with it. His backing consisted of a mere handful of Republican governors and congressional figures, all of whom faced tough reelection contests in northern and eastern districts. Scranton by now had given up on obtaining Eisenhower's formal public support.

The speculation and pressure on Eisenhower to take a public stand continued until the moment of the convention, but he refused to budge. In a letter to C. D. Jackson, Eisenhower complained about these pressures, quoting Lincoln from Stephen Vincent Benét's poem "John Brown's Body":

> They come to me and talk about God's
>   will
> In righteous deputations and platoons,
> Day after day, laymen and ministers.
> They write me prayers from Twenty
>   Million Souls
> Defining me God's will and Horace
>   Greeley's.
> God's will is General This or Senator
>   That . . .
> And, yet, if it is probable that God
> Should, and so very clearly, state His will
> To others, on a point of my own duty,
> It might be thought He would reveal it . . .
> Directly, more especially as I
> So earnestly desire to know his will.

"Straighten Up and Fly Right"

In late June, the movers arrived and worked into the night packing my family's belongings and stripping our Gettysburg home bare. I carted several suitcases of my clothes the half mile to my new summer home, the guest house on the northern end of the circular driveway in front of my grandparents' house. The guest house was equipped with two single beds, a small desk, bathroom, and a private telephone, granting me enough self-sufficiency to be able to come and go at will without disturbing my grandparents' routine. After a week of job hunting, I went to work as a salesman behind the counter in a battlefield tour shop connected to Gettysburg's brand-new Holiday Inn.

I discovered that Gettysburg had awakened from its mood of complacency about national issues. One year earlier, when Governor George Wallace of Alabama had traveled to Gettysburg for the dedication of an Alabama state monument, his presence was interpreted as a highly symbolic act of reconciliation. Five months later, the Kennedy assassination had shocked the community, especially the younger people. One could detect throughout our small town a strong desire to redeem that tragedy. Since

Granddad had been a political opponent of Kennedy's, I sensed a vague tone of reproach in some of the letters I received from friends as they pledged themselves to pursue the course set down by the fallen leader. As a few of my friends went off into service-oriented summer jobs, I would be whiling away the summer behind a ticket counter and "making money for local promoters."

Racial passions ran high. There were rumors of planned riots in Gettysburg's sleepy black quarter. Scuffles and incidents between Gettysburg's invisible black ghetto and the neighboring children of Appalachian farmers multiplied. Politics even pierced the genial atmosphere at the tour shop.

All summer I had a good-natured argument with Don Bickel, my high school football and basketball coach, who moonlighted as a driver for a commercial bus tour of the battlefield. Though a lifelong Democrat, he was my personal hero. He had once been drafted by the Baltimore Colts to play football, as one could guess by his enormous frame and broad shoulders. By now, his waistline sagged considerably. His left cheek bore a long scar that reminded everyone who knew him of a tragic automobile accident that had cut his career short. He was a Truman man and delighted in razzing me about the Goldwater fiasco brewing that summer.

"Well, Eisenhower," he would begin, stepping off the bus after unloading a group of tourists after the hour-and-a-half ride through the battlefield. "Looks like Goldwater might carry Delaware this fall, maybe Idaho and if he's lucky, Arizona."

"Might do as well as Truman could," I replied.

"Watch that," he'd say jokingly.

Once he stood next to me as two customers, bedecked with cameras and pamphlets about the battle, strode in demanding a refund because two blacks had been allowed to board the bus. The coach explained the company's policy of permitting everyone to ride the bus. A refund was impossible. "That's robbery," the man drawled, "and I intend to talk to your superior about that."

"You do that," the coach replied, pounding a Joe Louis–size fist into the ham of his left hand.

As the couple hurriedly left, the coach turned to me.

"What do you think of your old pal Barry Goldwater now?" he glared. I blushed, speechless.

I usually arrived home from the tour shop shortly after five o'clock and disappeared into the guest cottage to read, phone friends, and plot my nocturnal escape after dinner. Granddad would arrive back from the office at around five, climb the stairs to his room, shower, shave, dress, and wander back downstairs for a cocktail before dinner. Mamie spent most of her days at home answering correspondence and watching soap operas in bed. In time to greet Granddad upon his return from the office, she would dress and resume the perpetual solitaire card game she kept spread over her wrought-iron card table next to Granddad's easel on the porch.

Evenings were uneventful. Social hour usually involved watching the nightly news or a favorite television program. Dinner was served on trays promptly at 7:30 in front of the television.

Friends kept the Eisenhower home generously stocked with gadgets, fix-its, and useless electronic "time-savers" that fascinated my grandparents endlessly. Granddad and Mamie seemed to assume that within several more decades of the kind of progress they had witnessed in their life, the world would be full of electronic card shufflers, talking clocks, and singing coffeemakers.

Granddad's favorite new gadget was the remote control television channel selector that, unfortunately, was the source of most of the disagreements around the house. His switching back and forth between his favorites and Mamie's every ninety seconds or so was a habit that upset Mamie.

At the beginning of social hour, Granddad would take his customary position in a compact velvet upholstered rocker next to the sliding glass door, set at an exact distance from the television screen to avoid radiation. Mamie sat in a large stuffed armchair several feet behind. Granddad would punch the channel selector "on" button, and the argument would begin.

"Now what is it the two of you would like to see," he would ask cheerfully, examining the television guide through the bottom section of his bifocals. Mamie always had a choice. Granddad would check Mamie's channel suggestion against the television listing, turn with displeasure, and canvass me for my choice. I perfected a technique in which I would draw up as though about to respond, hesitate, and wait for Mamie to interrupt and deflect the decision away from me. Mamie would indeed take over, and the two would argue over what "young people" liked to see on television.

Granddad, with a gesture of resignation, would turn to the set and begin experimenting with the remote. He was anything but skilled. As often as not, he would punch the remote and the television set would begin to run through the VHF and UHF bands until Granddad managed to catch the desired channel. First *Rawhide.* Then *Donna Reed.* Then *Perry Mason.* Back to *Rawhide.* Then another quick pass over the entire UHF and VHF bands.

"Ike," Mamie would plead, "make up your mind." Granddad often played deaf. He sat with his right leg draped over his left, his head cocked slightly to the left, his mammoth hand rising to his face while he ate, then falling away while punching the remote. Mamie's plea would finally register and he would turn to me again, casting a hard look through his bifocals. I tried to be inscrutably enthusiastic about everything. Mamie would interrupt, and Granddad would resume punching the remote.

Despite the tranquil rural Pennsylvania setting beyond the sunporch and the aimless activity at dinnertime, evenings were tense. Granddad's tinkering with the remote control was nervous activity. Throughout dinner, he sat in constant motion, punching the switch, chewing on the frame of his tortoiseshell glasses, bouncing his crossed leg in impatience.

I felt the need to slip away at night. I had passed the driver's test, and taking up Granddad's offer, I had purchased Mamie's car at a discount. As advertised, the '62 Valiant had sat in pristine condition in the garage at the farm beneath the hayloft for four years until I acquired it on my sixteenth birthday. Unfortunately, the car's engine block had ossified owing to disuse and it required constant maintenance. But I was glad to have wheels, albeit with "Mamie Doud Eisenhower" written in large gold script across the glove compartment.

Granddad had allowed me to purchase the car upon the one condition hinted at in his letter: I was not to drive it over 55 miles per hour. Solemnly I agreed but with several mental reservations. Since I would rarely return before Granddad and Mamie turned in for the night, I said my good nights before revving up and roaring off. I spent many evenings that summer cruising through town, dragging along the new I-15 bypass of Gettysburg and calling on friends. The car was independence. I loved driving, floating through the countryside with the windows down and radio blaring.

In time, I gained a reputation around Gettysburg as a "cowboy" in my '62 Valiant. I even gathered a few invitations to drag at the U.S. 30 Drago-Way. But soon I had to slow down when a warning was passed to me at the Tour Center that the state police had been keeping tabs on my driving habits. If caught, the warning went, there would be no second chances.

I usually returned to the guest cottage around midnight. Morning came early. Granddad was usually awake shortly after six, as had been his habit in the White House and the Army. To avoid him and questions about the previous evening, I slept until seven, disrupting the routine around the farm by causing Sergeant Moaney to cook breakfast twice.

Even when awakened by the sound of Granddad departing for the day at the office, I lay awake in bed waiting for the noise of Granddad's departure and the sounds of Moaney's humming and slow tread across the gravel driveway toward the guest cottage for the announcement of "seven o'clock."

Moaney was always humming a song of his own, familiar-sounding but uncategorizable. He carried a tune that resembled a Stephen Foster melody or a spiritual, but the words were improvised. "Good Lord, I'm going away," he sang, morning and night, waiting on the table, or setting up trays, vacuuming the rugs or polishing the silver.

Moaney sensed I stalled in the morning to avoid inspections or last-minute instructions from Granddad on his way to work. Knocking at the door, he always seemed to be laughing. "Master David, time to get up," he'd announce, knocking loudly.

"Thank you, Sergeant Moaney," I would reply groggily.

"Yessssir, sure is time to get up," he would repeat, knowingly.

"Thank you, Sergeant Moaney, I'll be right in."

"Yes sir, time t'rise and shine," he would giggle.

"Be right there," I would reply. He knew something, I thought. Probably the hour I came in last night.

"Take your time, the General is gone," he'd say with a laugh, turning to walk back to the residence. Over the crunch of his slow gait, the sound of his humming would resume.

I wondered that summer how Delores and Moaney, both African-American, viewed the Republican Party nominee. Their permanent home was in nearby Washington. Delores was a constant radio listener in the kitchen while preparing lunch and dinner.

Both were undoubtedly well informed about Goldwater's outspoken opposition to the Civil Rights Bill. I hoped they knew of Granddad's efforts to lobby Republicans on behalf of passage of the bill.

Moaney seemed jovial, with a roly-poly walk and a ready laugh that was really a giggle. But his demeanor masked sadness over a frightful automobile accident that had killed his children and first wife. His happy marriage to Delores helped heal the scar of his earlier tragedy, but Moaney promised himself he would never again drive a car.

With the passage of years, as the stream of guests to the farm began to diminish, Moaney had more time on his hands and began gardening in a field below the kitchen. He spent evenings sitting on the back steps to the kitchen. Before going out to race my '62 Valiant, I would visit him and trade jokes about one of Granddad's moods that day or perhaps a frustration Granddad was experiencing in training the bird dogs. At times I felt I was interrupting a melancholy thought because his eyes glistened. But on seeing me, he would draw up and assume his good-humored posture.

"The general sure was mad with you today," he would say, amused.

"Guess I haven't seen him that worked up in some time," I would reply.

"Yes, sir," he continued, "time to straighten up and fly right." He'd heave in laughter.

"Time to straighten up and I mean yesterday!" I would add.

The Moaneys loved Dwight Eisenhower, and the respect and affection was reciprocated. Sergeant John Moaney would be one of eight honorary pallbearers at Granddad's state funeral. Emulating his boss, Moaney took up several of Granddad's hobbies. He began painting. He loved fishing and hunting. He spent six months once weaving a tapestry of the White House, which he proudly presented to me on my birthday. It was revealed at his funeral in 1978 that Sergeant Moaney contributed a substantial percentage of his income to the maintenance of his church on the Eastern Shore in Maryland. And after Granddad's death, the Moaneys honored their promise to look after Mamie. Out of respect, partly out of superstition, for nine years Moaney refused to enter the small bedroom Granddad had used for naps, which adjoined Mamie's pink and green suite.

Granddad also felt the compulsion to get away every now and then. Sometimes after work, he would ask me to take him for a ride, or if I could put off leaving for the evening, to join him on his stroll along the lane leading from the residence to Waterworks Road. When he asked to go along on a drive, it was under the pretext of needing something at the store. I scrupulously buckled my seat belt while he fastened his, and the two of us would crawl down Route 15 with the speedometer stuck on 40 to the town square. He spent most of the time monitoring the speedometer. We usually said very little.

I enjoyed the reaction of townsfolk in front of the drugstore. The parking spaces on the town square were side-by-side instead of end-to-end. After parking, Granddad would give me a brief list of items he wanted, then drop his head and stare at the radio to avoid recognition. Before walking into the store, I always looked behind to check the expressions of the people alongside the '62 Valiant. Some glanced aimlessly around, impatient, others applied lipstick, checking themselves in a mirror, looking at a watch. In moments the scene would be transformed. A small crowd would form, all eyes glued on Granddad, staring in disbelief at the familiar profile.

We played golf about once a week. By now

I was inured to Granddad's "giving up" on my golf swing, and constant complaining that it was like my baseball swing. I was free to enjoy the spectacle of an Eisenhower golf game for what it was, a hilariously emotional event. Granddad played golf with fierce concentration, complete humorlessness, as a perfectionist, and with mixed results. Occasionally, he broke 80. More often, he shot in the mid to high 80s.

Granddad was an authority on many of the game's fine points by the time he left the White House, owing to years of playing in the company of the finest pros at Augusta, Blindbrook, and other famous courses around the country. He was a stickler on putting technique and an expert on sand-trap shots. Above all, he played to win and disliked raw power with no finesse. I hit a long ball inaccurately. The drive, he said constantly, is "pure exhibition."

Granddad never threw clubs or pounded them shapeless after poor shots. Instead his face would wrinkle up like a prune, his eyes glint, his body shudder then stiffen as he bellowed an oath. His anger was always directed at himself, but with such ferocity that it struck fear in anyone playing with him. Would he have a coronary? Could he control himself? His doctors kept insisting that his blood pressure reacted positively to a regimen of golf, yet playing with him always made me wonder why. He was mercurial. His worst rounds were often his most serene, his best round the most agitated. One afternoon he shocked my mother for eighteen holes with unpredictable and terrifying outbursts of wrath, agony, and self-reproach. In the car returning to the residence, he sat studying the scorecard, tabulating the numbers and then rechecking. "Barbie," he beamed, "this was the best round I've shot in over six months."

Some — my mother in particular — had a pacifying effect on Granddad. Former White House aide Kevin McCann, who had rejoined Granddad's staff in Gettysburg, recalled that Eisenhower regarded his daughter-in-law with "the pride of Abraham." Granddad used to refer to her as "perfect," once remarking to McCann that "when Barbara was born, the mold was broken."

Mom was an Army brat. Her father, Infantry Colonel Percy Thompson, our grandfather "Daddy Perc," was a veteran of both world wars and Korea. In 1943, he had earned a Silver Star with Oak Leaf Clusters in service with the U.S. First Division. Like the Eisenhowers, the Thompsons had a talent for picking up stakes and mastering the social amenities necessary in Army life, like golf. Granddad spent hours coaching Mom with her golf game and developed a prize pupil. My mother swung a club fluidly and aggressively. With Mom, Granddad was patient.

His Washington minister, Dr. Edward R. L. Elson, claimed that Granddad had only a dim awareness of the chilling effect his outbursts on the golf course had on others. In fact, Elson told me years later, Eisenhower had been unaware of the force of his temper altogether until he sat in the congregation of the National Presbyterian Church one Sunday and listened to Elson deliver a sermon titled "The Love of Christ Controlleth All Men." Letting Christ work through you, Elson argued, you can control all emotions.

Granddad had always shown great interest in sermons, but, according to Elson, this one struck an unusually responsive note. Granddad asked Elson to drop by the White House for a parish call to explain it. He was intrigued by Elson's thesis, suspecting it spoke to him in ways he had not considered before. As Elson reminded me, great men are seldom clever about themselves and Granddad was no exception. Elson added,

"The control I spoke of he had achieved long before in his life."

Granddad made a real effort that summer to encourage me to think about my future. Soon I would be selecting a college, a major, and committing myself in a direction that would open some doors and close others. When he joined me on walks after dinner down the lane, he attempted to counsel me, draw me out about what I had in mind.

Years of exposure to the most successful men in the country had stamped his notions of how a young man should pattern himself to get along in the world. But like the businessmen around him, Granddad tended to equate what he valued in a subordinate with what he felt brought about success and enrichment in a profession. He stressed education and professional degrees, early exposure to corporate life, and loyalty to superiors, and, above all, fastidious homework and ceaseless study. "You want to know more than your boss," he insisted. "Always know more, always anticipate the problems of your superiors. Never take shortcuts."

What Granddad valued about himself were his "Germanic" traits — persistence, hard work, and thoroughness. These qualities had undoubtedly equipped him well in the Oval Office. But they did not get him there. Indeed, as Dad pointed out, Grand-dad's boldness and independence as a middle grade officer had distinguished him, and his intuition and self-confidence had advanced him in ways that higher education and refinement could not. For the most part, he and his colleagues were unfettered personalities, eccentrics, individualists — far cries from the bland corporate types that they held up as examples of model officers.

Our evenings were rarely disrupted by politics since Granddad avoided discussion of the Goldwater situation during hours away from the office. One night my best friend, the son of a Gettysburg College professor, called asking whether it would be possible for him to bring his brother and an Indian foreign exchange student to the farm for a chat with my grandparents. Since the call came before social hour, I thought I should check. On my private line from the guest house, I called Granddad and Mamie.

Mamie picked up the phone next to her solitaire table. With a bullhorn speaker and a long-stemmed earpiece, the phone was a decorative piece and inherently defective in the transmitter and receiver.

"Hello," she shouted.

"Mimi?" I said. She paused, unsure of the

voice she had just heard. Gunshot noises faintly rang out from Granddad's television set at the far end of the room. I concluded my grandparents were dressed and having a cocktail. "Mimi, is it okay to bring a few friends to meet you all?"

"Oh! David! One moment. Let me check with your grandfather."

Pause, blam, blam, zing.

"C'mon over," she cheerily replied.

Fifteen minutes later when we entered, Granddad started, glanced at us, and punched the remote control channel selector switch that began to dial the television set through its entire frequency band. Slowly he unfolded his body and rose with a warm grin, waving my friends to a seat.

My friends had come to quiz Granddad about politics. For a half hour or so, he patiently answered their questions about the Republican Party, Goldwater, and the success of the Johnson administration. Yes, Goldwater would have to broaden the base of his appeal to win. No, on the contrary, Goldwater had been, in his experience, "an honorable senator," and of great help to his administration. Yes, Johnson had been an effective leader to date. No, the election was not a foregone conclusion. No, the election of Goldwater would not mean the United

States would withdraw diplomatic relations with nations all around the globe. Granddad spoke matter-of-factly, though at times evasively.

The questioning was surprisingly hostile and direct. I grew extremely uncomfortable by the expressions of outright skepticism worn by my friends and the Indian visitor. In sheer nervousness, at moments I turned to watch the snowy static on the empty VHF frequency. When the questions finally ceased, I followed closely behind the visitors, anxious for them to disappear.

At dinner, Granddad seemed slightly depressed. He said nothing about the visit, and afterward he exhibited less than his usual interest in the television set. I wondered whether Granddad understood how bizarre his handling of the Scranton-Goldwater problem appeared to members of his own community in Gettysburg. There had always been a separateness about Eisenhower's existence in Gettysburg. Republicanism that summer seemed to enlarge the existing gulf between Eisenhower's manorial life on his farm and the currents of opinions in Gettysburg.

I had learned early on that Granddad did not like to talk business or history with outsiders and the uninformed. For instance, although I grew up surrounded by wartime mementos, decorations, and a library of war memoirs, I was never encouraged to ask Granddad about the war. I did ask questions, however, on a few occasions, most memorably that summer of 1964. I had seen a documentary about World War II and the German V rocket program, which had been taken over by the United States and converted into a space program under the direction of chief Nazi scientist Dr. Wernher von Braun. I was curious why the Germans did not produce more of these rockets in greater number. "The rockets were a stupid misappropriation of resources to begin with," Granddad snapped. "The missiles made little difference; they were prestige weapons at best. If the Nazis had had any damn brains, they would have produced more jet fighters. The V-1 and V-2 programs proved the total stupidity of the Nazi dictatorship."

COW PALACE

Eisenhower attended the 1964 Republican National Convention in several roles: as a commentator for ABC News; as a senior statesman of the party; and as a supporter "by implication" of the Scranton cause. In the latter two roles, Eisenhower was a failure, a reminder that he had never felt completely comfortable with political life. In August 1952, as his first presidential campaign drew to a close, he had written Ann Nevins, wife of his Gettysburg farm manager Arthur Nevins, "Politics is particularly bewildering for a man who was raised in the simple concepts of army existence. Personalities — particularly personal animosities — are seemingly far more important than are issues, ideals and principles."

When he arrived with Mamie in San Francisco for the Republican convention following a four day cross-country trip by train aboard the "Convention Special," he was unprepared for the passions felt on all sides in San Francisco. Eisenhower had not yet grasped Goldwater's purpose — to court martyrdom and to seize the party to secure a forum for expanding his views, not to win the presidency.

Milton attended the convention as a Scranton delegate and ultimately delivered the nominating speech placing Scranton's name before the convention. My father, an avowed Scranton supporter, flew into San Francisco aboard his Piper Comanche following a four-day flight across the country. Dwight Eisenhower took up quarters in a suite at the St. Francis Hotel to act as a conciliator between the angry conservative and moderate factions. But with the exception of a short passage in an address he delivered before the convention, Eisenhower's impact on the convention was negligible.

Even as Eisenhower arrived in San Francisco, the platform committee under the direction of Goldwater forces was busy drafting a document that repudiated many of Eisenhower's presidential policies. Although the conservatives had conceded a number of items to the Scranton forces, including platform planks that softened Goldwater's stand on foreign aid, Cuba, Social Security, agricultural subsidies, and urban reconstruction, they refused to budge on a number of additional proposals. They vetoed a plank affirming presidential control of nuclear weapons, which was designed to blunt Goldwater's vow to delegate control to NATO commanders. They also vetoed an anti-extremism declaration aimed at fringe groups of the right and left, mostly the right, designed to force Goldwater to repudiate the John Birch Society. They refused a civil rights plank that would include a forthright declaration of support for the Civil Rights Bill Goldwater had opposed. Lastly, conservatives rejected a preamble placing the convention on record as praising the record of the Eisenhower administration.

Goldwater arrived in San Francisco in the wake of the publication of the full transcript of an interview he had given the German magazine *Der Spiegel*. In the interview, Goldwater had significantly enlarged the body of ill-considered and radical-sounding remarks that had plagued his campaign from the beginning. On the Cold War: "Any foreign policy that this country adopts should not be afraid of war." On the recent passage of the Civil Rights Bill: "If they could have locked the door to the Senate and turned the lights off, you wouldn't have gotten twenty-five votes." In a televised appearance in June, Goldwater made remarks that permitted viewers to infer that he would look favorably on a proposal that had appeared in an Air Force journal calling for the use of low-yield nuclear weapons to defoliate the Ho Chi Minh Trail, thereby exposing the North Vietnamese and their supply convoys to attack. And in June at a commencement address, Goldwater had denounced "the illusions of détente."

The bitterness between Scranton and Goldwater quickly boiled over. On the eve of the platform debate, Goldwater received a communication purporting to have been signed by Scranton that thrashed "Goldwaterism" in uncompromising language. In part it read:

> You have too often casually prescribed nuclear war as a solution to a troubled world.
>
> You have too often allowed the radical extremists to use you.
>
> You have too often stood for irresponsibility in the serious question of nuclear holocaust.
>
> You have too often read Taft and Eisenhower and Lincoln out of the Republican Party. . . .
>
> In short, Goldwaterism has come to stand for a whole crazy-quilt collection of absurd and dangerous positions that would be soundly repudiated by the American people in November. . . .

Scranton's staff had drafted the letter without his knowledge. But when the communication became public, Scranton, while disagreeing with some of the wording, refused to apologize. The floor debate over the "extremism" amendment provoked some of the wildest scenes in convention history. "Some of you don't like to hear it, but it is the truth," Rockefeller declared, referring to the existence of hate and prejudice in America. Rockefeller smiled in derision as the convention floor erupted into a pandemonium of shouting delegates, catcalls, clenched fists, and boos. The spirit of a lynch mob prevailed over the convention.

At first Eisenhower attempted to arrange Scranton's withdrawal from the race in exchange for platform concessions. He raised the possibility with Goldwater by phone and received a friendly though noncommittal response. On Monday, when Lodge called on him at the St. Francis, he asked Lodge to relay this proposed agreement to Scranton. Lodge refused. Eisenhower next called Goldwater again and suggested he name Scranton as his vice presidential candidate. Goldwater voiced desultory interest. He had already privately decided that the compliant William Miller, chairman of the national Republican Party, would be his running mate.

After failing to arrange a deal between Goldwater and Scranton over the platform and the vice presidency, Eisenhower spent his time attending a round of candidate dinners, shopping, and playing bridge in his suite at the St. Francis with Slater, Gosden, and several Augusta friends.

Eisenhower's turn to address the convention came late Tuesday. He spoke to a sea of strangers, delegates, many of whom had dissented quietly throughout his years in the White House and had resented his linking the Republican Party to the UN, civil rights, Social Security, and to the basic reforms of the New Deal. There was a tepid response when he urged support of the Civil Rights Act: "With the passage of this law, Republicans should now take upon themselves a moral commitment: to do their utmost to see this law is implemented not merely by the powers of legally constituted enforcement agencies, but by the hearts of a determined and free people."

One key passage, however, inserted on the advice of Bryce Harlow and regarded by some historians as marking Eisenhower's "turn to the right," ignited one of the most frenzied ovations of the convention. Seeking a point on which all Republicans could agree, Eisenhower emotionally warned against allowing Republicans to be divided by "those outside our family, including sensation seeking columnists and commentators who couldn't care less about the future of our party." The convention floor rose, as though on cue. Shouting lustily, the delegates gestured angrily at the television booths, cameras, and anchormen located above the convention floor. Observers noted that Eisenhower broke into an uncomprehending smile that was lost in the swirl of a demonstration he did not expect, but seen by television viewers, who must have shared his amazement.

The rest of his speech did not elicit much excitement. "It is my conviction," he urged in a vain plea for unity, "that the disappointed among us should strive to improve the party, not desert it." As Slater's diary records: "In the late afternoon on Tuesday we went to the Cow Palace to hear General Ike's talk which was well received — but it's rather plain to see that 12 years and even 8 have taken their toll and these delegates are looking to new leaders. It's so often the case, that a man who is a leader fades into dimness soon after he leaves the public scene."

The next day, July 15, on the first ballot, Goldwater forces mustered 883 votes to win an easy victory. Scranton manfully strode to the platform to urge the convention to make the vote unanimous. The Romney, Rockefeller, and Scranton delegates promptly fell in line without protest.

The next morning, however, several prominent northern Republicans declared their independence from the national ticket. The *New York Times* on the editorial page described Goldwater as "totally unfit, on the basis of his views and votes, to be President of the United States. . . . The nomination of Barry Goldwater for the Presidency is a disaster for the Republican Party and a blow to the prestige and to the domestic and international interest of the United States." When Goldwater announced his choice of Miller as his running mate, the *Times* acidly observed that Goldwater's selection "at least had the virtue of consistency."

On Thursday evening, the delegates assembled to hear from the candidate himself what kind of country he envisioned and how he would run his campaign. In a carefully worded section of his acceptance speech, Goldwater replied to the demands that he reconcile the defeated wing of the party:

Anyone who joins us in all sincerity we welcome. Those who do not care for our cause, we don't expect to enter our ranks in any case. And let our Republicanism, so focused and so dedicated not be made fuzzy and futile by untimely and stupid labels. . . .

I would remind you that extremism in

the defense of liberty is no vice — and let me remind you that moderation in the pursuit of justice is no virtue!

Eisenhower was angry with Goldwater's performance. He permitted newsmen the next day to quote him saying that the party had not fielded its strongest candidates and had overlooked his "personal choices." From San Francisco, he drove to the Monterey peninsula for several days of golf at the exclusive Cypress Shores. To friends, he seemed downcast.

Eisenhower went through the motions of supporting Goldwater for the remainder of the campaign. On August 6, he hosted a "unity" meeting with Goldwater in Gettysburg. Still smarting over Goldwater's exclusionary tactics and his implied repudiation of the Eisenhower administration, he arranged for Goldwater to meet him at his office instead of at the farm. He also asked Nixon to attend. In his presidential *Memoirs,* Nixon recounted the meeting:

He [Eisenhower] began the meeting with some straight talk. In fact I had seldom, if ever, heard Eisenhower lay it on the line the way he did in this session. He told Goldwater that he ought to stop shooting from the hip. He suggested that Goldwater give a speech discussing the charges of extremism that had been made against him and admit that he may have encouraged them by the language of his acceptance speech.

Goldwater responded just as candidly. He said that it was not in his nature to be cautious. He could understand that Eisenhower was particularly sensitive about those of his comments that had been taken to be critical of the Eisenhower administration, but he had not meant anything personal by them. On the whole, however, Goldwater took a conciliatory line. This . . . seemed to bode well for the success of the upcoming [GOP] summit meeting.

Goldwater returned to southern Pennsylvania six days later for a highly touted "summit" meeting in Harrisburg. On hand along with the Republican nominees were Eisenhower, Nixon, Rockefeller, Romney, and Scranton. Following a genial meeting, Goldwater emerged to meet the press, which had been assembled in order to give the candidate an opportunity to clarify his statements on extremism and demonstrate party unity. Instead Goldwater stubbornly refused to say that he had made any "concessions" for the sake of unity.

Perhaps Goldwater recalled the humiliating publicity that Republican nominee Eisenhower experienced after his "summit" with the defeated senator Robert Taft at Eisenhower's Morningside Heights residence at Columbia in 1952. Taft had walked away from that encounter gloating over Eisenhower's capitulation on point after point. Or perhaps Goldwater believed that no one should be able to accuse him of compromising his principles.

As Nixon related:

The rest of the press conference was a typical Goldwater performance. He himself brought up his controversial statement that he would consider giving military commanders in the field control over the use of tactical nuclear weapons and, under intense questioning, refused to back away from it. When one reporter asked about his policy toward Germany, I saw Eisenhower wince when Goldwater replied, "I think Germany originated the modern concept of peace through strength."

Eisenhower was infuriated by Goldwater.

On the drive back to Gettysburg he sat silently for most of the ride. Finally he said, "You know, before we had this meeting I thought that Goldwater was just stubborn. Now I am convinced that he is just plain dumb."

Eisenhower would limit his barnstorming for Goldwater to appearances in Ohio, Illinois, and Wisconsin, where statewide candidates battled to survive the pro-Johnson tide. In Gettysburg, in mid-September, Eisenhower and Goldwater sat down for a televised discussion about national security issues, which was broadcast as a half-hour advertisement. But the general election campaign had been doomed from the start, and by October, Republican-leaning newspapers across the country — with few exceptions — announced for Johnson. To C. D. Jackson, a man with impeccable credentials within the Rockefeller branch of the party, who lay terminally ill in a New York City hospital, Eisenhower wrote:

> The political situation beggars description. Frankly, I am bewildered, particularly to find some of my oldest and staunchest friends and supporters deserting to the opposition camp. I do not, of course, believe

that any man should vote against his conscience, but I do think that we are forgetting the real importance of having two strong parties under the American system of government. I believe that too many of our people have succumbed to the great battle cry "something for everybody, for nothing."

But with equanimity, Eisenhower excused the desertion of nearly every moderate leader in the Republican Party, including the public defections of New York senator Kenneth Keating, New Jersey senator Clifford Case, Romney, and Rockefeller. The Republicans would have to live to fight another day — and in Eisenhower's opinion, there would be another day.

On the weekend before the balloting, Eisenhower decided to skip the Election Day photographs and vote absentee. He flew to Georgia, where he vacationed for two weeks, playing golf and bridge, and serving up quail hash breakfasts. Eisenhower and his friends discussed ways of contributing to a Republican comeback in 1966. Everyone agreed that there should be a moratorium on assigning blame. Eisenhower drew up a plan for writing articles in which he would expound general principles around which the party could unite, and offer views on key issues such as public debt, increased centralization of political power in Washington, inflation, education, and civil rights.

The Republican cause was about to sustain a major but perhaps not permanent setback. In the spring of 1964, Bryce Harlow, also one of Nixon's closest associates in Washington, had written a perceptive assessment of President Johnson for Nixon's use. Harlow pointed out a speech given that spring by the political scientist Samuel Lubell, who predicted that any support for Johnson deriving from the powerful affection felt for the slain President Kennedy would prove to be "superficial." Indeed, Harlow contended, the Johnson and Kennedy wings of the Democratic Party were "on a collision course" over a host of domestic and foreign policy issues. Harlow warned, however, he was not sure the GOP would be able to take advantage of this schism in the 1964 campaign. "The question as of the first of May," he wrote, was "whether or not the American public will voluntarily await the collision after November . . ."

On Election Day, 1964, Lyndon Johnson won the greatest popular vote landslide in

American political history. In the aftermath, Nelson Rockefeller issued a statement asserting that Goldwater and his wing of the party had been repudiated by the balloting. By implication, Rockefeller positioned himself for the nomination in 1968 and read Goldwater and his supporters out of the party. In retaliation, Nixon held a press conference on November 5. He called Rockefeller "a spoil sport and a divider," because of his postelection comments and his refusal to aid the national ticket.

The lines of the contest for the presidential nomination in 1968 were drawn.

Meanwhile, the Eisenhowers postponed their departure for Palm Desert and spent a quiet December in Gettysburg. Shortly after Christmas, they took time out for a poignant farewell.

Progress had continued to invade the Appalachian environs of Gettysburg in 1964. The U.S. Route 15 highway bypass, begun under Eisenhower's interstate highway program, was complete and had reduced overnight stays in the town center. Several old buildings along the easterly boulevards pointing toward York were razed. Gas stations and fast-food chains bought the empty lots and erected stores.

The Gettysburg Hotel had long been the tourist and social hub of Gettysburg's traditional downtown area. Dwight Eisenhower had dined with his young bride, Mamie, in the restaurant on special occasions almost fifty years earlier. Eisenhower had used the hotel as an office during his recuperation from his heart attack in 1955 and again temporarily in 1961 before the Gettysburg College campus office became available. But, due to competition from the new Holiday Inn and fast-food places, in 1964 the Gettysburg Hotel failed financially.

The passing of the hotel was sentimental for the Eisenhowers. For its grief-stricken owners, the Scharfs, the old building had provided a livelihood and a home. When the hotel closed on December 14, 1964, the Scharfs received a call that afternoon from John Cummings of the *Philadelphia Inquirer,* asking them if they would mind if he had the last drink served at the bar. The Scharfs agreed.

At five, Mrs. Scharf received another call, this one from Mamie Eisenhower asking whether she and Ike could treat the Scharfs to dinner. They agreed, after a brief and friendly argument over who would treat whom.

The five converged on the hotel at dinnertime. The conversation was light. Eisenhower recalled that when the hotel served as his temporary office space, there had been one obstacle that nearly prevented him from doing any work at all. Though newly licensed by the state of Pennsylvania to drive a car, Eisenhower had not been dexterous enough to parallel-park the huge Chrysler Imperial. Scharf cooperated by saving a space in front of the hotel. Then, when leaving for the day, Eisenhower would alert Scharf and Scharf would alert General Schulz. Schulz would bound down the stairs, rush outside into the town circle, and direct traffic for several minutes while Eisenhower revved up the six-ton buggy to drive home. The five laughed and reminisced some more, basking in the warmth and poignancy of the farewell. Mrs. Scharf calmly announced she had removed her possessions and was not returning to the hotel.

The check arrived.

"Please, General, sign the check," Mrs. Scharf asked.

Ike gazed at her warily. "I know what would happen, and my money is as good as yours."

Twenty-year-old Dwight David "Ike" Eisenhower with his parents, Ida and David, and younger brothers, Milton and Earl. *Eisenhower Presidential Library and Museum.*

Ike in Chicago in 1911, en route to West Point, in a photo taken by his then girlfriend, Ruby Norman. *Eisenhower Presidential Library and Museum.*

Northward view of Eisenhower Farm. Barbeque pit in right foreground; residence in center, with barn behind. Putting green to right of residence. Evergreens from the fifty states line the lane leading to the Waterworks (now Millerstown) Road. *Eisenhower Presidential Library and Museum.*

ABOVE: David Eisenhower and Julie Nixon at the 1957 inauguration. David's sister Anne is next to him and Julie's sister, Tricia, is next to her. *Getty Images.*

RIGHT: David and Julie with Julie's parents at the International Debutante Ball in December 1966. *International Debutante Ball.*

BELOW: The Eisenhower family, Christmas in Eldorado, 1965. Front row, left to right: Anne, Mamie, Susan, David, Mary Jean, and Barbara Eisenhower. Second row, left to right: Milton Eisenhower, Uncle Joel Carlson, Dwight Eisenhower, and John Eisenhower. *Eisenhower Presidential Library and Museum/Zeni Photography.*

Harry Truman and Eisenhower at the Truman Library in Independence, Missouri, November 10, 1961. *Eisenhower Presidential Library and Museum.*

Eisenhower meets with President Kennedy in Palm Springs in 1962. *U.S. Navy.*

President Lyndon B. Johnson confers with Eisenhower aboard
Air Force One. *White House Photo.*

Eisenhower preparing to eulogize his
old friend Winston Churchill, London,
1965. *Eisenhower Presidential Library
and Museum.*

Eisenhower with his best friends: George Allen (left) and Freeman Gosden, Palm Springs, 1966. *Eisenhower Presidential Library and Museum.*

Eisenhower and Sergeant John Moaney grill steaks, mid-1950s. *Eisenhower Presidential Library and Museum.*

Eisenhower at the bridge table with (left to right) General Alfred Gruenther, "Pete" Jones, and Barry Leithead. *U.S. Navy.*

David and his grandfather at the Gettysburg farmhouse just before David left to start college, 1966. *Family Collection.*

David, Ike, and Mamie on the sunporch at Gettysburg in 1967 with Ike's most recent painting. *Photo by Julie Nixon.*

Julie and David in the '62 Valiant, 1968. *Getty Images.*

Eisenhower at Fort Gordon, pointing to the logo on his robe, 1965. *Eisenhower Presidential Library and Museum.*

Eisenhower at Walter Reed Army Medical Center with newly inaugurated President Richard Nixon. *White House Photo.*

■ ■ ■ ■

PART II:
GRANDDAD

■ ■ ■ ■

4
ELDER STATESMAN

AN OLD FRIEND

On a wall facing the street in Averell Harriman's Georgetown home in Washington, D.C., hangs an oil landscape of a village in a valley, evidently Sun Valley, Idaho. The painting is almost lost in the dazzling spectacle of signed portraits and photographs of the Washington and international luminaries Harriman played host to in over fifty years of high-level diplomatic and political service. There is no identifying plaque next to it.

When I interviewed Harriman in 1977, I thought the painting looked like one of Granddad's, the variety of greens, the distinctive brushstrokes, the prominence of the hills enveloping a cluster of small structures. I was about to ask the ambassador when we were interrupted by a phone call from the Carter transition headquarters in Plains, Georgia. With Harriman gone, I went over to examine the painting more closely. In the lower right-hand corner, the letters *DE* identified the painting as one of Eisenhower's early efforts, perhaps in 1950 or 1951.

Years of ill will and misunderstanding preceded me through the doors of Harriman's Washington home. In late 1951, Eisenhower and Harriman broke bitterly over politics, shattering an association that had been personally and professionally intimate throughout World War II and the Truman administration. The painting was a relic from the intimate days; giving away one of his paintings was Eisenhower's most genuine token of friendship. I compared the effort poured into that canvas with the flowery inscriptions on the photographs of the famous and near famous from the Roosevelt, Truman, Kennedy, and Johnson administrations.

When Harriman returned from his call, I pointed out the painting and asked him how he had gotten it. "Oh yes, you noticed," he replied cheerily. "You know, your grandfather and I were quite close once."

As we sat down, Harriman described first meeting Eisenhower in June 1942 aboard a C-47 returning to Washington from London. Eisenhower had been in London to explore conditions on the island for an American military buildup. Harriman, the Lend-Lease coordinator, was returning to Washington to make the case for more guns, ships, and food for the British and Russians until the full might of U.S. ground and naval power could be transferred into the theater.

Though Eisenhower did not make much of a first impression on Harriman, they eventually became close friends. When Harriman became ambassador to Moscow, he made a point of visiting the Supreme Commander's headquarters in Algiers and then in France when traveling to and from the Soviet Union. He also hosted Eisenhower during a triumphal tour of Moscow in August 1945.

The two men had been friends and neighbors in New York. As president of Columbia, Eisenhower coaxed Harriman into contributing his family home, Arden House, to the university in order to provide the needed facility for Eisenhower's pet project, the American Assembly. Founded by Eisenhower in 1950, the Assembly was a forum for leaders in business and government "to reconcile divergent views in order to accomplish a common purpose." Eisenhower and Harriman were both sent to Europe in 1950 to form NATO. The story of their friendship ends in 1951, when Truman dispatched Harriman to Paris to sound out Eisenhower, then commander of NATO, on his intentions regarding the presidency in 1952. Harriman, upon learning Eisenhower was a Republican, told him that it was his duty to run and prevent Taft from winning the election, but he warned, "As a Democrat, I will be out to lick you."

Eisenhower said he understood and assured Harriman that he would not take criticism personally. "But," Harriman told me, "Ike found it wasn't so simple. He just didn't understand politics. He had no idea of the difference between opposing a man politically and personally."

Kevin McCann, who had been working with Eisenhower in Paris in late 1951, recalled a heated argument between the two men. The subject was politics and the "blow-up" occurred one night at a dinner party in full view of all the guests. The familiarity between them ended. "It used to be 'Averell' and 'Ike,' " Harriman continued, "and then suddenly it was 'Governor' and 'Mr. President.' " In the 1950s, the two men saw each other only on official occasions during business hours.

When Harriman ran for the Democratic nomination for president in 1956, he campaigned with Truman's backing and emerged as a strong critic of Dwight Eisenhower's first term. Eisenhower grew so angry with Harriman's criticism that doctors added Harriman's name to the list of forbidden topics of discussion in Eisenhower's presence, a list doctors gave the vice president and members of the cabinet.

McCann had always admired Harriman. During the late stages of writing the second volume of memoirs, Kevin left the presidency of Defiance College and joined the staff in Gettysburg. Around the office, he promoted Harriman. He liked to remind Eisenhower of Harriman's contribution to Columbia and of their early association, and urged his boss to find a way to befriend Harriman again. Eisenhower would "hear nothing of it." McCann persisted. Eisenhower decided he had been a bit too harsh and unforgiving, but pride was involved. He lacked a pretense to approach his onetime friend.

Then, on January 24, 1965, Winston Churchill died. Eisenhower attended the funeral at the invitation of Queen Elizabeth. Harriman, who attended as a member of the official delegation, traveled with Eisenhower aboard an Air Force plane. During the flight, Eisenhower sat in the middle compartment. Supreme Court Chief Justice Earl Warren and Secretary of State Dean Rusk, representing President Johnson, sat in the rear, while Harriman sat in the forward compartment. For several hours, Eisenhower avoided everyone, feigning fatigue. Finally, he ambled forward and sat down next to Harriman.

"He began by greeting me as 'Averell,'" Harriman recalled pleasantly. The two men talked about old times over scotch. In the hours remaining on the flight, they attempted to explain away the thirteen years of silence. Harriman complained that Eisenhower's aides had suppressed the nice things Harriman had said about him, and poisoned him by showing him comments taken out of context. Eisenhower supposed this was true, and regretted they had ever come to words.

The Churchill funeral was an ideal chance to repair the slights and misunderstandings of the past. It served to remind both men of the momentous war years. For several days, all that had come between them must have seemed petty before the grandeur of Churchill's life and the pageantry of the state ceremony.

The state funeral proved to be one of the most difficult ordeals of Eisenhower's retirement. He revered and idolized Winston Churchill, and considered knowing Churchill to be one of the highlights of his life. Eisenhower had agreed to deliver a eulogy of Sir Winston during the live BBC broadcast as Churchill's bier was placed aboard a barge at Tower Hill Pier, to be transported up the Thames and, ultimately, to burial in the quiet English village of Bladon.

The atmosphere in London was electric. Hundreds of the world's famous and powerful streamed past Churchill's black coffin mounted on a catafalque in Westminster Hall. The *New York Times* noted: "The thousands who watched at street corners and the millions who watched on television knew they were seeing a moment of history."

For peace of mind, Eisenhower had requested General Leonard Heaton, commander of Walter Reed Army Medical Center, to accompany him to London. Since his stroke in 1957, he had deep-seated doubts about his ability to cope with stressful situations. He was convinced that his speech was slurred because of the stroke, which accounted in part for his uncertain handling of press conferences toward the end of his administration.

In his years at Walter Reed, Leonard

Heaton earned the absolute trust of the most powerful men in America. His knowledge of their fears and insecurities was firsthand. He had performed surgery on two presidents, several secretaries of state, and military and congressional leaders. He combined the conviviality of a southern gentleman with a reassuring professional manner.

On the night before the funeral and the satellite telecast that would reach an estimated 325 million viewers worldwide, Heaton stayed up late with Eisenhower in his room at the Dorchester Hotel. As he recalled, "General Eisenhower was under great stress and tension." He was afraid "he would choke."

"I hope I don't stammer over 'honored,' " Eisenhower said as he practiced delivering his handwritten text in front of Heaton and a mirror.

"You won't," Heaton replied firmly. But Eisenhower repeated, "I hope I don't have any difficulty tomorrow, Leonard. I hope I don't have any difficulty saying these words."

Heaton sat and listened while Eisenhower read through the text flawlessly, without hesitation. "Why, you're not going to have any difficulty at all," Heaton said. "You're doing fine. It's a wonderful, wonderful tribute. I can tell you are not going to experience a bit of hesitancy."

At the funeral the next day, there was a noted contrast between the dignified procession of honors rendered Winston Churchill and the comparative improvisation and anguish of the traumatic state funeral fourteen months earlier for John F. Kennedy. The *New York Times* observed that "disorder" had been the meaning of Kennedy's death; "fulfillment . . . a more evident theme today."

The mourners and the curious watched the ceremony in a spirit of appreciation and awe for the varied accomplishments of Churchill's long life. Fortified by Heaton, Eisenhower delivered a graceful and acclaimed tribute. Introducing himself as someone with "no charter to speak for any nation — only myself," he called Churchill

the epitome of the British and their defiance of threat and their tower of strength in adversity . . . a great maker of history . . . but his work done, the record closed, we can almost hear him, with the poet [Tennyson] say:

Sunset and evening star,
And one clear call for me!

Twilight and evening bell,
And after that the dark!
And may there be no sadness of farewell,
When I embark . . .

Eisenhower continued: "With no thought of the length of time he might be permitted on earth, he was concerned only with the quality of service he could render to his nation and to humanity. Though he had no fear of death, he coveted always the opportunity to continue that service. . . . In the coming years . . . there will ring out through all the centuries one incontestable refrain: here was a champion of freedom. . . ."

As the bier passed beneath the London Bridge, Eisenhower closed with the words: "And now to you, Sir Winston, my old friend, farewell."

Eisenhower and Harriman returned to the United States aboard the same plane that had transported them to the ceremony. The Churchill funeral had brought them together to commemorate the man many believed was the century's greatest leader. Deplaning, the two men parted as friends.

But I detected in Harriman a sense that their reconciliation had been less complete. I asked him whether they had ever corresponded after the funeral.

"Well, no," he replied. "Had no reason to. But I think of him as a friend, and I am happy that we rectified some of the misunderstandings."

I told Harriman that Eisenhower had looked for a way to make amends, and that for several years he had simply lacked a pretext.

"Is that so," he answered thoughtfully. "I hope that is true. I sincerely hope so."

TOUGH SPOT

President Lyndon Johnson rapidly forgave Eisenhower for supporting Barry Goldwater in the fall elections. The President had a hunch that Eisenhower's heart had not been in the campaign, and that his secret desire had been fulfilled when Goldwater lost the presidency in a landslide. Attempting to pierce any artificial barriers posed by partisan politics, Johnson ordered helicopters to transport Eisenhower to and from his Gettysburg farm, and issued a standing invitation to Eisenhower to use Camp David and the presidential suite at Walter Reed. He invited the Eisenhowers to attend his inauguration and to occupy a seat of honor on the podium. But, scheduled to be vacationing in Palm Desert in January, Eisenhower declined Johnson's gracious invitation.

Johnson was motivated by sincere admiration. With journalists he praised Eisenhower generously, once telling Arthur Krock of the *New York Times* that history would "make a great mistake" if it overlooked Eisenhower's talents, industry, and wisdom. He also told Krock that in conferences Eisenhower was the sharpest mind at the table, who consistently saw critical points and consequences that eluded "the 'whiz kids' in his administration and in Kennedy's."

In turn, Eisenhower was personally fond of Lyndon Johnson, liking him but with reservations about his ability to handle the presidency, the reverse of how he had felt toward Kennedy. Eisenhower had long delighted in quoting Johnson's pungent, expressive stories to friends. Throughout 1964 he had been flattered by the President's calls and special courtesies. He also recognized that Johnson's appetite for approval, his heavy reliance on polls, and his conservative instincts though the leader of a liberal party were likely to bring him to grief in the White House.

At the moment of his inaugural, Johnson

faced momentous decisions about the future of American involvement in Vietnam. That involvement had deepened significantly since Johnson's assumption of office in 1963, a month after the ouster and assassination of the beleaguered Diem. Throughout 1964, the leaderless Saigon government had been racked by coups and indecisive leadership while trying to identify a successor to Diem. Implicated in the overthrow of Diem, the United States had assumed the preponderant role of organizing the nation's economy and fighting forces. The involvement had grown deeper in August 1964 with the passage of the Gulf of Tonkin Resolution by Congress in response to clashes between American and North Vietnamese naval forces.

McGeorge Bundy returned from Vietnam in February 1965 with a pessimistic firsthand assessment. "The situation in Vietnam," he informed Johnson, "is deteriorating." A Vietcong offensive in 1964 had nearly overrun the country. The "pacification" program was a failure as more and more of the countryside fell into communist hands. American economic aid and military advisers had not succeeded in building a confident and self-reliant South Vietnamese army. Bundy noted that the American policy of "self-imposed restrictions" on naval and ground operations had contributed to a situation in which the United States could not negotiate its way out of the conflict without a defeat. At the same time, he said, "the American investment is very large, and American responsibility is a fact of life which is palpable in the atmosphere of Asia."

With Bundy's report in hand, the Johnson administration dusted off contingency plans drafted a year earlier that contemplated a bombing campaign to halt infiltration through the DMZ, the demilitarized zone between north and south, and supply lines down the Ho Chi Minh Trail in Laos. For several weeks following Bundy's return, the administration debated feverishly how to salvage the war.

Meanwhile, Soviet premier Aleksei Kosygin had visited Hanoi in the first week of February 1965, a gesture interpreted as signaling the end of Soviet neglect of the region, and as a sign the Soviets were positioning themselves in anticipation of a North Vietnamese victory. During the Bundy visit, Vietcong units staged a raid on the American barracks at Pleiku, inflicting heavy casualties on American ground soldiers and support personnel. Escalation of the conflict was imminent.

Driven by Saigon's instability and by the provocation at Pleiku, Lyndon Johnson ordered the first of several reprisal strikes north of the 17th parallel on February 7, 1965. On February 13, Johnson approved "Operation Rolling Thunder," a campaign of continuous bombing of North Vietnam, set to begin in early March.

It was with great reluctance that Johnson had authorized the bombing in February and a partial buildup of American ground forces in March. Though as vice president he had advocated strong American backing of the South Vietnamese, calling President Diem the "Winston Churchill" of Southeast Asia, as president he bore actual responsibility for the consequences of action or inaction in Indochina. He agonized over the unattractive options he had inherited from John F. Kennedy: to accept a communist victory or to fight a war in Vietnam.

Johnson feared that a foursquare American intervention on the ground backed by bombers and ships would provoke a Chinese intervention comparable to the Chinese counterattack into Korea over the Yalu River in 1950. At the same time, he feared that without intervention Vietnam would be lost, which could unleash new political attacks similar to those in the McCarthy era.

Thus, while cautiously applying ever greater levels of American force in Vietnam, Johnson systematically undertook to guard his political flank by implicating Republicans in his policy. The most important member of the political opposition to him in cementing bipartisanship in Vietnam was Dwight Eisenhower.

Facing difficult decisions in Vietnam, Johnson plainly believed that the man who had said no to U.S. ground troops in 1954 would say yes in 1965. As Senate majority leader, Johnson had been privy to Eisenhower's thinking in 1954 when the question was intervention on behalf of the French. Johnson had supported the compromise reached at Geneva, which had made the best of a bad situation. The South Vietnam that emerged in 1954 had weathered ten years of crisis and had been fully accepted as a "free world" ally.

Eisenhower's views on Vietnam in late 1964 to early 1965, on the eve of U.S. ground intervention, were somewhat ambiguous. With his business friends, most of whom were skeptical about the looming conflict, Eisenhower was empathetic toward Johnson, who found himself in a "tough spot" in Vietnam. To his brother Milton, who was convinced that intervention would be a "colossal mistake," Eisenhower acknowledged the military hazards and the perils of "going it alone" in Southeast Asia. His views seemed somewhat clearer to Dad. When I asked Dad what Granddad, if president, would have done in 1965, he replied, "I don't know whether he would have gone in or not, but had he gone in, he would have gone in with everything."

"Win" was the essence of Eisenhower's advice when Johnson began soliciting it in earnest in early 1965. On February 17, Eisenhower and Johnson met for several hours in the Cabinet Room to discuss Vietnam and the various options before the President. According to Johnson, Eisenhower endorsed Operation Rolling Thunder and encouraged him to "shift from retaliation to a campaign of pressure." Eisenhower also "saw merit" in Johnson's decision to station an American division south of the DMZ, adding that if more troops became necessary in the future, "so be it." As yet, the question of full-scale ground intervention was not before the President.

Eisenhower wrote Johnson on March 12: "I think your policy of applying pressure, discreetly, on North Vietnam is having some beneficial effects. Certainly I hope so. More than this as I told you on the telephone, I think you had every right — indeed the obligation — to protect our important bases with some of our own troops."

Eisenhower had definite misgivings about the use of conventional forces in Vietnam deployed in a defensive or pacification role. His administration's "New Look" foreign policy had been drawn up on the theory that America would never again fight extended ground campaigns in either Europe or Asia. The "graduated response" policy of Kennedy-Johnson was the brainchild of Maxwell Taylor, one of Eisenhower's most ardent defense critics and currently the ambassador in South Vietnam. The major problem with "graduated response," in Eisenhower's view, was that the doctrine contemplated extended wars of attrition fought overseas and invited doubts about American firmness. Any intervention had to be quick and overwhelming and leave no doubt about the will to succeed, he believed.

In the present case, Eisenhower thought that the congressional passage of the Gulf of Tonkin Resolution, with its promises that the President take "all necessary steps" to defend Southeast Asia, settled the question of whether the United States was committed to the defense of Vietnam. He therefore resolved to say nothing publicly that would undercut or second-guess the President's moves that might deter the communists.

Returning from California by train, Eisenhower was besieged at every stop by newsmen seeking comment about the Marine landings at Da Nang and the bombing of North Vietnam. Back in Gettysburg, he wrote Johnson explaining his press replies:

I have consistently said (and shall continue to say) that, first, we should all understand that there is only one spokesman for America in conducting our current Foreign Relations, the President of the United States. Secondly, I expressed the conviction that under the circumstances as I now understand them I believe that you are employing a policy well calculated to serve the best interests of the United States.

As the bombing and buildup of U.S. forces proceeded, Wisconsin Republican congressman Melvin Laird delivered a speech that June in the House of Representatives in which he declared that "in several public utterances, Administration spokesmen have implied that the ground force buildup in Vietnam is Eisenhower or Republican policy. Such an implication is just the opposite of the truth."

Lyndon Johnson swiftly wrote Eisenhower a letter enclosing a *Philadelphia Inquirer* column by Marguerite Higgins titled "Laird Flunks as Historian." She refuted Laird by quoting a 1954 letter Eisenhower wrote to Churchill in which he had emphasized the critical need for action to stop communism in Vietnam, stating that in the event of a French defeat, "the ultimate effect on our and your global strategic positions with the consequent shift in the power ratios throughout Asia and the Pacific would be disastrous." In Johnson's cover note about the column, he wrote:

I send you the attached memo from a trusted member of my staff who I put to work immediately on the letter you called about yesterday. It confirms what our friend, Dirksen, said about the impetuosity and hotheadedness of Mel. This is given to you in confidence because I knew you were disturbed yesterday.

But Laird had not exactly flunked. Nor had Johnson and Higgins read Eisenhower's

344

letter to Churchill carefully. Eisenhower had continued in his letter to urge a coalition of American and British forces, adding, "I do not envisage the need of any appreciable ground forces on your part or on our part. . . ." Eisenhower's cautionary letter, however, had concerned a distant time. He decided not to comment publicly about Laird's speech in the hope of encouraging a united front in Congress that might induce the enemy to quit.

Johnson's net soon grew tighter. In mid-August of 1965, the White House readied a pamphlet documenting the history of American support for Vietnam. It cited a letter Eisenhower had sent Premier Diem in late 1954 pledging economic aid as a basis for current U.S. military actions. Pressed for comment about the Diem letter, Eisenhower, in the words of the *New York Times,* "demurred."

Johnson chose to regard Eisenhower's reaction as an endorsement of current policy. He dispatched a courier to Gettysburg bearing a copy of the pamphlet and a cover letter:

My Dear General:
    I cannot tell you adequately of my deep

gratitude for the unhesitating support you give to the needs of your country.

I watched you on television and I read your statement in the newspaper. No one knows better than you the accumulated demands of the Presidency. No one gives more attention than you to the best interests of our country. Whatever course of action you believe to be right is the course to which you give your approval and the massive weight of your prestige and wisdom.

No one of us is prescient enough to predict the verdict of the future. But history will surely record that President Dwight D. Eisenhower, both in and out of office, never swerved from what he believed to be the truth nor from giving his courage and his energy to the people he serves as patriot, soldier, President, and now as wise counselor to the nation.

Flattered, Eisenhower replied:

Dear Mr. President,

It is sheer understatement to say that I most deeply appreciate your personal letter expressing gratitude for the support I have been able to give you in your efforts to solve the problem of Vietnam.

As you say, none of us knows what history will finally say about our successes and failures in life; but I am surely going to put a copy of your letter with my papers in the Presidential library at Abilene so that some future historian, 100 years from now, will be given an opportunity to read it, and be impressed!

By the fall of 1965, Johnson was providing regular briefings for Eisenhower in Gettysburg. Through General Andrew Goodpaster, now secretary of the Joint Chiefs of Staff, Johnson kept Eisenhower informed in advance of bombing halts and troop level increases, and his efforts to enlist allied support and to open conversations with the communists. The President also telephoned frequently and invited Eisenhower to lunch at the White House periodically to discuss Vietnam and foreign policy.

While supporting Johnson publicly, Eisenhower suppressed misgivings about the stops and starts and the appearance of indecision at the top. At some level, Eisenhower recognized that he was being taken "captive." In the 1970s, Bryce Harlow told me about several of Eisenhower's private lunches and coffees at the White House with Lyndon Johnson. Usually Eisenhower would arrive in Washington and go first to Harlow's office, where the two would talk over matters they expected Johnson to raise, then climb into Harlow's limousine for the brief drive to the White House. "All the way over," Harlow remembered, "the General would bitch and moan and groan that 'Johnson is using me.'" Eisenhower would work himself into such a state of indignation that Harlow feared he would turn around and leave for Gettysburg. Practically at the White House gates, Harlow would attempt to quiet the General so that he would not be discourteous. "But at the Diplomatic Reception Room, he would see the President and a change would come over him," Harlow continued. "Suddenly he was all smiles and the picture of affability." Eisenhower's conversations with Johnson were invariably warm and friendly and "underneath it all," Harlow explained, "the General loved it — at least initially."

Eisenhower was impatient with uninformed criticism of Johnson. He could be surprisingly angered by opinions that very nearly reflected his own if, in any way, he detected that these sentiments, whether critical or supportive, revealed bias or a lack of sensitivity for the nuances of the Indochina situation.

In the summer of 1965, I declined Granddad's offer of the minimum wage plus ten cents to return to work on the farm. I spent most of the summer in Mexico as part of the People to People program. That summer, the American force level in Vietnam rose from 50,000 to 175,000. Approaching draft age, I followed administration pronouncements closely and became concerned about the open-ended and vague nature of official statements on the war. It was not comforting to learn that ten times more people were likely to die on American highways in 1965 than in Vietnam. Most unsettling of all, the administration itself seemed as yet undecided whether the United States was in a war or not. I agreed with most people my age that we either should get in the war with guns-a-blazin', or stay out. So did Granddad.

One day after returning from Mexico, I expressed my doubts at length at lunch with my grandparents in the family dining room. I related all the critical views I had heard expressed in Mexico. Seated at the head of the table, Granddad listened intently, coiled for the first careless word.

I concluded, wishing that Johnson would

do something, anything. "Maybe, he ought to threaten North Vietnam with atom bombs — see if that works." Granddad had listened in dead silence, his hard gaze forcing me to avoid eye contact. His face grew red. Upon hearing the final remark, he thumped a fist on the table and leaned forward in his seat. "Young man," he said evenly, "you never, I repeat *never* threaten an enemy with the use of atomic weapons unless you mean it." He paused. "And then you make it a promise."

Throughout the buildup, Eisenhower's advice to Goodpaster had a theme: the United States was "not going to be run out of a country we helped to establish." Since the President had "appealed to force," the United States "must win." Thereafter, Eisenhower confined himself to strategic military advice in his capacity as a five-star general, with the goal of bringing the war to the quickest possible conclusion. He stressed the value of sustained and heavy bombing to destroy North Vietnamese airfields and fuel depots. In meeting after meeting, he advised against attempts to wage the war from Washington and urged greater latitude for General William Westmoreland. Above all, he said, "we should not base our action on minimum needs but should swamp the enemy with overwhelming force. We should err on the side of putting in too much rather than too little."

In late fall, Eisenhower advocated a blockade of North Vietnamese ports, which in his opinion would require a declaration of war — which he favored. In December, he raised serious objections to Johnson's decision to order an indefinite pause in the bombing and to dispatch emissaries to more than forty international capitals in hopes of sounding out diplomats about a compromise outcome. "If they do not respond," Eisenhower observed, "where will that leave us?"

Meanwhile, Johnson continued to reassure Eisenhower, through Goodpaster, that Westmoreland had the latitude he needed and that the Pentagon was complying with all of his requests for logistical and troop support. Eisenhower was grateful for the assurances, but not entirely convinced that the President had set his mind to the task of doing what needed to be done in order to win.

COLORS

By the summer of 1965, in accordance with a statute passed by Congress and prompted by the assassination of President Kennedy, former presidents were provided full Secret

Service protection and a detail of agents reestablished the old command post in the annex next to the barn. Several of the agents were veterans of the Eisenhower White House. Life at the farm seemed to take a step back in time. Granddad was ambivalent about the necessity for so much security. As he had written Dad more than a decade before, commenting on a cascade of "threatening letters" in the spring of 1953, "For myself and the members of the family living with me, I have not the slightest concern. In fact, life for me personally would be much happier if I had less of this so-called 'protection.' Certainly I think that one faithful fellow going along with a six-shooter — possibly reinforced by one in my own pocket — would be ample." Now, however, the Secret Service was once more in charge of public events for Granddad and Mamie. Private times indoors at the farm became even more precious.

Granddad was slowing down. He began dictating his reminiscences and spending more hours painting at his easel on the sun-porch overlooking his eastern fields, though he did not seem to finish paintings as regularly. Painting continued to provide a handy excuse to sit apart from the constant activity on the porch while remaining close enough to monitor; it still relaxed him, permitting him to experiment with color and texture and to satisfy his compulsion to observe.

In the White House, Granddad had often painted during his post-lunch rest mandated by doctors after his 1955 heart attack. His White House studio was a small room next to the elevator on the second-floor family quarters. The room, with its northern light, overlooked Lafayette Park. As a boy, I was often invited to the painting studio to keep Granddad company. Although he was absorbed in his painting, he also enjoyed chatting. His conversation wandered from subject to subject, triggered by the images on the easel. First a dab of yellow, then a dab of blue. Mix. Mix. Pause. A comment. Granddad's stream of consciousness covered whatever was on his mind.

Since the rest periods were supervised by doctors, assistant White House physician Major Walter Tkach was one of Granddad's most frequent companions when he painted. Years later, Tkach re-created for me those hours of conversation in the White House, beginning one afternoon when the President was mulling over Secret Service reports of a threat to his life and a recommendation that he cancel a planned trip to Richmond,

Virginia. In to check the President's blood pressure, Tkach was waved to a chair by Eisenhower as the latter took up his paint-brush. While painting, Eisenhower ruminated about the Richmond business. It reminded him of several incidents just before D-Day. An uncanny look-alike of Montgomery, his living double, had been sent to Gibraltar to be detected by German intelligence in order to lull the German High Command into complacency. Eisenhower also had had a double when he was confined to a villa near Versailles during the Ardennes counteroffensive. "It was like a prison," Granddad recalled.

"Mr. President, it was necessary," Tkach volunteered.

"Walter, nothing can really be done to prevent anyone intent on 'getting someone,' " Granddad replied. "And if someone were ever to get killed in my place, it would not be fair."

At their frequent midday sessions, Tkach listened to the President discuss many subjects, but especially the war and its leaders through the rose-tinted glasses of time. He referred to his wartime associates by their first names or nicknames: Churchill was "Winston," Patton was "Georgie," Eden was "Anthony," and Bradley "Brad." Occasionally Tkach picked up bits of history. During one painting session, Granddad intimated that there had never been the slightest chance that Patton would be fired for the so-called soldier slapping incident in Sicily, "which did not stop me from putting him on ice to let him cool off," he added. "Georgie always came in contrite."

Tkach's impression was that an important influence in Eisenhower's life — someone he rarely discussed except when painting — was Douglas MacArthur. As a middle grade officer, Eisenhower had served on Mac-Arthur's staff for nearly a decade and he had admired the general lavishly. Despite everything, he still did, though they had long since parted ways politically and personally. Throughout Eisenhower's presidency, MacArthur had sat in his glory in a suite at New York's Waldorf Towers. There were rumors that the general wanted to run the Department of Defense. But it was a relationship that could not work again. The rumor was that in 1956, MacArthur had almost endorsed Stevenson, refraining in the end only because such an act would have been regarded as professional jealousy. Eisenhower also was aware that MacArthur had disparaged him, calling him "the best clerk I ever had," referring to his nine years of service with the general, and had made light of his contributions to the war. "At times it was nauseating," Granddad said about his years with MacArthur.

"But, Mr. President," Tkach protested, "under MacArthur you must have learned a lot about command."

Brush to paint, brush to canvas.

"I learned a lot about dramatics," he said, repeating his by now famous rejoinder when MacArthur's "clerk" comment surfaced in print.

Granddad disclaimed any skill at painting or any motive in doing it other than the pure enjoyment of reproducing scenery and people, whether accomplished by an original sketch or by re-creating a postcard scene. He specifically eschewed introspective art, and was uncomfortable with the idea of painting to express himself. Despite his modesty about what he called his "daubs," and his penchant to give away whatever was on his easel to whoever admired it, be they a cabinet official, White House usher, or Navy chief, Eisenhower took a measure of pride in his work.

In 1959, it was a poorly kept secret that one of the contemporary artists to be featured at the United States Exhibition in Moscow was President Dwight D. Eisenhower. American officials in charge of the cultural exchange had notified the White House that the Soviets had requested a painting by the President. Surprised but delighted by this news, Granddad had carefully selected a painting he had done of me, age five at Augusta, gripping a nine iron from a set of children's clubs that had been designed for me by golf legend Bobby Jones.

Along with the Eisenhower painting, the committee choosing art for the exhibit had decided on works ranging from abstracts to nudes to paintings with contemporary "social themes." When news of the selections reached print, the House Committee on Un-American Activities had opened an investigation into the political affiliations of the artists involved, only to learn that thirty-four of the sixty-seven American artists had had communist or communist front affiliations at one time or another. In the midst of the controversy, Eisenhower commented on one of the artworks in question, a caricature by Jack Levine of a corpulent businessman and an overstuffed soldier — a grotesque lampoon of greedy American capitalism and militarism. Asked about it at a news conference, Eisenhower responded by expressing the wish that the U.S. exhibit in Moscow contain more "representational works." In response, the *New York Times* quoted Mrs. Edith Halpert, owner of the Downtown Gallery in New York, and exhibit curator, who had a few words to say about the President's failure to defend the Levine painting: "some people think the President's paintings are not so good either."

Despite the discreet efforts of the staff, Granddad saw the story and was furious. He buzzed his secretary Ann Whitman with precise instructions. Director Abbott Washburn in Moscow was to be called. The painting of David was to be crated and returned to Washington immediately.

Whitman hurriedly reached Washburn, who told her that it would not be diplomatic to recall the painting since Soviet exhibit officials had already decided to hang it in the main office of the pavilion. Whitman called Dad and asked him to present the situation to his father.

Dad interrupted Granddad poring over a stack of papers. Thump.

"What is it?"

The Oval Office door swung shut, blocking out Whitman's ability to hear.

Dad emerged a few minutes later.

"How did you do?" Whitman asked.

"I'm afraid I ignored empirical rule number one — 'the President is always right.' "

The painting was crated and quietly returned aboard a government plane in August.

Occasionally, Eisenhower tried to create moods with his work. *The Deserted Barn,* painted in August 1955 and given to Chief Walter West, was an imaginary scene from his childhood. He described the painting in a letter: "In order to make the exercise of some interest to myself, I wanted also to represent desolation or hopelessness if this could be done in a structure." Granddad undoubtedly referred to the desolation and hopelessness he saw in many of the abandoned and poverty-stricken landholdings in Kansas left behind by the migrations westward. This desolation was among his reasons for venturing east, and into the Army.

His paintings reveal the unequivocal character of his thought and his passion for order and absolutes. Typical are his paintings of the Alps and Rocky Mountains in which his contrasts are notably exaggerated. The valleys are lush and pastoral, the mountains fiercely jagged and ominous.

One of Granddad's favorites was a painting of the Byers Peak Ranch in Fraser, Colorado, the home of his longtime friend Aksel Nielsen, which he had visited often before his heart attack. Eisenhower once said that being in Fraser was a religious experience. The mountains brought him closer to the mysteries and intangibles in life than anywhere else. In the painting, he converts the ranch scene into a bold juxtaposition of sensations that Colorado evoked in him. Aksel Nielsen's ranch house is sheltered protectively by thick, prosperous pine trees. The adjoining fields are richly productive. The cottages appear to be large and comfortable, set back from distant neighboring mountains, which tower into the heavens like the Himalayas of *Lost Horizon,* impenetrable barriers between the ranch and the outside world. The colors are vivid and bold. Yet in reality, the Byers Peak ranch house and surrounding cottages are small and primitive. Fraser sits on a plateau near the timberline, and therefore the air is thin and the trees are small.

Elsewhere Eisenhower's tendency toward absolutism is even more pronounced. In *Snowbound,* he portrays a bundled woman, carrying a load of firewood, returning to her home in a snowstorm. The bleakness is total. The little cottage is nearly covered by drifting snow. The lights from the windows, which act as a beacon, are almost swallowed up by the storm. The sky is a relentless gray-black. The entire painting bends against the impact of the storm. Likewise, Eisenhower's autumnal landscapes are alive and exhilarating in the way he regarded the season. Every tree leaf is bright red or orange; nothing is muted. There is no hint of rain or mud. Autumn is an explosion of colors and crisp sensation. The world he painted, like the world he saw, was one of sharp distinctions, of orderly and unmistakable transitions from one mood to the next, a world of right and wrong.

One can learn a great deal about Dwight Eisenhower through his artwork. Although he commanded five million troops during World War II, spent a lifetime in the military and politics, and led the nation at the height of the Cold War, his work is pastoral and devoid of violence. His portraits of Lincoln and Washington, of his family and friends, are straightforward and spare. Eisenhower's artwork, as art critic Frieda Kay Fall put it, was seemingly oblivious to the "rising and falling tide of civilizations in mortal conflict. By painting he was not striving for the moral improvement of his fellow man nor the world in general, and in his work was a conspicuous absence of any influence of the recent historical past in which he played such an important role." Painting "brought a certain validity to his basic tranquility."

SETBACK

The fall of 1965 marked the tenth anniversary of Eisenhower's heart attack. He had thus reached the informal deadline placed on his ability to lead an active life pronounced by Paul Dudley White and the doctors at Fitzsimmons Hospital in September 1955. Eisenhower approached the deadline with a sudden passion for living, as if time had become precious.

Granddad began keeping a log of his daily regimen of eating and exercise for reference when consulting with his doctors. No egg yolks; no fancy seasonings on his food; a one-mile stroll after dinner to improve digestion; golf to improve circulation; one scotch before dinner; the strict avoidance of unnecessary excitement and trauma, hence the continued ban on watching Army-Navy football games on television. At seventy-five, his scrupulous self-regimentation, his powerful physique, his dynamic presence, and his abundant nervous energy lent the impression of immortality despite the succession of major illnesses that had become national issues while he served in the presidency. At night he dictated personal reminiscences for his next book, *At Ease,* an informal memoir that would highlight the prewar years and his life outside politics.

Eisenhower had a busy fall in 1965. His second volume of presidential memoirs, *Waging Peace,* was published. He traveled to Denison, Texas, to visit his birthplace and address a high school convocation. In October, the Republican Party celebrated his seventy-fifth birthday by organizing a series of fund-raising dinners in major cities around the country, at which Eisenhower appeared. And Augusta National decided to open its 1965–66 season by scheduling a party commemorating the Eisenhowers' fiftieth wedding anniversary six months in advance.

It was in Augusta, however, that Eisenhower's health faltered, this time decisively, bringing him to the state of old age and permanent semi-convalescence that had seemed imminent for years but that he had until then successfully defied. The Augusta season's opening in November was an unmistakable reminder of advancing years not only for Eisenhower, but also for many of his friends. George Humphrey, scheduled to present Ike and Mamie with an eighteen-carat gold Asprey bowl engraved with the various homes of Eisenhower's career, had to cancel at the last minute because of heart trouble. Golfing great Bob Jones, who was to act as master of ceremonies, arrived in Augusta after an automobile trip from Atlanta and went directly to bed on doctor's orders.

Following the evening of tributes, the presentation of the bowl, the thousand pink carnations for Mamie, and the humorous toasts taped by sound technicians for the enjoyment of future generations of Augusta National members, Eisenhower decided to linger at the club for three weeks. Ninety "close friends" had traveled to Augusta for the anniversary party, and a dozen remained for golf and bridge in the pattern of the presidential days.

Eisenhower had an understanding with Augusta's Cliff Roberts that he would not accept social engagements off ground while staying at Augusta. A day or so after Roberts left to attend to investment banking business in New York, Eisenhower broke the agreement for the first time and traveled to Aiken, South Carolina, several miles away, for dinner at the winter home of businessman Barry Leithead.

Returning shortly after midnight, he began suffering acute chest pains, a probable coronary. Within the hour, a medical team from Fort Gordon arrived at Mamie's cottage at Augusta to diagnose and assume responsibility for his treatment. Early in the morning, Eisenhower was transferred by ambulance to Fort Gordon. A defibrillator stabilized his heartbeat and saved his life.

Eisenhower's second heart attack came as a shock. Though he recovered sufficiently to return to Gettysburg by early December, he lost more of the jaunty self-assurance first shaken in 1955 by his heart attack and later by his stroke. Now he monitored the dull pains and uneasiness in his chest anxiously for signs of an emergency. He began withdrawing from politics and confined himself to social affairs involving fewer people and less mental and physical exertion. That winter, Eisenhower grew noticeably more mellow on personalities, while unbending in his criticism of campus turmoil and the growing protests against the war in Vietnam. Convalescing in Gettysburg, Eisenhower seemed at times depressed and uncertain.

One afternoon, secretary Rusty Brown drove to the farm to deliver the late mail. Eisenhower was often working half days, and not returning after lunch to his office on the campus of Gettysburg College. As she climbed the staircase leading up to the small bedroom Eisenhower used for napping, she saw her boss propped up against several pillows. Mamie was sitting in a chair at his bedside, clasping his right hand with her left and chatting audibly. Rusty was unnoticed.

"Why you old so-and-so," Mamie repeated several times. "You've always had the most masculine hands, and you still do." Rusty stepped back, deposited the papers on a sofa, and slipped away.

Eisenhower aged visibly. His powerful presence, which had always been faintly frightening, evolved into a kind of grainy charm. To me, Dwight Eisenhower had always been imposing and at times unapproachable, and I had never understood why people thought of him as so genial. But the onset of old age revealed a warmth and humanity in his features that had not been obvious to me before — like cutting through the outer rings of a tree stump and discovering a core. A weight loss changed his physical appearance in a pleasing way. His neck and shoulders diminished, thus accentuating his most unusual features: his large gnarled hands and big ears. His thinned face highlighted bushy eyebrows and softened the expression in his piercing sky blue eyes.

As Kevin McCann once put it, Eisenhower, like most people, was a sphere revealing parts of himself to different people. As he grew old, we were to glimpse the side that had been withheld from the grandchildren but had been apparent to so many others. One of my sister Anne's favorite possessions is an old textbook of Granddad's given to her several years before he died. Scrawled in pencil in one of the margins is the word *damn.* "Until I saw that," she recalled later, "I wasn't sure he was human."

Eisenhower's friends detected a new resignation and wistfulness. Whereas in the past Eisenhower could be aroused by criticism of his presidency, he now grew philosophical. In an unpublished article, Eisenhower wrote simply that disagreements involving his own conduct had never interested him as much as the more numerous examples of his abilities to get along with people and win their cooperation. The generally tepid reviews of *Waging Peace* were disappointing but aroused little response or desire in him to keep setting the record straight. He enviously cited Nixon's 1962 *Six Crises* as an effective book, and once wrote that with a chance to do everything over, he might have patterned his replies for history along the lines Nixon had chosen. Finally, Eisenhower simply stopped reading political books and responding to criticism altogether.

Granddad's health caused him to rethink the farm business. That winter he told Arthur Nevins that he would probably be getting out of the purebred cattle business in 1966. He was doing so for financial reasons, and because hiring farm help was getting harder. In lieu of a highly advertised herd sale, Granddad would inform representatives of the American Angus Association and the editors at the *Aberdeen-Angus Journal* that he was "receptive" to an offer for his herd. A private auction was set for March 17, 1966, and a second one for late 1966.

In mid-March of 1966, while Mamie visited the Main Chance spa in Arizona, leaving Granddad "alone" with his bridge and golf-playing friends at Eldorado, John Toland's best-selling *The Last Hundred Days* was published. It contained highly critical observations about Eisenhower's refusal in the closing days of the war to counter Soviet political moves throughout Eastern Europe, particularly during the race for Berlin.

Toland's book was just one of many that had appeared in recent years criticizing Eisenhower's skill and foresight as a commander. Montgomery's, Alanbrooke's, and

Eden's memoirs had criticized Eisenhower not only as a general, but also as president for fumbling the politics of the cold war.

In his diary Slats Slater offered this observation: "The General had not seen the book and I doubt that he will. His general comment was 'it's awfully easy to look back from twenty years and see what should have been done. And the historian, no matter how careful, can never feel the tension, the uncertainty, hear the rumors — and put himself in the situation existing at the time of the action.' "

The task of answering Toland would devolve on others, namely Dad, who had left the Freedoms Foundation and was hard at work on a history of the Ardennes counteroffensive of 1944, *The Bitter Woods,* the first of several books he would write on the war. With Dad's encouragement, I had written my Exeter senior thesis on the Yalta Conference of 1945, held in the wake of the German Ardennes counteroffensive. Dad had given my paper high marks, and engaged me at length on the subject. He followed up by presenting me with Eugene Davidson's *The Trial of the Germans,* a searching and exhaustive account of the Nuremberg trials complete with in-depth profiles of the Nazi defendants. Like the Bible I had received at age ten, *The Trial of the Germans* was one of the most treasured gifts I had, signifying my admission to a circle within the family who were beginning to study World War II.

Dad's book would stand as a definitive account of the Ardennes campaign and inevitably, an answer to the revisionist books like Montgomery's 1958 memoir, which had questioned Eisenhower's strategic decisions in late 1944 and early 1945. In writing the book, Dad was drawing on his direct experiences in the war, which he seemed to be reliving that summer.

Dad had graduated from West Point on June 6, D-Day, and after several months of infantry training at Fort Benning, had deployed with the 71st Division to Europe, arriving in January 1945. Detached from the 71st upon his arrival, he had been sent to a Signal Information and Monitoring (SIAM) unit attached to General Bradley's headquarters, a job that involved assuring the flow of accurate information between headquarters and the battlefronts. Work with the SIAM battalion had given him a front-row seat during the final stages of the German collapse, and, knowing Granddad better than anyone, he had been privy to his thinking on the final phase of the war for over twenty years.

The controversial decisions of the European campaign weighed on Dad's mind as though they had been decided yesterday: the validity of Eisenhower's "broad front" strategy in 1944–45 and insistence on unconditional surrender; the agreements reached with the British and Soviets in the closing days of the war, which shaped the future of Europe; and the horrors of the conflict and eventual trial of the Germans at Nuremberg and at lesser tribunals.

Having known many of the American command officers since his boyhood, Dad now traveled to Europe to interview the surviving German and British commanders in order to fill out his research on the war years. Along the way, he developed a certain admiration for several German commanders. But like Granddad, he found it difficult to reconcile the admirable qualities of the German enemy with the horror of what he had seen and the history he was researching. The war experience bound Granddad and Dad tightly. Vignettes of their shared experience appear throughout Dad's writing, including his stark account of April 13, 1945, the day after Franklin Roosevelt's death:

That evening Dad, General Bradley, General Hodges, a group of aides, and I sat around talking. Dad had just sent his message of condolences to President Roosevelt's widow. But the thing most on his mind was the horror camp near Gotha that he had gone through only the day before. The scene of atrocities had left him visibly shaken and he had not yet adjusted the entire episode in his mind. With him on the visit was the reputedly rough-and-tough George Patton, who had become physically ill. Dad had cabled home to ask for a contingent of reporters and legislators to come immediately to witness.

"Well, the only speck of optimism I can see," Dad said that evening, "is that I really don't think the bulk of Germans knew what was going on. When I saw that camp yesterday, I ordered the mayor of Gotha to turn out the townspeople and make them clean up the mess. Last night he and his wife went home and hanged themselves. Maybe there's hope after all . . ."

THE HOUSE OF DURABLE ROCK

In the spring of 1966, four long years of prep school drew to an end. I had a summer to look forward to and a fresh start in college. And along with everyone my age that year, I was aware of a great change coming over America's campuses. It was something unforeseen when we had entered school four years earlier, unanticipated by the parents who had sent us away, and difficult to communicate to anyone on the outside of an increasingly self-conscious community of students and professors.

Civil rights had been the catalyst. Great leaders like Martin Luther King, Jr., had made the fate of the black underclass of America, uneasily ignored and patronized for a century, a question of conscience. Popular music adopted the idea of change and preached the notion that the generation of students coming of age had the opportunity and the obligation to break established patterns and guide the country away from the perpetuation of prejudice and the horrors of war. John Kennedy's death had impressed many with the delicate balance between good and evil, and it galvanized a new social awareness, especially on campuses. The concept of the university acting as the vanguard of the conscience of the nation took hold.

The ferment sweeping universities between late 1964 and 1966 was paradoxical.

Student organizers canvassed campuses to recruit volunteers on behalf of the poor, but attracted the support primarily of millions dissatisfied with a life of abundance. This dissatisfaction with society took root first among the most idealistic students. The earliest radicals seemed set apart in a world of their own, admired and fabled as guerrillas. But soon the spirit of protest pervaded all quarters of campus life. At Exeter we often read English themes aloud in class, and in 1966 the themes were distinctly political and social. Students from privileged towns such as Greenwich and Brookline endeavored to describe life in Roxbury as they gleaned it from black literature, political workshops, and field trips into the ghetto to teach underprivileged youngsters how to read. Artists and athletes, heroes in my first two years, fell from grace. Musicians ascended as linguists of the new political culture. Nearly everyone experienced an "identity crisis" — natural for some, obligatory for the rest.

In letters home, I made no attempt to explain what was happening at Exeter. My parents received the school newspaper, and I knew they were drawing their own conclusions. I learned that Granddad began to question my parents about the kind of environment his grandchildren were growing up in. Unlike my teachers, school administrators, and friends, Dwight Eisenhower had no ambiguous feelings about "campus unrest." In "Afterthoughts," an appended section to *Waging Peace,* Eisenhower confessed bewilderment with the manifestations of "outright wickedness" and "laxity of morals" apparent to him as he wrote in 1964. At that time, he was addressing petty theft, cheating on exams, and loose sexual morality on campuses. When by 1966 the students were advocating draft resistance and civil disobedience, Eisenhower became truculent in opposition.

The spring before graduation was a time of great anxiety at Exeter and high schools throughout the United States. Seniors planning to attend college were supposed to take an exam administered by the Selective Service. As I recall, receiving a certain score qualified one to go to college with an exemption from the armed services; a point less than passing meant boot camp.

Canada is not far from Exeter, and a number of students were rumored to be planning an escape there if Vietnam still raged at graduation. Shortly before commencement, I registered for the draft, which was obligatory for young men turning eighteen. Taking no chances with my common sense, Granddad sent me a card, twenty dollars for a night out on the town, and a note: "Now you are signing up for the draft. I am not at all well informed on the policies affecting selective service but if you should become one of those called upon to serve actively in the Armed Services of our country, I know you will do so efficiently and cheerfully."

Protests against the war proliferated across the country. At Amherst College, where I had been accepted as a freshman in the fall, Secretary of Defense Robert McNamara's commencement address was interrupted by a noisy walkout led by faculty members and student firebrands, setting the pattern for the treatment of Johnson administration officials on university campuses thereafter.

In January, I had invited Granddad on behalf of the Exeter school administration to address the commencement. Because of his precarious health, Granddad at first was reluctant to accept. He eventually decided to honor the invitation. He wrote to me on May 20: "I am going to talk largely about 'character' rather than education, professions and so on. I have read a draft to your Dad and Mother and they thought it was O.K., so possibly I am on the right track. I assure you that I will make a great effort to avoid 'preaching.' "

Sitting in the audience on graduation day, June 12, I compared the scene before me with the memory of Granddad's visit in 1962. Then, the autumn weather seemed to crackle in anticipation of the Cuban Missile Crisis. Eisenhower had been a curiosity, a magnet, a reassuring symbol of the kind of statesmanship that would bring victory in the Cold War, a good-natured opponent of the young president. Graduation day 1966 was, like October 1962, incomparably beautiful, but in a different way. Rich sunlight created a cathedral-like effect through the tall trees shading the commons, where the outdoor ceremony was held. The ritual of graduation seemed inward and pensive, part wedding, part baptism, part funeral. In the audience were parents, restless little brothers and sisters, and babies crying at awkward moments.

The program was designed to honor achievement and to inspire graduates with thoughts about the future. But in that ceremony, the guests and students were facing an uncertain future, and the speeches highlighted the familial and protective bond among Exeter graduates. Vietnam dominated everyone's thoughts.

Granddad's theme was indeed character. He told the graduates:

Suppose we liken the career of an individual to a house — a lifetime home built of his own deeds, words, mistakes and accomplishments, growing continuously through the years until the day comes when the final piece is fixed firmly in place, and the occupant lies down at last to rest. If the house is to be strong, rather than weak, beautiful instead of mean, useful instead of worthless, its foundation must be sturdy and solid. You will recall the Biblical parable of two houses, one built upon sand, the other upon durable rock. When the winds and floods struck them both, the one was demolished and swept away — the other, on rock, withstood every shock of wind and wave.

The "building blocks" of character were hard work, worthy ambition, loyalty, common sense, integrity, and moral courage. He spoke of the continuum in American history that posed my graduating class with similar challenges and unavoidable responsibilities to those that had fallen on his West

Point class fifty-one years earlier. He cautioned the graduates against influences that would lure them away from the values that mattered most. He stood solidly with the leadership that was asking the country to sacrifice in Vietnam.

Granddad did not mind sounding old-fashioned. He did not address the subjects that electrified campus life — dissent, Cold War revisionism, Black Power, or even his own farewell address. His talk was a reminder that there was no escaping a clash between the values of his generation and the amorphous, mushrooming community coming to life across the nation's universities.

My sister Anne had a similar experience. A year later Granddad addressed her commencement at the Shipley School in Bryn Mawr, Pennsylvania. As at Exeter, he spoke about the essential character traits of sound citizenship. Concluding, he startled Anne and delighted the audience of female prep school students with a Victorian thought. "Remember," he said referring to the mini-skirts coming into fashion around the country, "ankles are always neat, but knees are always knobby."

Dwight Eisenhower was proud of the

commencement addresses at Shipley and Exeter. He had the latter reproduced and sent to several friends, and referred to it frequently in answering public correspondence that questioned the student "revolt" and campus dissent against the war. In *Waging Peace,* he had made it clear that he believed that student unrest and other social problems would be resolved in time, and that "freedom in an orderly society" would endure. In "Afterthoughts," he had written: "The great ideas of the West will continue their outward journey in concentric circles until one day they cover the entire globe. Our cardinal concepts of human dignity, of free enterprise, and human liberty . . . will become so strong that as they crash against the conflicting currents of Communism, they will overcome and demolish dialectical materialism and the ideology of regimentation."

GOLDEN ANNIVERSARY

Dwight and Mamie Eisenhower celebrated their fiftieth wedding anniversary at my parents' home in Phoenixville on July 1, 1966. It was a strictly family affair. Edgar and Milton Eisenhower traveled thousands of miles to be on hand for the festivities.

The day was one of many moods: nostalgia, poignance, hilarity. About twenty members of the Doud and Eisenhower families gathered at midday at our home on the outskirts of town. As caterers arrived to prepare the dinner, the older folks rested and napped while the younger members of the family escaped the crushing July humidity in the icy water of our unheated swimming pool. My swim was interrupted by a summons from Granddad to drop by the family room, where he rested on a foldout bed, for a discussion about my future.

Granddad seemed weary and serious. He explained that he had decided to simplify the farm operation and confessed that he no longer felt strong enough to cope with the myriad details involved in farming. He was concerned that time was slipping away, and that he had not taken all the time he wanted to make himself available for advice about my future.

In that moment, something changed between us. I sensed that he was hoping I would indicate whether he had succeeded in instilling values and a spirit of enterprise in me. There were long awkward pauses. I repeated a familiar litany about my conscientious state of uncertainty about my future. He listened with skeptical silence.

Toward evening, everyone gathered for hors d'oeuvres, drinks, and photographs. When the young Eisenhowers had married in Denver in 1916, the highlight of their wedding reception, held in the drawing room of the Doud home on Lafayette Street, had been the entertainment of a local harpist. Sentimentally, my parents hired a harpist to re-create the event of fifty years earlier. In 1966, the harpist arrived in a Volkswagen van. She weaved melodies in air-conditioning under electric lights, and the faint roar of a jet passing overhead in a landing pattern for Philadelphia International Airport occasionally interrupted. Mamie had provided a list of the music performed at the reception fifty years before. Their favorite in 1916 had been "Home on the Range." Our harpist's rendition interrupted the lively conversation and everyone joined in the song.

For my sisters and me, the real curiosity was great-uncle Edgar Eisenhower, Granddad's older brother. Over the years we had seen very little of him, but we had been virtually raised on tales of his driven obsession with work and of the bare-fisted rivalry between himself and his brother Dwight. Even now, more than seventy-five years old and the leading lawyer in Tacoma, Washington, millionaire Edgar remained half big-city lawyer and half cowboy.

As men in their sixties, Dwight and Edgar's reunions had often degenerated into heated arguments about which family in Abilene had been a better ally of the Eisenhower family, and who had been tougher, Edgar or Dwight. Because of this rivalry, there was none of the affection between Edgar and Dwight that was so evident between Dwight and his younger brother Milton.

Dwight had the upper hand in marriage. Edgar had been married several times, "a success," as Dad put it, "in everything except marriage." Edgar thus stood on the periphery of the celebration that afternoon and evening, his sunburned, lobster-red face striking against his white dinner jacket. After Milton delivered a moving toast, in the silence that followed Edgar piped up for the first time. "Very touching," he said irreverently. "Makes you kind of want to try again!"

In conjunction with their fiftieth anniversary, Granddad and Mamie granted a joint interview to *Parade* magazine's Rosalind Massow in which they discussed the secrets of a happy marriage and a rewarding and productive life. Early in the interview, Massow asked the big question: if

General Eisenhower had to do it over again, would he marry the same girl? "That's the worst question I ever heard," Eisenhower laughed. "There's only one possible answer." Then he grew philosophical and added: "As a matter of fact, I wouldn't want to live life over again. I've made my mistakes, my errors and blunders like everyone else, but to go back and start again at, say 20 — no. Look what I would have missed. Everybody has to live his own life and take his share of the problems."

In an interview with United Press International about their half century together, Eisenhower was asked if he still painted.

"Well, yes, I try . . . and none of 'em are good."

Mamie chimed in, "He's good."

Back in Gettysburg, Eisenhower finalized the details to shut down his purebred Angus operation and convert the farm into a feeder operation. This meant leasing his ground to other cattle owners and buyers for the temporary feeding and maintenance of their herds. Granddad also told Art Nevins that he would sell or give away the horses that he had maintained for his grandchildren.

Granddad had offered my father the chance to inherit the property. Dad declined on grounds that the farm would be too difficult to maintain. Granddad subsequently decided to deed the property to the government for eventual incorporation into the National Park Service upon his death. With the liquidation of his Angus herd and the disappearance of the horses, the empty acreage of grassland in the north and eastern pastures of the farm gave the entire complex an unaccustomed, uncultivated, run-down look.

At Ease

The Gettysburg office had also undergone changes. With the departure of the memoir staff, Kevin McCann had arrived to assist Granddad with *At Ease.* Kevin and Rusty Brown became the anchors of the office. Rusty contributed serenity and a good-natured nonpartisanship to the occasionally strong personality clashes. She had been a WAC (member of the Women's Army Corps) during the war and later had acted as secretary for General Matt Ridgway at the Pentagon before joining the White House staff. Despite her years in Washington and abroad, Rusty never lost her midwestern flavor. She was a fit woman who loved the outdoors and horses. In another life, one can easily imagine Rusty Brown managing a large and boisterous Kansas farm household.

Rusty's White House experience had reminded her of the war, which she spent in the Pacific. The pace, the emotional highs and lows, the underlying sense of danger about one's work, the communal atmosphere of mutual aid and comfort, the purposefulness were characteristic not only of war but also the presidency. "The one thing everyone needs is a purpose," she told me. "During the war and the White House, I participated like I had been taught by my four brothers doing chores and playing war games as children — pitch in, do your part, and bring fudge, cookies and soda to the troops in the field."

But Rusty was not romantic about war, the White House, or life in Gettysburg. As a WAC, she had learned that war was not glamorous. She had endured shocks, ranging from the petty to the indescribable. She had been disillusioned at the beginning to discover that many GIs thought Red Cross women and WACs were "whores." And although not actually allowed to enter Nagasaki, she had seen the nuclear-flattened city from a distance aboard a passenger ship. "I was not able to integrate the sight of that city with a single bomb."

The rewards in a job for Rusty were the people she worked for. She was fond of both Granddad and Mamie. In them she found two people with "great warmth that dissipates awe and commands respect," a considerate couple who treated her with fairness and respect. She likened her experiences to joining a family "because you shared moments of intimacy with the Eisenhowers — saw them as they were."

The year before, Rusty had taken on an assignment that brought her as close to Dwight Eisenhower as anyone. Eisenhower was enjoying working with Kevin McCann on *At Ease.* He did much of the writing at the farmhouse, often dictating his reminiscences into a tape recorder he kept by his bed. Rusty Brown did the transcription. She recalls: "Listening to the tape, one felt that one understood Dwight Eisenhower. There he was, his voice, rumbling along talking about the things he had done as a child and as a young man. At times, he seemed to lose himself and just ramble. You can hear the chuckling on the tape when he thinks back over some of the pranks and fights — he couldn't restrain himself."

Granddad ordered Rusty to destroy the

dictations, but Rusty had grown too attached to the personality revealed in them. She stored them secretly in the office and later turned them over to the Eisenhower Presidential Library in Abilene, Kansas.

Eisenhower dropped his guard considerably when he agreed to write *At Ease* for Doubleday. He also relaxed his "rule against discussing personalities." He answered a few personal criticisms by Truman, Montgomery, and others. In addition, before beginning his dictations, he handed McCann a list of individuals he wanted to praise:

General Omar Bradley
General Alfred Gruenther
General Bedell Smith
General Lucius Clay
George Humphrey
John Foster Dulles
Admiral Alan Goodrich Kirk
General William Simpson
General Carl Spaatz
General Royal Baker
Herbert Brownell
William Rogers
General Courtney Hodges
General Leonard Gerow

General Lucian Truscott
James Mitchell

The preponderance of Army people on the list shows that Eisenhower's mind was ranging back to his formative experiences in the Army, which had prepared him for the supreme tests of North Africa, Italy, D-Day, and the European Theater command. The people on the list are evidently individuals who contributed enormously to success in the war but whose contributions were in danger of being slighted by history. Bradley is the only famous general on the list — by including him, Eisenhower evidently wanted to emphasize in *At Ease,* as in his book dealing with the war, Bradley's crucial role as an Army group commander in the European campaign. Marshall, MacArthur, Patton and Mark Clark, all famous generals, were not in need of special mention, though each figures prominently in Eisenhower's retelling of his war and prewar years. But whether listed for special mention, or simply covered, Eisenhower's military associates were to be shown in *At Ease* as remarkable people. They did not always agree, and in some cases their paths diverged after the war. But there was deep mutual respect rooted in friendship and shared experiences, and in shared convictions about the rightness of their cause, about the significance of America, and the task incumbent on Americans, in Truman's words, "to bind up the wounds of a suffering world — to build an abiding peace, a peace rooted in justice and in law."

Perhaps the most interesting sections of *At Ease* are those dealing with Eisenhower's education and experiences as a middle grade officer between World War I and 1941. He would dedicate the book to General Fox Conner, a high-ranking veteran of Pershing's Allied Expeditionary Force staff who became Eisenhower's mentor when he was stationed in Panama in the early 1920s. More than anyone, Conner guided Eisenhower in his professional development as a strategic thinker and operational officer. More than anyone, Conner persuaded Eisenhower of the inevitability of a second world war. At the outset of war in Europe, though American opinion was divided fifty-fifty on most war issues, there is no doubt that Eisenhower favored intervention in Europe and was prepared for it. In a journal on September 3, 1939, from Manila, where he was about to leave MacArthur's staff, he somberly wrote:

This evening we have been listening to broadcasts of Chamberlain's speech stating that Great Britain was at war with Germany. . . . If the war, which now seems to be upon us, is as long drawn out and disastrous, as bloody and as costly a war as the so-called World War, then I believe that the remnants of nations emerging from it will be scarcely recognizable as the ones that entered it. . . . Hundreds of millions will suffer privations and starvation, millions will be killed and wounded, because one man so wills it. He [Hitler] is a power-drunk egocentric, but even so he would still not do this if he were sane. He is one of the criminally insane, but unfortunately he is the absolute ruler of 89,000,000 people. And by his personal magnetism, which he must have, he has converted a large proportion of those millions to his insane schemes to blind acceptance of his leadership. Unless he is successful in overcoming the whole world by brute force the final result will be that Germany will have to be dismembered and destroyed.

Following his second heart attack, on doctor's orders Eisenhower took a fifteen-minute break from his office schedule twice a day. Mamie kept the office supplied with bouillon and tea for the break. Each full day Eisenhower spent at the office, at mid-morning and at four o'clock, he drew the shades over his window, slumped back into his chair, and elevated his legs on an ottoman. At the sound of his buzzer, Rusty, like a registered nurse, arrived with bouillon or tea, placed it on a small table next to his desk, and on doctor's orders drew up the chair to talk lightheartedly with the General.

At first he seemed embarrassed by the enforced rest and Rusty's required presence, but eventually he looked forward to it. The two had much in common. Rusty's grandfather had been a Kansas cowboy before the Eisenhowers and Stovers (Eisenhower's maternal family) moved into the state. Thus Rusty had a link to the central Kansas of adventurers, prostitutes, and gunslingers who had moved on by the time the Eisenhowers settled in Abilene. The Abilene of Granddad's youth had been a pastoral farming community, but the memory of Abilene's glory as depot and transport center for Texas beef being sent north to market and of Wild Bill Hickok ridding the town of outlaws lived on and excited the imagination of every young boy. Eisenhower was proud of his Abilene background. Its heritage had sparked his fondness for history and legend, the two often indistinguishable in his mind.

Rusty and Granddad also talked football and horses, particularly Granddad's horses. Well-mannered Sporty Miss was "everyone's favorite." Eisenhower bemoaned the wasted potential of Doodle de Doo and her foal, Doodlin', also a fine physical specimen. Doodlin' was a high-strung, nervous animal like her mother. Though Doodlin's birth had mellowed the mother somewhat, she still had streaks of uncontrollable wildness. Eisenhower listened carefully to Rusty's ideas about horse breeding. As she recalled years later, "he accepted that you knew what you were talking about unless you proved you didn't. He didn't second-guess me or anyone he talked to — never ridiculed anyone's ideas, including mine. He wouldn't have told an idiot he was an idiot."

Eisenhower eventually gave Rusty and her niece the horses.

She also discovered in their twice-daily chats that Eisenhower had high standards for everything — horses, staff, family, himself. "His highest praise," she recalled, "was 'very able,' " because, she explained, "among other things, he was trying to apply

393

the brakes on overindulgence in language, morals, and money." Occasionally Eisenhower would reminisce about the White House years, although rarely the war. As president, he told her, he knew he had done "an able job."

He also enjoyed spinning a yarn from time to time about Blackie, the wonder horse in Panama he described in *At Ease,* which he had trained to do everything except fly and speak foreign languages. For the most part, Eisenhower and Rusty spoke seriously. Many of the stories Eisenhower told were fables with a point or moral. His favorite saying, repeated each time with the passion of a first telling, was "There is no black and white except in morals and exact sciences." Rusty never pursued the thought with him and simply listened. "After all," she laughed later, "what's left?"

"Girls today," Rusty concluded, "would think of him as old-fashioned. He knew his place, and everyone else's who had anything to do with him." When talking to her, he skipped the "damnations" and "hellfires," deferring to her femininity. He behaved differently when he dealt with others. "Talking to General Schulz," she recalled, "you could hear him all over the building."

Eisenhower also made a habit of spending

thirty minutes each morning in McCann's office drinking coffee and working on the current writing project. They talked about the presidency. His most difficult moment? The Rosenberg clemency decision, which Truman had dumped in his lap at the outset of his administration. He had never been comfortable with the circumstantial nature of the case. To allay these doubts and satisfy himself that the verdict had been just, he listened to hours of evidentiary presentations by Herb Brownell on the material that had been excluded from the trial itself. In the end, he decided, but not without hesitation, that the evidence upheld the verdict. His personal secretary Ann Whitman called the Rosenberg decision the "most trying crisis of the entire eight years."

Complicating the Rosenberg trial was the fact that the codefendant was a woman. Eisenhower had authorized the execution of Private Eddie Slovik for desertion during the war. He had refused clemency many times as president. But, according to Whitman, he had never stood in judgment of a woman.

Furthermore, he disliked judgment in principle and to illustrate this point he often talked about a character he had known at West Point named John Markoe. Markoe was an unbridled rake who, like Eisenhower, found the Army disciplinary routine onerous. Also like Eisenhower, Markoe was brawny and physical, and indifferent about academics. The two used to "slip over the wall" on Saturday nights for a beer or two.

Markoe was a legend in his time at West Point. In 1914, Granddad's third year at the Point, Markoe reputedly sparred with the light heavyweight champion of the world in a ring in front of a vast gallery of cadets. Midway through the sparring bout, Markoe decided that the punching was getting too serious. In Granddad's telling, "Markoe just came off the floor and knocked the man cold." As the champ sank to the mat, Markoe supposedly knelt next to him and recited the rosary.

Ultimately, Markoe also knocked the captain of the cadet guard unconscious on a Saturday night following a few beers, and found himself about to be expelled. Aware of Markoe's natural leadership ability, however, the academy administration decided instead of expulsion to place Markoe in the "custody of his class." His classmates thus undertook the responsibility of protecting Markoe from himself. Markoe graduated with a reputation as a brawler and wild man, and, in Eisenhower's eyes, "the best potential officer" he had ever seen. He left the Point described, like his friend Dwight, as "born to command."

Markoe went from West Point to the head of an all-black regiment on the Mexico border during the punitive expedition against Pancho Villa in 1916. As the story goes, one night he got involved in a barroom fight over the refusal of one of his lieutenants to drink with black soldiers. A man was killed and Markoe was accused of manslaughter and discharged. "He was ahead of his time," Eisenhower remarked. "He stood up for his Negro soldiers." Markoe went on to become a Jesuit priest. The two men met briefly again in 1941 when Eisenhower traveled from Fort Lewis to San Antonio just before the outbreak of the war.

Markoe reminded Granddad of characters like George Patton, a mix of talent and immaturity that was both valuable and exasperating. A thin line separated Eisenhower from these types. And, when called upon to judge others, Eisenhower, mindful of his past friendship with Markoe, always had a feeling about his Army career of "there but for the grace of God go I."

The conservative influence of the Army had tamed the swashbuckling and uninhibited Ike Eisenhower from Abilene. Over the years, he had learned techniques to curb his instinctive combativeness. For instance, he noted the futility of hatred. "Instead of hating people," he told McCann, "and wasting all that energy in a self-destructive way, I forget." Well into his retirement years, Eisenhower maintained a "black book," a registry of the living dead containing the names of people who, as far as Eisenhower was concerned, simply had ceased to exist.

Eisenhower and McCann had similar backgrounds and notions about life, both stamped by their rural upbringings. To McCann, Eisenhower often reflected on what had drawn him to Gettysburg. "In the big city," he once remarked, "everyone is covered with a veneer. You have to be pompous, a stuffed shirt." The two men liked the unvarnished characters, the "oddballs." Human nature comes through in a small town. In *At Ease,* Eisenhower recalled a meeting at his Columbia University office with a well-connected, well-heeled, fourth-generation heir. When McCann briefed the General on his visitor, using his full name, Eisenhower muttered under his breath, "God help that man."

Eisenhower was not unconscious of his heritage. As a child, he knew the Eisenhowers were from the wrong side of the track. As a young man, he had fervently identified himself as an American in the way of an immigrant seeking acceptance. Though his family predated most of the other settlers in the United States, the Eisenhowers had not tried to assimilate. Not until his father, David, decided that German would not be spoken in his household did the Eisenhower family shed its strong German influence. Dwight and his brothers were the first generation not to speak German in the home.

Eventually Eisenhower developed considerable pride in his German heritage. He respected German fighting qualities exhibited during the war. But his abhorrence for Nazi atrocities also forced him to be selective. To McCann, Eisenhower often referred to his ancestral region in the Palatinate as "good people, sound people — who, even among those who stayed, rejected Nazism."

In *At Ease,* Granddad idealized his boyhood in Abilene. He called his years in Abilene a "golden time," the happiest of his life. He talked often about his mother and the happenstance that she had been born in Virginia, the beloved home state of Robert E. Lee. Mindful of her, Granddad told McCann that he in every speech on civil rights had tried to curb the "rowdyism and hooliganism" of die-hard segregationists by appealing to southern pride.

"The biographies will never capture Abilene," Granddad complained once. He was surprised by how his biographers had inflated his boyhood scrapes into epic confrontations. For instance, the story of how he had stared down Wes Merrifield before entering seventh grade was embarrassing. "Sure we fought hard," Granddad admitted; "we were just kids." And there were the stories of Dwight's showdown with legendary town bully Dirk Tyler. The facts, Granddad told Kevin, were that people in Abilene were not afraid of Tyler as the biographies alleged. "I was sitting in a barber chair one day and a bunch of people stormed in claiming Tyler says he can beat the hell out of you. Tyler knew nothing about fighting. I was taken in by a bunch of bored people who wanted to see a fight."

In the course of helping Eisenhower write *At Ease,* McCann took time away from the office to visit many of the places covered in the book. He spent several days in Abilene talking to Eisenhower's former neighbors, learning important facts about the Eisenhower family, including their social and religious heritage as members of the River

Brethren Church, which had migrated westward in the late 1870s from southern Pennsylvania and Virginia.

On his trip to Abilene, McCann got a vivid picture of the realities behind the legends; of the many hardships endured by Ike's grandparents when they left Pennsylvania, and the struggles of Ike's father, David, in Kansas as he tried to make a life for his sons and wife. His grandparents' consolation had been their River Brethren faith in the face of "repeated personal tragedy," including the loss of several children.

McCann understood. He and Granddad had an important fact in common. Both had lost a son, the Eisenhowers in the 1920s while Granddad had been serving at Fort Meade. McCann had never gotten over the loss of his son, and he knew that the Eisenhowers had never gotten over Icky's death at age three of scarlet fever. Indeed, a picture of Icky was displayed in the guest bedroom on the second floor of the Gettysburg residence, maintained as a permanent shrine to Icky.

But sadness is a part of life, and the Eisenhowers were able to cope because of the lessons learned from Ike's mother, Ida. In *At Ease,* he would devote an entire chapter to Ida, recalling the nightly Bible readings and the friendly competition she promoted among the brothers to become conversant in the Good Book. When he completed a full reading of the Bible at age twelve, his mother gave him a gold watch. Eisenhower often said later, "To read the Bible is to take a trip to a fair land where the spirit is strengthened and faith renewed."

Just fifty miles north of Gettysburg, in Elizabethville, McCann visited the site where Eisenhower's grandparents bought and worked a farm and where several generations are buried. In *At Ease,* Eisenhower quoted the still visible inscription on his Aunt Lydia's limestone marker:

Lydia A.
Daughter of
Jacob F. and Rebecca
Eisenhower
Born Aug. 27, 1857
Died Nov. 15, 1874
Aged 17 Yrs. 2 Mo &
19 Days

She gave her heart to Jesus
Who took her stains away
And now in Christ believing,
the Father too can say
I am going home to glory

A golden crown to wear
O meet me meet me over there

No Pains

Before entering Amherst College in the fall of 1966, I made plans to spend the summer in Phoenixville working as a surveyor. I had again declined Granddad's offer to work at the farm. In January he had written me: "I hear you have a job lined up for next summer at $1.25 an hour. I understand your plan is to join a survey team; I assume as a rod man or one of the chair men. I hope you like it, particularly if you think you will be learning something. But, if you want a farm job, I can always use an extra hand in the summer and I would pay <u>slightly</u> more than the offer you have now."

But I had contracted mononucleosis shortly after graduating from Exeter and eventually had to leave my surveyor's job after two months because I could not stay awake. My grandparents were sympathetic. One day, returning from work, a letter arrived from Granddad marked "Personal–Confidential–Top Secret–Eyes Only."

Dear David,
    I have just been talking to my doctors and after describing my own condition and

403

symptoms, I remarked that you were now a victim of mononucleosis (spelling is not guaranteed). This was their comment:

"Mononucleosis is a disease that normally attacks young people. Among members of the medical profession it is called the 'kissing disease.' We recommend David pick his clients with greater care."

Devotedly, Granddad
Personal–Confidential–Top Secret–
Eyes Only

I spent the rest of the summer commuting between Phoenixville and Gettysburg, where I continued to date several old girlfriends. On the pretext of helping me "monitor my clients," Granddad asked me to bring my dates by the farm for a Coca-Cola in the evening. My grandparents had a Brownie camera that we used to take snapshots of the four of us for their albums.

Granddad and I watched baseball on Saturdays. Though he had been known as a football player in college, I felt that his favorite sport was baseball. Through him, I had learned to love the game. Its strong attraction for him, I suspect, was nostalgic. Baseball's season evolves over the spring and summer months, each game as random and unconnected as a day at the office. Following baseball is like keeping tabs on the neighbors. Attending a game is like dropping by for a visit to see how everyone is getting along. Sustaining interest is easy because of the ever-present potential for an abrupt change of fortune.

Most seasons blend together but good years stand out with dazzling distinctiveness. A fan awaits a championship series in his hometown like a big promotion in business or a move. In 1966, however, baseball's popularity was threatened. Granddad blamed baseball's troubles on the home run era of the 1960s. He sermonized about the folly of the parade of .230 hitters who went to bat with the single thought of driving the ball out of the park. It was selfish and self-defeating. Run production required ingenuity as well as skill and the capacity to be flexible. When Eisenhower and his contemporaries played at the turn of the century in the dusty summertime leagues for spending money, a run was the product of a four- or five-man effort. The first man reached base, and the second man moved the first man along with a grounder to the right side of the infield or a bunt. The odds now improved for a hit to bring the lead runner home. Perhaps a break would materialize. An alert player capitalized on breaks, mitigating the need for a hit. Should the lead runner advance to third, a sacrifice fly got the job done.

Granddad's favorite ballplayer was the legendary Honus Wagner of Pittsburgh. Wagner was the greatest shortstop in history, an acknowledged master of fielding, bunting, the stolen base, and the hit-and-run. Second on the list was Tris Speaker, the gifted centerfielder whose positioning techniques Granddad emulated as an outfielder at West Point.

I tried to interest Granddad in the "modern player." I was frank. I called Roger Maris's sixty-one home runs in 1961 "sport's greatest achievement." Maris achieved this milestone under so much scrutiny by television and writers that he had lost much of his hair that season. He had to fly jets, crisscross the country and time zones, play at night under lights, and endure many things unknown to ballplayers forty or fifty years earlier. But Granddad recalled damningly that Maris had once labeled Ty Cobb a "Punch and Judy" hitter. "Why, they tell me Roger Maris can't hit .300," Granddad observed, peering sternly through his bifocals. "What good is he?"

Granddad was similarly disparaging of the great Ted Williams. I pointed out that Williams had proven the superiority of the modern player by combining tremendous home run power with a .344 lifetime average. Granddad disapproved of Williams's spitting at fans. "They tell me he could not field," he remarked once.

As he liquidated his farm operations and completed *At Ease,* Eisenhower faced a certain aimlessness. Doubleday had a number of ideas for future books, but each one sounded like a rehash of the volumes Eisenhower already had written. He gave some thought to undertaking a major project on the Atlantic alliance of World War II, in which he would explore his relationships with Churchill and Marshall. Sam Vaughan, now Eisenhower's principal editor at Doubleday, suggested a catch-all volume that would include much of Eisenhower's correspondence. Vaughan believed the General's lucid and detailed letters sharply revealed his ideas and personality. Eisenhower also had several ideas that might be appropriate for this book. For instance, as late as 1969, he planned an essay about John Markoe through which he would tell a parable about the pain of pronouncing judgment.

But Eisenhower had reached the end of

the line in writing. His sporadic attempts to begin the new book would suffer from a sustained lack of interest. His attempts at an essay on the Cold War foundered. His efforts on the Churchill-Marshall project were repetitious. Eisenhower's memory was playing tricks. Gone was the subtlety that had made him the master diplomat of the war and master politician of the postwar era.

That summer, at the request of his doctor, Eisenhower began another medical diary to record symptoms. Inevitably, he commented on articles he read, politics, and visitors. He noted with gratitude the arrival of summer thundershowers over southern Pennsylvania relieving a three-month drought. Since he had been told by well-meaning friends that his eating habits were partially responsible for his two heart attacks, he kept track of his reactions to various foods. He recorded meticulously his consultations with physicians. On August 23, 1966, he wrote: "Walking this morning, early, I decided to do nothing more than saunter — unless I take things very easy, I get some chest discomfort. As usual it is difficult for me to describe symptoms but there develops a sort of ache with some shortness of breath. . . ."

On the 24th, Eisenhower flew to Philadelphia to present a trophy to the winner of a benefit golf match for cerebral palsy. On the 25th, he wrote: "Nothing to report. Colonel Parsley [one of Eisenhower's doctors] called me and after listening to my story said he thought I was doing 'as well as could be expected.' "

On Friday, August 26, Eisenhower noted a visit to the White House for luncheon with Lyndon Johnson, Bob Anderson, Eisenhower's former defense secretary Neil McElroy, and presidential aide Tom Watson, to "plump for Eisenhower College." In 1966, Congress had recognized newly established Eisenhower College in Seneca Falls, New York, as "the permanent living memorial to the life and deeds" of Dwight D. Eisenhower.

In late August, Eisenhower addressed the Army War College in Carlisle, Pennsylvania. On September 10, he drove to Latrobe, Pennsylvania, for a private dinner with Arnold Palmer and several friends celebrating Palmer's thirty-seventh birthday. On September 24, his entry marks his customary observance: "September 24. My first son's birthday. He would have been 49 today."

Notable in his journal is the absence of

political activity. In late September, Eisenhower flew to Chicago for a visit with his brothers Earl, Edgar, and Milton. There he attended the only Republican fund-raising dinner on his schedule that fall. The outing bolstered his spirits, and he returned to Gettysburg eager for work.

September 27. The past three days have been the best, overall, since I left the hospital. . . . Met with Ben Hibbs today — starting on a new article on "Improvements in Government Machinery." Filmed a short statement on Mountbatten.

A few days later, Eisenhower observed that his angina attacks were caused by "tension or over-activity." "By tension," he wrote, "I mean excitement — such as watching a football game on TV when I have a real interest in either team." In 1966, for the eleventh consecutive year, on doctors' orders Eisenhower took a nap and slept through the annual Army-Navy football game. His passion for Army football was so intense that it threatened his health.

In October, Nixon drew Eisenhower's attention to UN ambassador Arthur Goldberg's speech at the opening of the UN

General Assembly in which he stated that the United States was prepared to order a cessation of all bombing of North Vietnam "the moment we are assured privately or otherwise that this step will be answered promptly by a corresponding de-escalation from the other side."

"This statement it seems to me," wrote Nixon, "runs directly contrary to the principle that you and Foster Dulles insisted upon in dealing with the communists — that we should never rely on communist promises — but should always insist on guaranteed deeds. I tried to make that point in a speech at Columbia, South Carolina, a brief excerpt of which I am enclosing. . . ."

Eisenhower's response was immediate. In a letter dated October 7, he wrote Nixon that he had just sent a letter to Goldberg. "I decided that the Ambassador meant to emphasize the word 'assured' as a condition for cessation of bombing," wrote Eisenhower, who proceeded to express his frustration with Senators Mike Mansfield and Jacob Javits, who had criticized him, as he put it, "for saying that the first priority for the nation now is winning the war and that I would support any practical means that the President might have to use to win it." Eisenhower was annoyed that the two senators had interpreted the comments to mean that he was "urging" the use of atomic bombs. As he added caustically to Nixon, "I think that even such great military experts as these senators would know that you can scarcely use this kind of weapon in South Vietnam where friends would be as badly exposed as one's enemies. . . ."

In reply, Nixon sent his just-issued statement on President Johnson's imminent trip to Manila for the Asian summit, a journey timed, in the opinion of the Republicans, uncomfortably close to the midterm elections. Nixon proposed that the heads of government at Manila use the occasion to issue a Pacific Charter and "set forth a long range program for peace and freedom in Asia." Nixon was careful to assure Eisenhower, a stickler for bipartisanship, that his suggestion was a "responsible and constructive position for members of the Loyal Opposition to take."

Republicans were also on solid ground in suspecting that the Goldberg overture was both a signal of distress and linked to a behind-the-scenes push to start talks with the communists, which Eisenhower opposed. As Dad recalled, that fall, when Eisenhower was in Washington at Walter Reed for a physical, Johnson arranged for

Cyrus Vance (Deputy Secretary of Defense) and Robert McNamara to brief him on the latest developments in the war. Eisenhower in turn took the opportunity to serve notice privately that he felt Johnson's most serious error in Vietnam was procrastination; it was time to recognize the obligation to decide and act. When Vance and McNamara began their reports, Eisenhower asked a series of questions. What about the growing antiwar demonstrations? Explain the stream of public offers to negotiate, and the constraints Washington was imposing on Westmoreland. "Why don't you declare war?" he demanded. The two men had no answers.

The Manila summit was indeed timed to coincide with the closing weeks of the 1966 elections, handing Johnson the excuse to skip campaigning and thus minimize his association with the off-year losses predicted by the polls. In Manila, Johnson discussed strategy and troop levels with the leaders of South Vietnam, Australia, New Zealand, South Korea, the Philippines, and Thailand. He was joined by a pessimistic McNamara, who privately reported on his latest tour of South Vietnam. The twofold increase in the North Vietnamese army (NVA) since December was having an impact and there was no discernible progress in pacification efforts, which had actually regressed, in his opinion, since early 1965. He predicted a stalemate lasting well past the 1968 elections.

At the climax of the fall campaign, Republicans, galvanized by the sudden vulnerability of Lyndon Johnson, smelled a chance to capture a significant number of state and national seats lost in the Johnson tide of 1964. As usual, Eisenhower was inclined to take the rhetoric of the campaign with earnest literalness. In his diary, he wrote:

October 12. Political campaign is apathetic. Johnson goes to hustings with words that are far from inspiring. He calls Republicans "party of fear." When I recall his weak and cowardly actions when a Senator, I could laugh except that it is all so false.

When I was trying for a good Civil Rights bill he threw every roadblock he could. He argued for jury trials and contempt cases; he actually, at one period, asked for a secret appointment at the White House so that he could beg me to avoid pressing for continuation of the Civil Rights Commission!! Now — listen to the man!!

Earlier in the month, he had tried to get me interested in the campaign, writing me at Amherst to report:

Around here there does not seem to be developing much enthusiasm about the political campaign. I suppose that is because there is no President to be elected this year. If this is so, the reason seems to be faulty indeed. Too many of us are allowing too much authority and responsibility for our lives to become concentrated in Washington. I think it is just as important to develop enthusiasm for the election of a proper city council, a county board of commissioners, or statewide governor and legislature as it is to get the right man in the Presidency. Indeed, if we had better and stronger government at lower levels we would do much to reduce the risk that one day we are going to be governed by an entrenched and organized bureaucracy.

Eisenhower's attempt to maintain a diary ends around Election Day 1966, except for a closing flurry at the end of November before entering the hospital for gall bladder surgery. The election results buoyed his spirits considerably:

November 8. Election Day. Was out of office all last week with a nasty cold. . . . I hope results of election are good! It would be some evidence that we are recovering from 1964 debacle.

November 9. This morning the world looks better. In yesterday's elections the Republicans made significant gains in state houses, Congress and State Legislatures — apparently netted a gain of 1 in Senate. No pains.

November 10. The Republican victory has given us three additional Senators, 46 or 47 Congressmen and 9 more Governors. No pains.

5
"MOST ADMIRED"

"MORE COST ... MORE AGONY"

As 1967 began, America's Vietnam involvement, which was supposed to end by 1966, had swollen to a military presence of nearly half a million troops. Casualties soared and the "nightmare" of the protracted land war in Asia had become a reality.

Nothing worked. Johnson wavered between a policy of conciliation, by suspending the bombing of the north to entice the enemy to negotiate, and a policy of escalation. The American effort was extensive enough to inflame world opinion, yet too limited to achieve negotiations. In addition, Johnson's Vietnam policy opened an undeniable fissure within the Western alliance. In a speech shortly after New Year's Day, de Gaulle called upon the United States to end its "detestable intervention" in Vietnam.

The drive to unseat Johnson in 1968 began in earnest. In January, Arkansas senator William Fulbright published a book titled *The Arrogance of Power,* in which he denounced the corrupting strains Vietnam imposed on American society. In March, addressing a student gathering at Princeton, former Kennedy speechwriter Ted Sorensen issued a suggestion couched as a historical observation: "Johnson," he noted, "would be following the historical pattern not to run." A committee formed to draft Kennedy/Fulbright and opened an office in Washington.

White House visitors described the dark mood that enveloped the President and his staff. A defensive Johnson was widely quoted as saying he was determined not to be the first president to "lose a war." Stories circulated that the President had cast himself in the mold of Abraham Lincoln, assuming the tragic countenance of the Great Emancipator, who balanced the demands of achieving social justice in the United States with the costs of a just, though divisive and misunderstood, war. Johnson's movements away from the White House were increasingly confined to military bases, aircraft carriers, and familiar presidential retreats, safe houses against the armies of protesters who plagued his every appearance. In his January State of the Union address, Johnson defiantly answered de Gaulle and other war critics: the United States would persevere in Vietnam "notwithstanding more cost, more loss, and more agony."

Eisenhower, among friends, now spoke more often of his misgivings about Johnson's refusal to take what he deemed the necessary steps to achieve victory. He did not second-guess the decision to intervene, nor did he minimize Johnson's difficulties in attempting to wage a war opposed by many Democrats in the Senate. "But once the decision is made to commit American prestige," Eisenhower repeated endlessly, "all else must take a second seat to winning."

Specifically, Eisenhower felt Johnson had failed to reckon with the domestic implications of a protracted limited war. The President could not wage war in Vietnam while enacting massive social welfare programs without weakening the economy and setting the conditions for a crippling inflation. His policy of limited war excused vast segments of the country from the inevitable sacrifices and created obvious inequities.

Believing America to be in a de facto state of war, Eisenhower favored placing the economy on a wartime basis, a congressional declaration of war, and military escalation leading to a negotiated peace. But in his public utterances, Eisenhower either supported the President's policy or called for harsher measures against the North Vietnamese, which in the peculiar logic of the day meant one and the same. Hawkish criticism was regarded then as aiding the administration cause because such criticism did not challenge the basis of American involvement. Eisenhower further urged publicly that the American president must be the "sole spokesman" for the nation in foreign affairs. He argued that the information available to a president at a given moment was always superior to the information available to critics. Therefore, citizens, and particularly former presidents, had an obligation to stand behind their elected leaders until new elections provided recourse.

By 1967, an important factor in Eisenhower's thinking was the character of the dissent over Vietnam. In the course of two years, it had evolved rapidly from criticism of Johnson into something more fundamental. Vietnam had merged with the issues of social reform. The antiwar left questioned both the legitimacy of American leadership of the free world and the justice of the American social order. In the widespread campus and urban riots, the walkouts, university seizures, the March on the Pentagon in October 1967, and growing draft resistance, Eisenhower perceived the vague outlines of what in 1963 he had so derisively termed the "forced draft social revolution." A defeat in Vietnam would be yielding to communism abroad and to radical forces at home. As he wrote to me on October 5:

. . . the world has always had problems and, while I have faith that our young people and their successors will succeed finally in developing a better place in which all can live, I still cannot wholly control my temper when I hear about draft card burners and professors encouraging youngsters to refuse to comply with draft calls.

This nation has been good to all of us. Suppose we had been born in Spain, Italy, Sweden or even in the land of our good ally Britain? I am more than disturbed that so many people who had the good fortune of taking advantage of the opportunities this country provides are unwilling to meet the responsibilities that it necessarily has to look to its citizens to perform.

No one could hate war more than I, but I get very upset when I find people who are quite willing to enjoy the privileges and rights afforded by this country but publicly announce their readiness to flout their responsibilities.

Over coffee at the office in Gettysburg, Kevin McCann tried to persuade Eisenhower that Johnson's policy was folly. McCann favored Vermont senator George Aiken's approach: "Say 'we win,' and leave." Kevin was not impressed by the dissent sweeping over the country. There had been draft riots in the Civil War. Kevin reminded Granddad of the Bonus Army, the scraggly group of some twelve thousand World War I veterans who had gathered in Anacostia in 1932 over real grievances — starvation, poverty, neglect. For more than a decade, Kevin continued, the country had endured a depression. All had turned out well in the end.

McCann decided that what Eisenhower needed was a dose of the Vietnam War from the perspective of the junior officer and the noncommissioned officer. At that level, the war was stripped of its glamorous façade. Platoon leaders lived with the reality of the war. Perhaps they would offset the polished briefings from officers dispatched from General Earle Wheeler's office. Eisenhower met with several junior officers but they failed to have much impact on him. Mc-Cann blamed it on "stage fright." Soldiers just back from Vietnam could hardly be expected to level with a former president and five-star general about conditions in Vietnam as seen by field "grunts."

As the dissent deepened, Eisenhower began speaking more warmly about Lyndon Johnson around the office. McCann would not hear of it. Workers in adjoining offices overheard spirited discussions between the two. Regularly, Eisenhower's lusty voice would punctuate the conversation. "Kevin, damnit," he would howl, "why do you always have to bring up that 87 vote plurality," a reference to "Landslide Lyndon's" dubious senatorial primary victory in 1948, when Johnson's machine was accused of doctoring the final tally in rural precincts.

Johnson phoned Eisenhower often. Though most of their conversations focused on Johnson's detractors and trivial matters about political personalities, the link Johnson sought was spiritual and historical. He wanted the comfort of communicating with someone who could comprehend the unique pressures of the presidency. He also sought the sanction of a member of the presidential fraternity for his historic efforts to carry out a policy against the grain of elite opinion.

Lyndon Johnson became a frequent visitor when Eisenhower checked into Walter Reed for physicals and tests. Emerging one afternoon from Eisenhower's suite at Walter Reed following his gall bladder surgery in December 1966, Johnson encountered Dr. Edward Elson, now the chaplain of the Senate, in the lounge near the Ward Eight elevator, waiting to pay the next call on Eisenhower. Elson chattily asked Johnson how his talk had gone and how the general's spirits were following the operation.

For a moment the President seemed blank and unaware that Elson had spoken to him. Then a sadness welled up in Johnson's eyes. "Dr. Elson," he drawled, "when I need comfort, this is where I come and this is the man I come to see."

Robert Kennedy was Johnson's most persistent tormentor. Throughout 1966, Kennedy had maneuvered into a position to challenge Johnson for the Democratic presidential nomination in 1968 by taking up the causes of Vietnam, civil rights, and the amorphous issue of the promise lost by the slaying of his brother. From afar, Eisenhower regarded Robert Kennedy as a dangerous force in American politics. Twenty-four hours after John Kennedy's assassination, as Eisenhower and Johnson conferred in the small room adjoining the Oval Office, the General fervently pressed Johnson to curb Robert Kennedy's rumored abuses of the Justice Department and his use of intimidation tactics to silence critics of the Kennedy administration.

Eisenhower's memorandum of the conversation reads in part:

November 23, 1963 (Addendum to notes for the Pres.)

I stated that throughout the country there had been uneasiness, if not fear, because of the tactics employed by the Justice Department and the IRS in carrying out their duties.

Specifically, I said that I had heard some dismay expressed in business circles, in Universities, and even in Foundations, alleging a "political party" type of questioning by the IRS when supposedly engaged merely in examining financial accounts.

Another allegation has been that if any corporation or University submitted before a Congressional Committee any testimony unfavorable to the Administration that the head of such an institution would be promptly warned by the Justice Department that any contracts between that institution and the Government would probably be cancelled.

Eisenhower also suggested to Johnson in 1963 that after a period of grace he unload Kennedy appointees and form an administration with men loyal to him. But Johnson had kept most of the Kennedy advisers on, hoping to gain their allegiance. When, inevitably, strains between Johnson and Kennedy holdovers cropped up, many had become ardent critics of Johnson's Vietnam policy.

In subsequent years, Johnson often expressed to Eisenhower his fears about Robert Kennedy's designs on the presidency. According to Rusty Brown, one afternoon Johnson telephoned Eisenhower and confessed he was "terrified" of Bobby. "I never know what he's going to do, where he is going to strike."

Describing the conversation years later, Rusty Brown could recall nothing specifically that Robert Kennedy had done. "We are, I think, talking about a chill," she said. Johnson seemed blind to the fact that he was president and Kennedy the senator who had needed Johnson's last-minute help to win his seat in 1964 and who had ultimately run one million votes behind the Johnson-

Humphrey ticket. "I concluded," Rusty recalled, and so did the General, "that anyone who could frighten Lyndon Johnson was dangerous." As an afterthought, she added, "happily, nobody had that kind of power over the General."

In this period, Eisenhower was also in touch with Republican leaders, who sensed a rising tide of optimism about Republican prospects in 1968. Despite his bosomy relationship with the White House and memories of his bumbling of the 1964 campaign, Eisenhower remained a man whose support or opposition in the campaign could prove important.

The Goldwater rout had left the party without a titular leader, though not without able and attractive candidates. In 1966, Ronald Reagan, formerly a sportscaster and B-movie star, ran a highly independent and citizens'-minded campaign for the governorship of California, defeating the incumbent Pat Brown by a million votes. Although Reagan was widely perceived as a political neophyte, his electoral margin over Brown suggested that he had more than mastered the technique of winning. His success in California contrasted sharply with Nixon's failure four years earlier. Throughout early

1967, Reagan toured the country to test the waters on his "creative society" ideas.

George Romney would enter 1968 as the lone announced candidate for the Republican nomination. His claim, like Reagan's, rested on his demonstrated ability to win votes. Presenting a zealous and moralistic image, Romney would labor under the handicap of his televised admission in the fall of 1967 that he had been "brainwashed" on a trip to Vietnam by the official line of optimism. Few argued with Romney that the Vietnam War involved a massive public relations effort to exaggerate the odds of success. But Romney's choice of words prompted ridicule and reminded the public of his naïveté in foreign relations.

Nelson Rockefeller, despite a successful campaign for reelection in New York, adhered to his position of support for Romney and "no interest" in the Republican nomination. The bitterness of his hostile reception at the Cow Palace convention in 1964 lent credibility to the maxim that, though electable and qualified, Rockefeller would never be able to transcend the visceral hatred from his party's right wing and win a nomination. Eisenhower told McCann that Rockefeller had informed him in a telephone conversation that he had no interest in the presidency. "This time," Eisenhower related, "I believe him."

By 1967 the most intriguing prospect in the field was Nixon. Time had softened, though not erased, memories of Nixon's twin defeats in 1960 and 1962. Gradually Nixon was coming to be seen as a kind of modern William Jennings Bryan, a man who, with luck, might have served with distinction, but who instead found himself cast against great popular heroes. Articles appeared profiling a "New Nixon," now a prosperous Manhattan attorney broadened by his exposure to New York City and by his extensive foreign policy fact-finding trips. It was said he had mellowed and matured in defeat.

Eisenhower's ties to the Johnson administration peaked in July 1967, when he was in almost daily contact with the White House as urban ghettos from coast to coast experienced the worst riots in the nation's history. At various times during the month, riots erupted in Newark, Detroit, Milwaukee, Chicago, South Bend, Phoenix, Miami, and Sacramento. Smaller incidents, costly in lives and property, occurred in dozens of other cities.

Eisenhower was appalled by the specter of disintegration, anarchy, and the loss of control over the civilian population that urban rioting created. The riots climaxed on July 24, when Governor Romney of Michigan declared he could not contain the violence in his state without the aid of the U.S. Army. In Detroit, over a thousand fires broke out and forty-three people were killed, many by sniper fire. As federal troops took up positions in Detroit, fresh rioting erupted in Flint, Pontiac, Grand Rapids, New York's Spanish Harlem, Rochester, Toledo, and Cambridge, Maryland. Eisenhower spent the day in phone contact with General Goodpaster, passing along suggestions to the crisis control center at the White House.

He offered technical advice, telling Goodpaster about experiences he had had with riots in Columbus, Georgia, in 1919. When Columbus's mayor had appealed to Eisenhower for help, he recalled, "I had a little parade with tanks." He now recommended stationing military vehicles at central points around Detroit and sending them elsewhere as needed. Eisenhower also suggested Johnson declare martial law and that all windows be covered throughout Detroit to prevent sniper fire. Finally, he passed along a suggestion from Senator Richard Russell that the declaration of Detroit as a "disaster area" be stalled in order to make rioters consider what might happen should Red Cross and federal aid be withheld.

Throughout the week, Eisenhower cautioned the administration not to overreact. When he had heard reports that the FBI had become involved, he passed along remarks to Goodpaster that he and Senator Everett Dirksen felt that the Bureau had no jurisdiction unless investigating a "national conspiracy," only to learn that Director Hoover "disagreed" that the FBI had no business being involved.

Through Goodpaster, Eisenhower suggested that the President appoint a bipartisan commission to investigate the causes of the rioting and the question of "whether this is being masterminded." Johnson accepted the suggestion and named Governor Otto Kerner of Illinois to head the commission, which in its final report would blame the rioting on "white racism."

At the time, I was working in Chicago as an executive trainee for Sears, Roebuck. I lived in Evanston, close to Chicago's riot zone. Sears instructed employees to decline all inquiries from customers about rifles, handguns, and explosives, in compliance with federal directives requesting that private enterprise cooperate in preventing the distribution of weapons. I was a poor correspondent with home. And with each new episode of urban violence, I received frantic letters and calls from my parents and grandparents trying to find out if I was all right.

That summer, Eisenhower wrote an article for *Reader's Digest* titled "We Should Be Ashamed." In it, he deplored "the growing disrespect for law and order." The United States had entered "an era of lawlessness," despite "more opportunities, more resources, more talent and competence . . . more of the tangibly good things of this life than any other nation ever had."

Eisenhower called campus demonstrators "the wayward minority." He expressed amazement that adults, black and white, participated in riots. "This situation," he wrote, "is unacceptable in a civilized nation." Rioting, he continued, "must be handled without temporizing," and culprits prosecuted notwithstanding underlying grievances. American society had failed to instill discipline, restraint, and self-respect in its youth. When asked about his views on urban rioting, Eisenhower proudly referred to this article.

Months before, in the fall of 1966, Julie Nixon and I had entered colleges within seven miles of each other. She was at Smith and I was at Amherst. Granddad had written me just days after registration: "I had always secretly hoped that you might develop a yen for West Point but most certainly I have no criticism to make of your choice of your present school. It has a truly wonderful reputation." Again, thanks to Dad, I had never felt compelled to consider West Point and I looked forward to college.

On the bus trip from New York to Amherst just before classes began, I had overheard several people seated in front of me joking about Julie Nixon and David Eisenhower both being in the area. Since then, I had encountered more teasing about whether there was going to be a new Ike-Dick team. The speculation made me reluctant to visit Julie, despite my grandmother's urging.

Julie and I had met several times and played together as eight-year-olds in January 1957, at the time of the second Eisenhower-Nixon inauguration. On Inauguration Day, a photograph was taken of us on the reviewing stand with Granddad, Vice President Nixon, my seven-year-old sister,

Anne, and Julie's ten-year-old sister, Tricia. Julie, who had lost control of her sled the week before and crashed into a tree, had a skinned nose and dramatic black eye. At one point when the cameramen gathered to take pictures, Granddad had turned to her and whispered, "Look this way and they won't see your black eye." In the resulting photograph, I am staring intently at Julie and she is looking at me.

A year later, in 1958, her father made an even bigger impression on me. It was July 15, the day Marines landed in Lebanon. I had wandered over to the West Wing to see if the President's secretary, Ann Whitman, could type up the short story I had just written, "Janet's Stay," about my cousin Janet Thompson's trip east to visit us.

Mrs. Whitman did not seem to mind. She quickly typed "Janet's Stay" in the bold type used for Granddad's televised speeches and then ran off fifteen copies on the brand-new Xerox copier. I remember that Mrs. Whitman seemed tired and nervous and that her desk was buried under a mountain of papers, many stamped "Top Secret." At one point, the door connecting her office with the Oval Office swung open and I saw Granddad, dressed in a brown sport coat and light brown slacks, pacing restlessly in the company of several advisers.

About then, the vice president and several staff members swept into Mrs. Whitman's office. Mr. Nixon noticed me immediately and paused to say hello. I was excited when he was curious about "Janet's Stay." He purchased a mint copy for fifteen cents and two weeks later sent me a letter in which he said his entire family had sat in the living room for a reading of "Janet's Stay" and that everyone decided I was one of their "favorite authors." My parents promptly appropriated his note for safekeeping.

In the intervening years, my grandparents had seen the Nixons and their daughters several times, including the weekend at Eldorado in 1961. Granddad routinely signed his letters to his former vice president, "with affectionate regard for Pat and the girls." When Mamie and the Nixons saw each other in August 1966 at the funeral of family friend Raymond Pitcairn, Julie told my grandmother she was headed to Smith College, in Northampton, Massachusetts. Mamie told her I would be at Amherst. Immediately Mamie started urging me to call on Julie.

In late September, one chill evening shortly after Julie and I had a brief phone conversation about an invitation from the

Hadley, Massachusetts, Republican Women's Club — we both decided to decline — my roommate and I hitchhiked to Smith to pay a call. We took Julie and one of her friends out for ice cream. I was broke; my roommate had forgotten his wallet. The girls paid.

In the course of an evening together, Julie and I learned something about each other. Although we had similar backgrounds in having been brought up in the public eye, our experiences were quite different. I had spent my childhood in small towns and boarding schools. Julie had grown up in big cities. I did not know much about politics; Julie had been raised on the subject.

On the night of the 1966 elections, I returned to Baldwin House, Julie's dorm, to visit her. We had a good time together that night watching the returns come in, but I still hesitated about dating her seriously. Friends I consulted told me that if the obstacles getting in my way were insuperable, they would be more than happy to "look after her." Armed with this incentive, I summoned the courage to go back, and to keep going back. By December we were inseparable. Julie invited me to act as her escort at the International Debutante Ball in New York. The publicity was enormous. I received a note from Granddad:

Of course I am delighted that your squash is improving and even more that you are doing well in your studies. We had had a lot of people send to us pictures of you and Julie at the International Ball. One even came from Enrique [a White House steward in the fifties] in Guam. It was a full face of you both and I thought more attractive than some of the others. I have never heard about your New Year's party in New York. I had the impression that you and Julie were going out on the town but avoiding going to the "name" spots. In any event, I am sure you had a good time.

With the turn of the year, Julie and I were together as often as possible, often studying together weeknights. On weekends we frequently drove to New York and stayed at the Nixons' apartment on Fifth Avenue. It did not take long before our future became an unspoken assumption between us. We were young, but student marriages were not uncommon during the late 1960s. Despite different upbringings, our families were intertwined and we had similar views about the revolution under way in university life. Campus politics implicated her father and my grandfather in an "old order" targeted for replacement. We were among a handful of moderate Republicans at Amherst, including my best friend, Tom Davis, who like Fred Grandy was a future Republican congressman.

We had no illusions about the intensity of antiwar feeling. One evening that spring, we attended the showing of a film being presented on campuses by a Quaker peace committee. The audience of students, faculty, wives, older faculty children, many dressed in the uniform of the day — corduroy jackets with open collars and jeans — filed in solemnly and took their seats. Nobody called across seats to friends. Everyone sat intently and expectantly.

The film opened with an inscription cast against blood red. "On August 27, 1908, Lyndon Baines Johnson was born near Stonewall, Texas." The hall was silent. The words were displayed for twenty seconds or so to heighten the suspense. The film cut instantly to a scene of a cow giving birth. It mooed in pain as a rancher pulled on a calf's head stuck in the birth canal. The calf emerged slowly, bloodily shrouded in the blue placenta. The crowd cheered. "I want to leave," Julie whispered.

We stayed. From the nativity scene, the

film switched to video provided by the North Vietnamese of B-52 bombing runs over the outskirts of Hanoi. The camera zoomed in on the agonized faces of victims. The entire film was narrated through subtitles against the same bloodred backdrop. The crowd filed out just as it had come — stimulated, somber, intent.

As the year went along, the antiwar movement became more strident and single-minded. The "peace at any price" mantra put Julie and me on the defensive as we argued with classmates that America could not walk away from its commitment to Vietnam. Emotions on all sides ran high.

Increasingly, we created our own world of study, music, long walks, dinners, and outings through the western Massachusetts countryside. We regularly saw each other, and delighted in studying together in my room overlooking the quadrangle. At times we were interrupted by protests: a chemistry professor igniting home-produced napalm on the quadrangle lawn; flyers issuing invitations to carpool south for peace marches in New York City and Washington; pickets pacing the sidewalks in front of the Episcopal church; semicircles of students in short sleeves seated in the grass listening to guest lecturers speaking on Vietnam; chapel bells announcing the start of a lecture by a member of the State Department, who would explain the legality of the war.

Several days after the close of the spring semester, Julie and I traveled to Gettysburg. Granddad received Julie like a member of the family. He offered her a painting of the farm lane from among several propped along the wall near his easel. Then, with a broad smile, he produced the photograph taken on the reviewing stand at the 1957 inauguration with me staring at Julie and her black eye. Granddad had inscribed the photograph: "To Julie Nixon, who even then seems to have, unknowingly, acquired an admirer. Devotedly, Dwight D. Eisenhower."

Mamie had definite designs on Julie. Our age was no deterrent. Mamie had been only nineteen when she married, and her mother had been sixteen. She took us on a walking tour of the china on display and of her heirloom furniture in the seldom-used living room.

Before we left, Granddad asked us to visit him at his Gettysburg office. He had observed the rapport, and he had a serious purpose in entertaining us in a more formal setting — to discourage any thought of early marriage.

Dwight Eisenhower had a philosophy about such things. Years earlier, during one session by his bedside, discussing my future, we had talked about career paths. Generally speaking, he observed, men should complete college and several years of postgraduate education, be established in a profession and in a community, and only then decide on marriage. Though only twenty-six when he married Mamie, Eisenhower considered himself an established man — a West Pointer fixed in his occupation as an Army officer. Over the years, Eisenhower's views on this natural progression had calcified into a creed. He was buttressed by his conservative business friends, who likewise counseled their offspring against the kind of heady nonsense each of them had either contemplated or committed in youth.

In Julie's presence, Granddad drilled me about the use of my time: I was not concentrating on the right things; I was neglecting my health. He pointed out that my rather drastic weight loss in freshman year had to do with "irregular hours." I was oblivious of the long road, doing too much, planning too little.

Julie felt, and was supposed to feel, partly responsible. We were quiet on the drive back to New York City. I went on from New York to my summer job as a trainee for Sears in Chicago. Julie came to Chicago to visit me. On her nineteenth birthday, I flew to Key Biscayne to be with her and her family. I said little to Granddad about these meetings.

Shortly before the fall semester, Julie and I returned to Gettysburg. In a letter anticipating our visit, Granddad repeated the main points of our talk in June, juxtaposing several apparently unconnected paragraphs with an unmistakable meaning:

Of course, I am pleased to hear you speak of your fondness for Julie. She is a great favorite of Mamie's because she seems to have both feet solidly on the ground. The extremists, who command such attention in the papers and television will never, in my opinion, have any attraction for her. We shall be more than delighted to have the two of you here next weekend.

As I see it, you will have some six–ten years of education still ahead of you, depending on your choice of profession. If you go for law, or a business career, probably the shorter term; if medicine, the longer. In any event, no matter what profession you may select, the money that

Mimi and I have been setting aside in your name, is primarily for your education.

In the meantime I hope that, while your studies must always be first — and, indeed I believe there is real pleasure to be found in study and in learning — you will take available opportunity for exercise and to promote your health.

To do this, I suggest you should abolish worry; do your best on your work; but have a pleasant time doing it. By no means would I want you to abandon a social life, but at this stage it should not interfere with health and education.

The question of courtship was not as distant in Granddad's mind as I imagined. While I worked in Chicago, word reached Eisenhower in Gettysburg that old Abilene friend Ruby Norman Lucier was dying of cancer. Like all the women reputedly to have been among Eisenhower's flames, Ruby Norman's place in Eisenhower's life is unknown. Granddad rarely mentioned anything about being interested in women as a young man. His memory of those years centered around his self-portrait of the swaggering town Wyatt Earp, standing up for the rights of defenseless friends with his fists; one boy among six brothers surviving in a male world of scuffles, hard work, and athletics. I grew up thinking of Granddad as prudish. Indeed, Granddad hotly disputed accounts of his relationships with girls recounted by old friends in oral histories or in magazine articles.

Two facts point to Ruby as the girl Eisenhower liked best as a young man. First, she is the only Abilene girl he describes at length in *At Ease.* Second, for some unknown reason, Ruby saved several of Dwight's letters from West Point for more than twenty-five years before Eisenhower's rise to prominence, suggesting at least that young Dwight had made a strong impression on her.

According to *At Ease,* Ruby was one of the "pretty girls" from Abilene's south side, the poorer section of Abilene where Dwight and his brothers lived. She finished Abilene High one year behind Dwight. She dated him while he worked at the Belle Springs Creamery to help finance his brother Edgar through the University of Michigan.

Both Ruby and Dwight entertained thoughts of escaping the humdrum insularity of central Kansas. Ruby was a musician and dreamed of becoming a performing artist. Dwight and his brothers were inspired to follow the example set by his older brother Arthur, to leave Abilene for educational and business opportunities elsewhere.

But whereas Ruby had specific goals and a link to the larger world through music, Dwight's ambitions to leave town were vague. His decision to go to West Point was not based on a passion for the military. West Point was a way to achieve the break and get a free education.

Ruby was the first to leave. Upon graduation, she packed up and fled to Chicago, leaving Dwight behind as a second-year foreman at the creamery. Writing to Eisenhower at West Point, and presumably earlier in Abilene, Ruby alluded to the cosmopolitan way of life she had found in Chicago.

En route to West Point, Dwight stopped in Chicago to see her before continuing on to visit Edgar at Ann Arbor. After their whirlwind reunion, Eisenhower reported to West Point, where he took up writing Ruby passionate and beseeching letters. But his admission to West Point did not impress her. In her mind, Dwight had merely exchanged one cloistered rural environment for another. Her replies became halfhearted and sporadic. Eventually he wrote petulant and defensive notes scolding her for her lack of interest, but Ruby set the ground rules. The two could correspond, but only as friends. In desperation, Dwight agreed.

In one of the letters, Dwight proposed that he and Ruby travel together around the United States. Meeting rejection, he proposed instead that she travel to New York, the great city Eisenhower had come to know on weekends from the academy.

To no avail. Ruby Norman of Abilene was shedding her hometown, its cultural backwardness, its rough-hewn spirit and cowtown exuberance, and embracing the refined world of music and Chicago. Giving up on Ruby on the eve of an Army-Navy game, Dwight confessed the "blues." He wrote about some wild imaginings he had about what they could share if only she would become more responsive. He challenged her curiosity about what his imaginings were all about: "Although at one time I would have told you all, this business of being friends is difficult and I have to watch myself."

Dwight's last letter was postmarked "San Antonio, Texas." He reported in the letter that he had met a young, "society-conscious" girl named Mamie Geneva Doud. Dwight complained that Mamie seemed too wrapped up in parties, pretty jewelry, and clothes. But otherwise, he reported, "she seems kind of fun and okay."

The correspondence ceased. No words

passed between Abilene's "king of the roughnecks" and the town's south-side Cinderella for twenty-five years. Ruby drifted away from Chicago, met an Indiana businessman, shelved the dreams of being a performing artist, and settled into raising a large family and teaching music. With the outbreak of war and the appearance of Dwight's name in headlines, Ruby renewed the correspondence.

Eisenhower's early replies were perfunctory, signed "cordially" and "sincerely." Eisenhower answered one of Ruby's letters through Lieutenant Colonel James Stark, a member of his staff. Nonetheless, he answered, perhaps mindful of the irony that Ruby had been the one to retire into the obscurity of a midwestern town while Dwight had gone on to great heights. A year after the war, Ike and Ruby saw each other briefly in Abilene during Eisenhower's triumphal victory tour of the country, and again in Indiana at a whistle stop during the 1952 campaign. Thereafter they exchanged greetings on anniversaries, birthdays, and grandparenthood. Eisenhower met Ruby's husband and Ruby met Mamie. A youthful romance was gently converted into a friendship in old age.

In the summer of 1967, Eisenhower received word that Ruby had entered a hospital in St. Louis with leukemia. He arranged for a specialist at Washington University in St. Louis to look after her care. Eisenhower corresponded with Ruby every several weeks for news of her treatment and her response to medications. He sent her books, including the best-selling *At Ease,* which had been released in June. Eisenhower tentatively planned with several of her relatives to pay her a visit when he was in Kansas in November. His notes were cheery, brief, and warm, now signed "devotedly" and "affectionately." It was in November, however, that she died.

Thanking Eisenhower for his written condolences and an arrangement of flowers sent to her funeral, Ruby's son wrote a lengthy letter detailing what Eisenhower's kindness had meant to his mother. The last note she had read had been Eisenhower's relaying the news he had received from her doctors that she would soon be released. And the last book she had read had been *At Ease.* "The family outside her hospital room could hear her laugh out loud," her son wrote, "and many times she said 'this is the first one that really sounds like Dwight.' "

Just how involved the two had become, the extent of any promises exchanged in

Abilene, and the details of their visit in Chicago are all unknown. Interestingly, in *At Ease* Eisenhower mentions his rendezvous with Ruby in Chicago, but says little. He proceeds to describe a moonlight canoe ride with Edgar in Ann Arbor and two unnamed women as "the most romantic evening of my life." One can only wonder whether Eisenhower discreetly confused Chicago with Ann Arbor.

"ASIA AFTER VIETNAM"

In the summer and fall of 1967, Eisenhower was still being briefed regularly on Vietnam by Johnson, Goodpaster, and Chairman of the Joint Chiefs of Staff General Earl Wheeler. Increasingly he was alarmed by the defensive, defeatist mentality taking hold of the White House.

On August 10, Eisenhower was consulted about proposals to exchange a bombing halt of the north for talks. He endorsed a halt and talks *provided* the Soviets suspended all military aid to North Vietnam. In doing so, he warned Goodpaster about the dangerous "stalemate" theme he had noted in the press. Two months later, on October 18, at Walter Reed, he further told Goodpaster that his Augusta friends and associates were referring to Vietnam as an "endless war" and now questioned the point of it.

The written summary of the October 18 meeting reveals that Eisenhower was profoundly skeptical of any diplomatic strategy, having concluded that neither the Soviets nor the Chinese would pressure the North Vietnamese to cooperate in ending a war that was causing the United States so much distress. Complicating diplomacy, it was now obvious the Soviets and Chinese were antagonists, with Mao adopting a defiant attitude toward the U.S.S.R. Eisenhower began to sense that the United States had a stake in the Maoists, who were evidently committed to tossing off Soviet patronage.

But as usual, Eisenhower's specific recommendations for the President were confined to prosecution of the war. He recommended to Goodpaster that Westmoreland be permitted to form what he called a "Corps of Maneuver" to strike communist sanctuaries in Cambodia and Laos that were supplying North Vietnam. He told Goodpaster he had accepted an invitation to appear on television with Omar Bradley and was planning to share his belief that a majority of Americans favored "peace on an honorable basis" and that "peace at any price" was "no peace at all." He also was going to advocate "hot pursuit" into the sanctuaries and requested

Pentagon statistics from Goodpaster on how large the sanctuaries were.

But in the weeks to come, the word Eisenhower kept getting back from Goodpaster and Wheeler was that it was "inaccurate" to believe the United States was in a "stalemate" in Vietnam. Progress was being made, although, in the words of NSC adviser Walt Rostow, it was "agonizingly slow."

On August 5, Nixon sent Eisenhower an advance copy of an article he was writing for *Foreign Affairs* titled "Asia After Vietnam." He explained to Eisenhower, "It is a long range discussion of Asia, directed more to the intellectuals who read that publication than to the general public. It represents conclusions I have reached after my several trips to Asia over the years, most of which I have already discussed with you." Nixon added a personal note: "We were all distressed when we heard that you were going to the hospital this morning but greatly relieved when the later news reports indicated that you were resting comfortably."

In his suite in Walter Reed where he was in for a checkup, Eisenhower read over the Nixon article carefully and telephoned with suggestions on August 14, none of which, to Nixon's relief, disputed his foreign policy views. The General took no exception even to Nixon's forward-thinking China views, which were unfurled for the first time in this article.

The most significant new reality was not the stalemate in Vietnam but the Sino-Soviet split. And based on his discussions with Asian leaders, Nixon had little doubt that the Chinese would find it dangerous to shed their ties with the Soviets without tacit U.S. and Western support. In this context, the Vietnam War took on meaning not as a test of the credibility of American alliances, but as a test of America's interest in Asia and — by extension — America's interest in China's future. Should the United States accept a Soviet-sponsored settlement of the war or abandon the war altogether, the Chinese would know that for the indefinite future they faced the U.S.S.R. alone and had two choices: continued isolation or returning to a Sino-Soviet partnership.

Nixon thus perceived danger and opportunity in the Vietnam morass. In the language of geopolitics, Nixon could envision that an "acceptable" outcome in Vietnam would serve as the basis of an opening to China, which would formalize the breakup of the communist world and the breakup of an obsolete Cold War structure that had become a prop of the status quo, serving Soviet interests, not American.

October 17, 1967, was a crisp fall afternoon in Gettysburg. At 2:15, exactly on schedule, former vice president Richard Nixon arrived at the farm for an hour of conversation on the sunporch with Eisenhower. Two decades later, Richard Nixon would give Julie and me his detailed notes of the visit, written on a yellow legal pad.

Welcoming Nixon at the front door of the spacious farmhouse, Eisenhower guided his guest to the porch and seated him facing the sliding glass doors. Nixon glanced out, enjoying the view of fall corn in the far pastures and the carefully manicured putting green with its jaunty five-star flag flying from the cup.

Studying the General, Nixon noted that he looked surprisingly fit considering all of his heart problems. His sky-blue eyes were alert. Indeed, Eisenhower had been unusually active and in the news in recent days. On October 13, he had used the occasion of his annual "birthday" press conference to urge unity behind the President's war effort. A day later, his seventy-seventh birthday, he had gone to Washington to lay the cornerstone for the new National Presbyterian Church and had been honored at a Mayflower Hotel luncheon attended by a host of governmental officials led by Secretary of State Dean Rusk and Vice President Hubert Humphrey.

The activities had not seemed to tire the General unduly and he had made it clear in his note inviting Nixon to the farm that he did not want his doctor's stringent restrictions on his activities to interfere with their visit. "When you come to see me, please allow plenty of time," he had written. "Although it is true that I have to take certain amounts of rest time, I think I can still perform that little chore and at the same time have plenty of time for a long talk with you."

In keeping with the protocol of their periodic meetings, Eisenhower was, as always, in the position of host and mentor, and now with his advancing age, he was definitely mentor. In their last meeting in July, Nixon had reported on exploratory trips he had made to Asia and the Mideast. They had discussed Johnson and the war in Vietnam, and the organization of Nixon's burgeoning presidential campaign.

The intervening months, July to October, had been the proverbial lifetime in politics. On the GOP side, Governor George Romney of Michigan, backed by "moderate" Republican governors, including Rockefeller, had stumbled badly. The combination of his inability to quell July's massive Detroit race riots without federal troops and the controversy about his "brainwashing" remark on Vietnam had hurt him.

As Romney's star faded, Nixon's had risen. The mid-October polls confirmed that he was firmly in the lead among GOP voters and even narrowly led President Johnson among all voters. In July, Johnson had been basking in the good publicity of his summit conversations with Soviet Premier Aleksei Kosygin and the private assurances he had received from the Soviets that they would endeavor to influence Hanoi in the direction of a settlement. Then came the devastating urban riots. The recent Senate hearings on bombing policy disturbingly revealed that the Joint Chiefs of Staff (JCS) and McNamara had "sharply diverged" over the value and methods of Rolling Thunder, the bombing campaign against North Vietnam.

Sensing the disarray and potential catastrophe in the war effort, Eisenhower had taken a swipe at Senators Robert Kennedy and William Fulbright as well as Johnson's other war critics. He had castigated the so-called armchair experts for "assuming an expertise they do not possess." He implored critics on all sides to do "more thinking" and "a lot less talking."

Eisenhower's intervention in the politics of Vietnam had repercussions for Republicans. Still technically neutral in the race, he was warning Romney, or if Romney's candidacy was doomed, Rockefeller, against what *Newsweek*'s Kenneth Crawford called "the great temptation" to exploit war weariness by adopting the peace plank of Johnson's Senate critics. In a forthcoming *Reader's Digest* article, Eisenhower would promise to stump against any candidate, Republican or Democrat, who ran on a "peace at any price platform."

Explaining his recent public statements to Nixon, Eisenhower remarked that the GOP would forfeit its best chance to win if a peace plank were adopted since "many if not most Republicans support Johnson's goals even if they question the means he is using to achieve them."

Listening intently, Nixon concurred. As always, he took mental notes, which he would dictate or write on a yellow legal pad by day's end. It was a discipline he had developed as a way of making sure he did not miss nuances or information. These notes served as an informal diary of his latest adventure in national politics. Nixon's account of his visit with Eisenhower on the 17th was especially detailed, as their exchanges clarified two matters.

First, the General had come to a crossroads with Johnson on his conduct of the war. For two years, Eisenhower had been consulted by Johnson and the Joint Chiefs about every major move in Vietnam. He had been as helpful as possible, and patient, but his support had limits.

Second, Nixon was seeking Eisenhower's understanding, if not his blessing, for conclusions he had reached about Asia, knowing full well Eisenhower's views on nonrecognition of China and no retreat in Vietnam.

The war in Vietnam, in fact, overshadowed everything the two men discussed that afternoon. Eisenhower, the insider who talked regularly to the President by telephone, let Nixon know that he expected things to get worse. Briefed weekly by their mutual friend General Andrew Goodpaster, currently secretary of the JCS, Eisenhower was concerned about the President's negative state of mind, as well as the depths of the McNamara-JCS controversy and the malaise engulfing the war effort. Since July the North Vietnamese had been moving forces and supplies into the Laotian and Cambodian sanctuaries. The artillery battle at Con Thien on the DMZ was probably the opening of an offensive by North Vietnamese forces poised to strike at any point along the Vietnamese-Laotian frontier. Under the circumstances, Eisenhower argued, the endless public debates about the bombing and negotiations were academic, even subversive. "Who wants to stop the bombing?" he asked Nixon rhetorically. "The Communists do because it is hurting them. My answer to the bombing halt business is simple: does the enemy hate it?"

But Johnson was wavering on the bombing campaign. The President had directed the JCS to assemble a list of formal recommendations to be presented that very week as part of the latest reappraisal of the war. Johnson's options for intensifying the war were clear: step up Rolling Thunder; establish a blockade of Haiphong, a key North Vietnamese seaport; and expand the ground war into North Vietnam or into the sanctuaries. Eisenhower favored all three actions and had recommended them repeatedly.

Nixon noted a striking change in Eisenhower's demeanor and outlook since July. Gone was the customary jauntiness. Apparently Eisenhower, aroused by the obvious dissension in administration ranks and the defeatist mood in the country, felt that escalation of the war had become necessary to avert disaster and undue concessions to get negotiations.

Negotiations were coming as the apparent stalemate deepened. Johnson already had lost the Vietnam argument within the Democratic Party. In desperation, the President would let party considerations drive him toward talks and a peace of some kind in 1968. Having reported earlier that Romania and other "third force" governments were lining up to broker talks on ending the war, Nixon advised Eisenhower that he believed Johnson was holding back the bombing halt card to be played whenever peace talks might suit him politically.

In anticipation of the President's moves, Nixon had developed a position: he would support Johnson's official aims in Vietnam but criticize the indecisive strategy that had brought on the current impasse. And as a candidate, he would call for "de-Americanization" of the war and oppose a "wider war": a wider war that would ensue from a ground invasion of North Vietnam; the wider war that would result from use of tactical atomic weapons; and the wider war that would result if America agreed to a "false peace."

Nixon argued in his *Foreign Affairs* article that a settlement in Vietnam must in no circumstances come about in a process that linked the United States and the Soviet Union in an anti-China alliance. Eisenhower concurred.

Both men agreed that it would be difficult to chart the future course of the war no matter how clear the options were, because of the volatility of Lyndon Johnson himself. Johnson's problem, Eisenhower told Nixon, was that he lacked the inner pressure gauge that told him when to relax. He had no hobbies or interests outside of politics. For instance, their mutual friend UPI correspondent Merriman Smith had informed Eisenhower that President Johnson was often up at 3 A.M. phoning Honolulu, Saigon, and the Pentagon to get the latest word on the air strikes and ground actions. "He can't do that and possibly maintain the proper posture or frame of mind for basic decisions," Eisenhower had told Smith, promising the reporter that he would give Johnson a "real Dutch Uncle talking to." He had spoken with Johnson afterward, but it had made no impression.

Nixon noted Eisenhower's words carefully:

I told him [Smith] that when I was operations officer at the War Department I moved a whole division in and out of the country . . . reporting to General Marshall about it at the end of the week, and that was the way they wanted it. . . . For one thing, a war or combat situation is upsetting and that can . . . throw off judgment. The President's job is to know exactly what the problem is that he should solve and then decide how to solve it. Then he's got to find his lieutenants, his proconsuls, and then trust the men he picks and say "now you must do this within the limits I give you."

Do you go, do you send troops, say, to Lebanon or don't you. Now, it's up to somebody else to find where are the troops, exactly what kind, what's the date they are going in and so forth. The President of the United States must not burden himself with all of those things.

Johnson's decisions, he continued, had been compromises, always a "year and a half too late" on every major question to come before him: a year and a half too late to

461

commit troops, a year and a half too late to begin the bombing in earnest, a year and a half too late for measures to mobilize American opinion.

As their conversation drifted back to politics and mutual friends, the General relaxed, swaying gently in his gray velvet rocker. Eisenhower, Nixon noted to himself, was still an avid painter. An easel stood several feet away. Some canvases were leaning next to it, landscapes the General was painting from photographs stacked neatly on a small table. One of Eisenhower's snow scenes, *White Church in the Country,* hung in Nixon's bedroom in his apartment back in New York.

The discussion moved back in time to their days in Washington. Eisenhower brought up the spate of recent books about the Suez crisis in October 1956. He was particularly taken with the study that had documented the extent of British-French-Israeli military and political collusion before the Sinai invasion. "The truth always comes out sooner or later," he chuckled.

They talked on, going further back in time as the shadows began to stretch from the sunporch past the putting green and toward the grazing pastures and the woods that had sheltered Longstreet's Confederate corps one hundred four years earlier on the second and third nights of the Battle of Gettysburg. Seeing those very woods as a cadet in 1915 had inspired Eisenhower's lifetime interest in the battle and his later decision to buy a farm in Gettysburg. He had made the Civil War's lessons a theme in *At Ease,* each page sprinkled with gentle advice to the perplexing youth of 1967.

Two days before, police and students had clashed at the Oakland, California, induction center, the first event of "Stop the Draft Week," which would culminate in marches and disruptions in Washington that weekend. Eisenhower deplored the disturbances and the antidraft movement, recalling his earnest efforts as Army chief of staff to push universal military service through the 80th Congress when Nixon was in his freshman year there. "Maybe the hippie generation would benefit from a stint in the Army," he said with a smile.

As four became four-thirty, it passed through Nixon's mind that this was perhaps his last extended private talk with Dwight Eisenhower. The General seemed animated but frail, strong in spirit but translucent and, by late afternoon, suddenly old. As Nixon rose to leave, the General spotted a blue jay that had alighted on the bird feeder near the porch. He studied the bird intently as though making a mental note to have Sergeant Moaney replenish the feeder. Several seconds passed and then an awkward silence as Eisenhower appeared to be trying to pick up on a lost train of thought. "If only the time would come when men could sit down and rationally settle their differences in peace," he reflected sadly.

Just then, Mamie came bustling in, her full skirts swinging, and Nixon rose to greet her. For several minutes the three talked about Pat and the girls. The Eisenhowers told him about their plans to deed their farm to the National Park Service, which would maintain it perpetually as a historic site on the Gettysburg battlefield parkland. They described their upcoming weekend in Augusta, and the cross-country train trip they planned to California.

Mamie and the General walked with Nixon to his waiting car. As it pulled out, they waved; then they returned to the sunporch's glass sliding doors to wave broadly again as the vehicle rumbled along the lane past the flagpole. The car finally disappeared through the gate at the right turn onto Route 15, on the road to Washington.

By Thanksgiving, Julie and I had decided we wanted to announce our engagement to our respective families over the holiday weekend. At the farm, I informed my parents, sisters, and grandmother. I could not bring myself to talk directly to Granddad, knowing that he would argue that I should be more "established" first, and not knowing how to handle the advice. That Thanksgiving Day, between large family dinners and naps, the farm was a beehive of excitement and furtive conversation.

Mamie was thrilled. "She's a wonderful girl, comes from a fine family — you kids shouldn't have to wait!" Upon receiving the news, Mamie went directly to a jewelry box and retrieved an heirloom diamond her mother had worn through sixty years of marriage to her father. She gave it to me for Julie. My father and I had long and thoughtful discussions about the timing and how Julie and I would meet a budget. I knew that as soon as I graduated I would be drafted and would be serving several years in the military. Granddad had married Mamie and lived on a lowly lieutenant's pay of $141.67 a month for at least three years of his marriage. I wasn't worried.

Granddad was not miraculously in the

dark about the explosion of congratulations and plans swirling about him. Two weeks earlier, he had written Nixon a cryptic note asking him to call when he had time to talk about "some gossip that has reached my ears."

For two days, I awkwardly evaded mentioning the engagement in Granddad's presence. The wording of my intentions, rehearsed endlessly for precise, affirmative effect, deserted me. I considered breaking the news later by phone, or by telegram or letter. I cringed at broaching a subject as laden as marriage with loose strings dangling — our finances were vague, my career plans were uncertain. After lunch on the day we were scheduled to leave Gettysburg, Granddad summoned me to his bedroom, where he was preparing to take a nap. As I entered and sat down, Granddad removed his bifocals, set a pulp western down on his bedside table, and asked Moaney to pour me a Coke. Moaney swiftly drew the shades over the west- and north-facing windows and left. Granddad's demeanor did not betray knowledge of my news. He appeared tired, leaning back heavily into the stack of pillows as though to sleep.

Scarcely a hairbrush had been rearranged in that spartan room since it had been furnished. An olive-green scale stood at the foot of his unadorned mahogany frame bed. Granddad weighed himself to the nearest quarter pound each morning. A painting he had done of his grandchildren hung above the bed. His closet was stuffed with blue and brown three-piece suits, and dozens of highly polished shoes bridged by shoe trees. A small snapshot of Mamie rested on his bedside table. A photograph of me at birth with my parents and Granddad hung next to the window looking out over the circular driveway.

We sat in uneasy silence punctuated occasionally by comments about school and his plans for the desert that winter. He waited. For thirty minutes he waited. Finally, he relaxed into indifference. He asked the time and instructed me to have Moaney call him in an hour. Without excusing me, he fell asleep.

My mother had always been the first to assure me that behind his disciplined and austere approach to young people existed a tolerant, doting, and perceptive grandparent. I never doubted this, but knowing him to be tolerant and concerned with the best interests of those around him did not make communication with him any easier. Perhaps the real problem was my not knowing how to phrase personal thoughts to him.

Waiting for me upon my return to Massachusetts was a remarkable letter I shall always treasure:

Dear David:

For many years I have been struck by the virtual impossibility of men of the Nordic strain to express, in a face-to-face meeting, their affection, even when of the same family and when the ties of sentiment are strong indeed. A man whose family roots are in the northern European region may talk about another man in the most glowing terms, but in personal encounters, he usually conceals his feelings in a "Hi there" — or something like "how are you doing?"

I sometimes envy the Latins, who do not seem to be prey to these particular inhibitions — but I would not go so far as to favor the habit of men kissing each other.

At different periods of my life I have served under two men that I admired extravagantly and for whom I felt a great affection. They were Fox Conner and George C. Marshall. Though each had written to me commendatory letters and telegrams that were far more generous than I could possibly deserve, yet neither ever expressed to me, verbally, any compliment beyond, "Well, so far, you seem to be doing alright."

All this is an introduction of an effort of mine to speak frankly of the relationship that has developed between us. Because of ties of love and the respect for your mind and character, I value every contact I have with you — my only regret is that our personal meetings have become, from my viewpoint, too few. I like to talk to you, one reason being the deeper understanding I gain, through you, of the aspirations, ambitions and outlook of the intelligent college student of today. More than this, I find it fun to converse with you — although I am always diffident in seeming to pre-empt too much of the time available to you during Gettysburg visits. But we always seem to get some moments together — these I cherish.

Mamie told me of your telephonic report of the joy that you and Julie felt on her acceptance of your great grandmother's ring. I am more than delighted that the two of you feel such a deep mutual affection. You are both the kind of people who will, throughout your lives, enrich America. Moreover, a love, shared by two young and intelligent people, is one of heaven's greatest gifts to humanity.

Actually, the purpose of this letter is only to say that if at any time you think that I might be helpful to you, during whatever years that may be left to me, it would be a great privilege to me if you would let me know the matter.

Even if I could do nothing, it would not be for the lack of trying. This I mean very sincerely. I'm not only proud that you are my grandson, but my friend as well — to whom I give my deepest affection.

Devotedly,
Granddad

P.S. I started out this letter as a handwritten communication. I was promptly overtaken by so many blots and so many writing errors that I had to call on my secretary to type it into readable form.

P.P.S. The enclosed will help pay for a simple dinner for you two — but not at Twenty-One!!! Do not mention it, even to me. In fact, I've forgotten I sent it — D.

I replied immediately, apologizing for being fearful of his reaction. I had been wrong to assume that he would not approve. I had failed to discuss with him a family matter of prime importance. He waited several weeks to write back, and he disappointed me, erecting the wall I thought we had pierced by our exchange of letters:

In your reply to my letter of a couple of weeks ago you seemed to conclude that I was disappointed by your failure, earlier, to tell Mimi and me of the then imminent "engagement." I was quite astonished that you made such an interpretation of my letter, because my only purpose was to comment a bit on the natural shyness that seems almost invariably to develop in the personal relationship between any two Nordic males, who are bound together by a mutual affection.

I hope only to assure you that, while I could not seem to throw off my inhibitions when trying to express my fondness for my own grandson, I was certainly ready to stand by you in any case and at any time you might feel a need of my help. But it never occurred to me to imply a desire for any advance knowledge of your intentions, decisions, or plans, especially if these might involve another.

I had mistaken Granddad's intent. I later learned that he had written a similar letter to Dad years before. In deploring the distance he felt between himself and his son,

471

he had not been asking for anything or proposing changes. Though closer to Dad than to anyone, Eisenhower remained businesslike with his son throughout his life, as he did with me. Dad later remarked that it would be a strange world indeed if Granddad had suddenly started "letting it all hang out." I later learned that several weeks before Thanksgiving, Granddad had performed a solemn task. In early November, he had flown to Abilene for a day to be present for the transfer of the remains of his first son from a cemetery in Denver to a crypt at the foot of the spot he had chosen for his and Mamie's burial at the chapel on the grounds of the Eisenhower Library. The trip had been unsettling. Stubbornly and faithfully since his son's death in 1921, he had observed Icky's birthday each year. In *At Ease,* Granddad admitted that he and Mamie had never fully gotten over the loss of Icky. Looking back, I see clearly that Granddad was cheered by my news, and that he also had a lot on his mind.

Meanwhile, Granddad had resumed a journal. "Under orders of Doctors have started a diary on Oct. 21-1967 — to relate any physical difficulties." So begins Eisenhower's account of the final weeks of 1967.

In Augusta, Georgia, he wrote:

October 25: I don't dare practice [golf] because of chest discomfort. Find I'm using more n.g. [nitroglycerin pills] than ever before. 2–3 or even 4 a day. Apparently weakening somewhat. . . .

Back in Gettysburg, he continued:

November 10. Last eve went to a dinner at Alibi Club in D.C. hosted by Adm Jerry Wright (ret) and Bob Murphy (ex-state dept) of members of the Allied forces in the Mediterranean — in honor of first landing in Africa on Nov. 8-1942. Had a nice time but the day was long (got home at midnight & had to take total of 4 n.g. during the evening).

Just before Thanksgiving, while at Walter Reed, Eisenhower had an important meeting on Vietnam with General Westmoreland, one of his longtime favorites. He had championed the general's command for two years, urging the President to back Westmoreland's authority and restrain the "Pentagon civilians" so the soldiers could go about the business of winning the war.

As the artillery siege at Con Thien had ended, major new battles were developing on the Cambodian frontier, the largest near the town of Dak To in the Central Highlands of Vietnam roughly twenty miles from the Cambodian-Laotian borders and the terminus of the Laotian trails. What was new about the Dak To battle was that it focused attention on the existence of communist sanctuaries in Cambodia.

Several thousand NVA regulars moved into Dak To to secure the trail and eliminate a U.S. Special Forces camp in the area. Westmoreland, sensing a chance to defeat the NVA in open battle, rapidly moved elements of the 173rd Airborne Brigade and the U.S. Fourth Infantry into the area. In a major battle for control of the hills of the sector, the NVA forces were driven back into Cambodia amid reports that Westmoreland had "pressed" the White House for permission to pursue and destroy the entire network of Cambodian sanctuaries said to be housing as many as thirty-five thousand communist troops and serving as a conduit for supplies arriving via the port of Sihanoukville. So far, Westmoreland told Eisenhower, "no decision" had been taken by the White House on the sanctuaries.

Eisenhower had two questions for Westmoreland. First, what was the quality of the South Vietnamese army? Second, what progress was he making toward building up a "corps of maneuver" to eliminate enemy sanctuaries? Westmoreland responded that 50 percent of South Vietnamese units were "outstanding," 40 percent adequate, and 10 percent inadequate. As for the "corps of maneuver," Westmoreland "anticipated" that by spring First Air Cavalry would constitute a reserve in the two northern corps areas and the 101st Airborne would constitute a reserve in the two southern corps areas.

In the absence of administration decisions, Eisenhower decided to go on the air himself and urge greater latitude for Westmoreland and the Vietnam command. In a CBS television interview filmed at the Gettysburg farm, Eisenhower and his old comrade Omar Bradley appeared as spokesmen for the newly formed Citizens Committee for Peace with Freedom in Vietnam, which included former senator Paul Douglas of Illinois, former secretaries of state Dean Acheson and James Byrnes, and former president Harry Truman. Eisenhower's comments on Dak To and "hot pursuit" of communist forces into the sanctuaries made news. "This respecting of boundary lines," he observed, "I think you can overdo it . . . if you are chasing some people and they just step over into Cambodia or Laos. . . . I wouldn't. . . . It wouldn't bother me. . . . I'd just go right in. . . ."

The "ripple" caused by Eisenhower's CBS appearance was felt most strongly among Republicans, who took it as yet another attack on Romney's "independent" position on Vietnam, and an indirect warning to Rockefeller, who was reported that week to be "wavering" on the war. But the "hot pursuit" issue was also a problem between Eisenhower and Nixon. After a phone call and an exchange of notes, Nixon politely stepped out of the controversy. He released a statement in which he generously endorsed General Eisenhower's "military judgment" but added that "from a political point of view I would be very reluctant to take action that could be regarded as an invasion of Laos or Cambodia."

Thanksgiving came and went, and on Monday, November 27, the day after the holiday, Granddad recorded a big event in his diary:

Today Mamie and I took part in a ceremony in which we gave title of our farm to the federal government. Mr. [Stewart] Udall, Secretary of the Interior represented the govt. While we might have sold it, the fact is we hated to see it fall to private hands, while the govt. was anxious to have it as a portion of the 1863 battlefield and as a residence of a one-time President and First Lady. We are privileged to have lived in the house and to have use of the farm as long as both of us live — 6 mos. thereafter, possession goes to U.S.

At 4 P.M. on the 28th, Granddad and Mamie boarded a train in Harrisburg. Pennsylvania governor Raymond Shafer came aboard for a visit and to introduce several members of the Republican State Committee. The Eisenhowers were off to Eldorado by way of Chicago, Topeka, Abilene, Albuquerque, and Phoenix. Granddad would never see Gettysburg again.

From Palm Springs, Eisenhower recorded his second to last diary entry for 1967, dated December 21:

Mary Jean's 12th birthday. Sent her a telegram; Mamie sent a present. She is a fine little girl, rapidly growing up. We are indeed fortunate in our 4 grandchildren — David, Anne, Susan, and Mary.

X X X X X

No physical difficulties that I can feel;

indeed, at my age, I am most lucky. . . .

By January 1968, Lyndon Johnson was in serious political trouble, and his hold on his 1964 majority was all but gone. His administration labored under the shadow of a losing war. In April, Reverend Martin Luther King, Jr., had ended his silence on the war, calling Vietnam "an obstacle to civil rights," a war fought by the underprivileged that was absorbing the resources needed to finance social reform. In July, Congress had opened a new round of hearings on the alleged official deception surrounding the Gulf of Tonkin Resolution, in order to disassociate Congress from the conduct of the war. McNamara's leaked secret testimony before the House Armed Services Committee revealed that he did not think the bombing was curtailing enemy supplies and saving American lives. In November, McNamara announced his departure from the administration, reportedly over disagreements about Vietnam strategy and negotiations, contributing to the sense of disarray.

Shortly after the New Year, the Gallup poll would once again name Dwight Eisenhower the man most admired by the American people. Since the end of World War II, Gallup had been polling Americans on the most admired living American. The poll's significance is polemical and easily exaggerated. A professional politician will quickly point out that since respondents are not allowed to indicate a second choice, the "most admired" poll is naturally biased toward individuals with relatively narrow but zealous followings and not indicative of broad trends in public opinion. Likewise, the poll often registers the amount of publicity a person has received during the year, testing "name recognition." The president invariably leads the list.

Politicians watch the poll closely. It has proven to be prophetically accurate on at least one matter — forecasting the downfall of sitting presidents. Before December 1967, an incumbent president failed to lead the poll only three times. In 1951, Douglas MacArthur was the choice. In 1950 and 1952, respondents chose Eisenhower over Harry S. Truman. These polls signaled Truman's irreversible loss of favor with the voters. In 1967, the selection of Eisenhower indicated the end of patience with the incumbent administration. But unlike 1950, 1951, and 1952, respondents were not pointing to an individual who could offer a solution to the problems confronting the country.

In fact, the choice of Eisenhower was unexpected. He had spent the 1960s in the relative obscurity of retirement. After his presidential memoirs, his articles and speeches had focused on patriotism, family, common sense, and technical matters like governmental reorganization. Eisenhower had written and spoken from what *Time* magazine called "the remote past." His *Reader's Digest* article "We Should Be Ashamed" had revealed a rigidity about protest and the domestic impact of the Vietnam War that seemed eccentric among political figures of the day, who conventionally heaped praise on the "idealism" of the young. Eight years had not shaken the initial historical assessments that his administration had been, in Vice President Hubert Humphrey's words, "a bland diet" of do-nothingism. But somehow, Eisenhower's basic optimism and his confidence in the future as America's leading "soldier of democracy" was appreciated that troubled December, and Americans were beginning to look back on the peace and prosperity of the 1950s with nostalgia and affection.

6
HOMEWARD BOUND

WEDDING PLANS

The news of the Gallup poll about most-admired Americans coincided with stories from Palm Desert, where Eisenhower rested and vacationed, which quoted friends as saying that the General, burned by his 1964 experience, would withhold endorsement of a candidate prior to the 1968 Republican convention. According to a Christmas Day story in the *New York Times,* Eisenhower purportedly would actively oppose "any candidate proposing 'peace at any price.' " Eisenhower was quoted through friends as saying, "I don't regard myself as a missionary and I don't want to convert anybody. But if Republicans or Democrats suggest we pull out of Vietnam and turn our backs on the more than 13,000 Americans who died in the name of freedom there, they will have me to contend with."

The *Times* story placed Eisenhower once

again in the middle of Republican presidential politics. In an editorial, the newspaper took issue with Eisenhower's characterization of dissenters "as if they, and not the unsuccessful war effort, were the country's chief Vietnam problem."

On December 28, Tom Wicker wrote a column in the *Times* titled "Eisenhower Rides Again," in which he criticized Eisenhower's action as "significantly narrowing his party's room for political maneuver in 1968." Wicker pointed out that big-state candidates like Nelson Rockefeller had prudently observed silence about Vietnam for several years, preserving the ability to break openly with Lyndon Johnson's Vietnam policy. Wicker complained about the "remarkable bellicosity" of Eisenhower's recent remarks.

Some Republicans were reported to be upset with Eisenhower's collaboration with the Johnson administration. Throughout 1967, Eisenhower was accurately reported to be considering a request from Johnson to travel throughout Southeast Asia as a diplomatic representative of the administration. When newspaper reports in December quoted Johnson administration officials as now "weighing" the idea of "hot pursuit" into enemy sanctuaries in Cambodia and

Laos, Eisenhower was suspected of having floated a trial balloon on behalf of Lyndon Johnson during his joint appearance with General Omar Bradley on CBS. But in GOP circles, Eisenhower's views still carried significant weight, perhaps even more than in 1964.

As 1968 arrived, Eisenhower was friendly to the idea of a Nixon candidacy. He was impressed by Nixon's consistent high standing in the polls and by his persistence and intelligence. Eisenhower regretted that Nixon had suffered because of slights or public relations mistakes of his over the years, and the well-known opposition of some of Ike's business friends.

He also prized Nixon's friendship, as illustrated by a story told by Kevin McCann. In June 1967, the two men by coincidence found themselves staying just rooms away from each other at the Waldorf-Astoria in New York. Eisenhower was in town to attend a promotional event for *At Ease.* Nixon was at work on a speech he was about to deliver in the ballroom below. When McCann bumped into Nixon in the corridor near their respective rooms, he urged the former vice president to drop in and say hi to General Eisenhower. Nixon begged off, explaining he was preoccupied with memorizing his speech.

"The General would not understand if he knew you were fifty feet away and could not find time to say hello," Kevin suggested firmly. Nixon paused thoughtfully. "I guess you're right," he replied. According to Mc-Cann, Eisenhower was on "tip toes" for the rest of the day thinking that Nixon's gesture had been spontaneous.

There was also a matter of family romance. Our courtship initially caused as many political problems as it solved. Nixon found himself walking a tightrope by accommodating my desire to join the campaign trail while he was avoiding any appearance of pressure on Eisenhower to endorse him. I was enthusiastic about the Nixon campaign, convinced that he should, indeed could win.

Granddad, meanwhile, still viewed Nixon through the prism of the 1960 campaign. Only recently had he learned through published reports that Mamie, worried about her husband's health, had called Nixon in late October 1960 and persuaded him to decline Eisenhower's offer of additional help in the closing days of the race. Nixon endeavored to maintain a good relationship with the General, and his admiration for Eisenhower bordered on hero worship. He kept sending copies of his articles and speeches to Eisenhower for comment and suggestions. He called Eisenhower frequently with political intelligence and to solicit the General's assessments of the issues that would prove decisive in 1968.

Nixon took at face value Eisenhower's reported intention not to endorse any candidate prior to the convention. He reasoned that Eisenhower's refusal to intervene against Goldwater had hardened into yet another of the many laws by which he lived his life: permanent and undeviating neutrality in all prenomination battles involving Republicans in order to preserve the effectiveness of his support in the general election.

Should he bend this rule, it stood to reason that Eisenhower's endorsement would aid Nixon's campaign far more than it would help Reagan, Rockefeller, Romney, or any other Republican hopeful. Because of their long working association during the White House years, and the fact that their relationship had been the subject of so much speculation, a preconvention endorsement from Dwight Eisenhower would greatly bolster Nixon's claim of superior experience and competence.

Julie's diary entry of January 28, 1968,

written two days before Nixon's formal entry into the presidential campaign, reveals the sensitivity he exhibited toward Eisenhower. After dinner that evening, we had huddled in Nixon's study overlooking Fifth Avenue to discuss our idea of moving our wedding date forward to June:

Daddy mentioned that a June wedding would cause people to say it was an attempt to bind DDE-Nixon families closer together and to attract publicity. Somehow, however, David and I questioned D's [Daddy's] nervousness. . . . I just wanted him to speak frankly — I wanted to know what he really felt. I am still not sure but I think his main objection was the reaction of David's grandfather. . . . D finally said he was concerned, frankly, that if we married in June, DDE would blame Daddy. When we became engaged, DDE asked David to wait until graduation before we were married. D is afraid that DDE will think he pushed it and then make things difficult for RN. I can see D's point; it is likely that this would happen.

In the year-end newspaper stories, Eisenhower was described in reports from Palm Desert as a man of "boundless nervous energy . . . who can't sit still for five minutes . . . who still jumps out of the chair and paces to prove points." But these reports concealed a mild state of depression and illness. He and Mamie had arrived in California downcast after the visit to the chapel and Icky's grave.

Eisenhower had spent much of December in bed, unable to play golf and uninterested in the social activity that had characterized his previous visits. A photograph of him that winter that hangs in the men's locker room at Walter Annenberg's Sunnylands estate reveals him to be unmistakably somber. Hunched and preoccupied, Eisenhower is shown fishing alone at a small pond below the residence.

Following New Year's, Eisenhower had gotten out of bed and resumed shopping with Freeman Gosden, playing golf, and seeing visitors. At his office, still located in temporary quarters near Indio, Eisenhower met with California U.S. senator Thomas Kuchel, engaged in a bitter primary fight with right-wing educator Dr. Max Rafferty. Kuchel dropped by for a photo session and to receive an implied endorsement. Rafferty followed suit, arriving one morning and arranging for photos and a joint appearance outside the offices. Film mogul Sam Goldwyn paid a social call, as did former British prime minister Harold Macmillan and his grandson. Ben Hibbs arrived to discuss the outlines of an article in which Granddad would unveil his pet project for irrigation in the Middle East as a means of defusing the Arab-Israeli conflict. Governor Raymond Shafer of Pennsylvania visited on behalf of his favorite-son candidacy, which held the Pennsylvania delegation for Rockefeller, New York's favorite son. Ronald Reagan lunched with Eisenhower at Eldorado. Several of Eisenhower's Eldorado friends wished to attend the convention as delegates and Eisenhower asked Reagan if he could make this possible.

Most enjoyable were visits from Coach John McKay of USC, and writer Robert Danzig, who was writing a history of West Point football. Eisenhower noted in his diary that he doubted he had told Danzig much that he did not already know, but he had enjoyed the visit. Granddad and Mamie resumed a limited schedule in the community, attending the Palm Desert Community Presbyterian Church, receiving an award from the Port Authority of San Francisco, and a local "Respect for Law" citation. Eisenhower devoted some time to taping television advertisements for varied causes, including Republican fund-raising. In late November, McCann called on Eisenhower with particularly interesting news: "I told DDE that if things worked out and there was room for me [in the Nixon campaign] I was going to work in Wisconsin when I returned [from Africa]. He said, 'I am tied up with these money people who are against him . . . [T]he one thing you have to do is hammer away at the point that from your close association with me you know I am even stronger in my feelings now about his ability, etc.' "

Meanwhile, Nixon sent the General excerpts of an interview he had given Hugh Sidey of *Time* and *Life* about the organization of the presidency. Eisenhower replied:

I quite agree with your statement: "I'm not sure that any man can — by himself — be an adequate President . . ." The secret is adequate and skillful organization. You have described the necessity for surrounding the President with individuals of strong convictions, properly organized, so that necessary information and opinion come to him in usable form. Without such personnel and such organizations, errors of great magnitude are bound to occur in times of crisis. I think you have stated the case very well indeed. . . .

And as McCann departed to work for Nixon in Wisconsin, former congressman Robert Ellsworth, on behalf of the Nixon campaign, arrived to bring the General up to date on developments. He reported back to Nixon in New York that his friendly meeting with Eisenhower had lasted an hour instead of the usual half hour. Eisenhower expressed interest in every aspect of the campaign. He asked about the Nixon girls and whether Tricia would be campaigning along with Julie after her graduation from Finch College in June. She would be.

Discussion quickly moved to politics. Eisenhower made it clear that he had little regard for Governor Romney's "independent" stand on Vietnam, remarking that Romney seemed to have "a genius for talking about things he knew nothing about." How voters would respond remained to be seen. That raised the "stop Nixon" question and how it might develop. Who would lead it? Eisenhower did not think Rockefeller was interested in running but felt that he "could become involved because of the pressure on him." He also observed that the governor was being hurt in his controversy with New York City mayor John Lindsay over the sanitation strike in the city. In Eisenhower's view, Lindsay was on solid ground in resisting union terms, whereas Rockefeller's intervention on behalf of the unions was "a big problem and must be curbed." Eisenhower also did not expect Senator Charles Percy of Illinois, a personal favorite, to get involved unless the "campaign went too far to the right." That left Reagan, who continued to intrigue the General.

As Ellsworth reported:

First of all, he [Eisenhower] keeps telling Reagan that he has to stay as Governor for four years in order to prove he is not a right winger. His [Reagan's] people are always bringing him [Eisenhower] . . . documentary proof to show that he [Reagan] is not a right winger. Apparently Reagan has been having his people work hard on DDE. . . . The Reagan people tell Eisenhower that the Rocky-Reagan ticket would be the best. . . . He [Eisenhower] says that his response to them is that that is not a ticket that would appeal to anyone of any political principle. . . .

Eisenhower and Ellsworth ran down the list of potential vice presidential choices. Eisenhower "thought it would be a mistake not to have a Governor on the ticket." He felt positively about Scranton, his favorite, as well as John Love of Colorado, John Chaffee of Rhode Island, Daniel J. Evans of Washington, and John Volpe of Massachusetts. That reminded Eisenhower of a question he had about the progress Nixon was making in New Hampshire. He had seen a newspaper article that quoted Nixon as admitting he had to do well in New Hampshire, which Eisenhower took to mean "55%."

When Vietnam finally came up, Eisenhower was protective of Johnson. He expressed the hope the President might yet turn the crisis to his and the country's advantage. Kept thoroughly briefed by the JCS and occasionally Westmoreland, Eisenhower stressed, "The important thing in Vietnam is that we have to win, we have to succeed and we ought to send as many men as the commanders over there ask for to do the job." Ellsworth informed Nixon that Eisenhower apparently had inside information and believed Johnson was indeed on the verge of dramatic decisions and announcements, and was resolved at long last, in the General's words, to "end the war by winning it."

That winter, Granddad's Doubleday editors prevailed on him to start work on the "catch-all" book that would include a chapter on memoir writing, his favorite letters, more war stories, and a section summarizing the lessons of World War II. When Granddad, with some reluctance, dictated a prologue to the section on memoirs, he wrote:

. . . I do have many inhibitions about the role of a Monday-morning quarterback. There is, moreover, a capsule of wisdom on the subject.

"Never look back; something might be catching up with you."

According to Satchel Paige, the most durable of all baseball pitchers since Abner Doubleday allegedly devised the game, that saying was his life-long rule of conduct. It very well may have been mine too, through the first half century and more of my years on earth. Then, undoubtedly, the future with all its hidden wealth of surprise and challenge and change was far more exciting than the irreversible facts of yesterday.

In the last quarter-century or so, however, I have found myself intermittently looking backwards; putting down on paper or dictating on machine tape the record of deeds done, words said, goals attempted and sometimes achieved. Nevertheless, the future — what lies before my country and the world — is still my paramount concern. But for those who will be its shapers and leaders, I recognize the lessons of history can provide them guidance against repeating the mistakes of their forebears.

TET

On January 31, 1968, an ocean away, the first wave of a long-awaited communist offensive in Vietnam commenced on the Vietnamese New Year. In the next forty-eight hours, upwards of eighty thousand Vietcong troops attacked American and South Vietnamese forces for control of seventy-four South Vietnamese cities. The scale and coordination of the enemy assaults caught MACV by surprise and resulted in something bordering on panic, since the first wave was bound to be followed by a second wave of regular North Vietnamese forces,

494

which lurked in the DMZ and Cambodian sanctuaries. To maintain U.S. reserves, Westmoreland had to keep as many American forces as possible out of the city fighting and so the "clean up" depended on South Vietnam's army. But according to news reports, many South Vietnamese soldiers on leave for the New Year Tet holiday were slow to return, some deserting but many fearful to leave their homes and families. As the crisis intensified, U.S. battalions were inexorably drawn into the battles for Saigon, Hue, Kontum, Da Nang, and Quang Tri.

In Washington, Johnson met with reporters on February 2 to issue a brief statement of reassurance. But the confusion in South Vietnam and the fear of a second wave of attacks would cause Johnson to avoid any formal report to the nation for almost eight weeks. Despite two years of ground operations, the U.S. command had been clearly unprepared for the Tet showdown. *Newsweek* noted the "disquieting" fact that the coordination of over seventy city attacks by the communists required the acquiescence if not active cooperation of thousands of South Vietnamese. "The pacification program in the Vietnamese countryside," observed *Newsweek* at mid-month, "long asserted to be the real key to ultimate victory in Vietnam, had been dealt a blow from which it would recover slowly, if ever."

In Palm Desert, Eisenhower continued to receive briefings and reports. In his opinion, the Tet offensive was somewhat reminiscent of the German Ardennes counteroffensive in 1944. Viet Cong troops had emerged from their hidden defenses and had attacked a series of widely dispersed targets, their mistakes handing Westmoreland and the South Vietnamese an opportunity to gain a major tactical victory. But the President's prolonged silence in February and the pessimistic press coverage revealed a profound discouragement at the top with the course of the war. Fading fast was the likelihood Westmoreland would be allowed to exploit any victory in Tet as a springboard for long-overdue measures to win.

As February wore on, Julie chronicled in her diary the proliferation of antiwar speakers and seminars, fasts for peace, and petition drives at Smith. There also were fervent dinnertime discussions ranging from college rules about male visitors, Martin Luther King's Poor People's campaign set for summer, "Stop the Draft Week," and the legal proceedings brought against pediatrician Benjamin Spock, the Reverend William

Sloane Coffin of Yale and three others on charges of "aiding and abetting" violations of the Selective Service law.

Meanwhile, I became involved in the Nixon campaign. I had not been invited to take part in the formal kickoff of the campaign in New Hampshire in late January in order to avoid publicity that would appear to pressure Granddad to support Nixon. But when fog caused Julie's flight to New Hampshire to be canceled, I drove her from Smith to the opening reception. Once we had arrived at the motel, Mr. Nixon and I had a long chat about the pros and cons of appearing downstairs at the event. I volunteered to explain to Granddad the accidental nature of my trip to New Hampshire. That evening in Manchester, I attended the kickoff and became part of the campaign. My presence was reported, Granddad did not object, and in the weeks ahead, Tricia, Julie, and I would campaign together in the primary states of New Hampshire, Oregon, Nebraska, and Wisconsin. The grueling schedule, the tiny airplanes, and long hours proved to be an adventure and a challenge.

It seemed apparent in New Hampshire that the political consensus was shifting sharply in favor of disengagement in Vietnam. As Robert Kennedy fell into watchful silence, Eugene McCarthy attracted armies of volunteers and would nearly succeed in defeating Johnson in New Hampshire's Democratic primary. Yet Nixon, attracting a fraction of the publicity, would almost double the combined Democratic vote.

When the President visited Eisenhower in Palm Desert shortly before the primary for a golf game and lunch, Eisenhower noted in his diary Johnson's preoccupation with Kennedy and McCarthy, adding, "The President is obviously rusty in golf." The stage had been set for one of the most chaotic political years in American history.

"A RATHER REMARKABLE DAY"

The Coachella Valley is a natural shelter against anxiety and news of the outside world. As the campaign intensified, I feared that living in the desert isolated Granddad from the crushing problems that faced the country. In Palm Desert, he might find it easy to dismiss the intense emotions aroused by politics in 1968, because hard news is easily smothered by one's intoxication with the climate and the beauty. I reasoned that Granddad would not be helpful in the 1968 campaign unless an infusion of news from the outside focused his attention on politics.

I began writing him from school and calling from my campaign appearances along the primary trail trying to describe the depth of disillusionment with Johnson and the urgent need for change. Granddad's replies, as I feared, were dispassionate and cheerful. In early March he wrote:

I admit that the conduct of the Presidency during the last few years has created much doubt and unhappiness in our country, but we should never make the mistake of thinking that these problems are easy ones; there is no panacea, no short cut to hard thinking, considered judgments and prompt and firm decisions. The whole subject is one that I would like to talk over with you very seriously and at length.

Right now we have much of the country's unhappiness expressed by the candidacy of both [segregationist George] Wallace, on the one hand, and [antiwar senator Eugene] McCarthy on the other. The former seems to me to look like Captain Kidd with a shave; the latter seems to me as unsure of himself as a first grader trying to solve a problem in differential equations. Nevertheless, each seems to have a certain following. Here in California, both got the necessary number of signed petitions, about 100,000 each, to get themselves on the ticket for this year. At the very least, I am delighted that you got excited about these matters. I cannot stand anyone who is apathetic about our nation and the political and economic situations of the moment and what they portend for the future.

Incidentally, this reminds me that while Mr. Nixon is supposed also to have little appeal for the "young generation," I was delighted to see the report of his appearance before a student body of some 3,000 in New Hampshire. Probably he should make it his business to get to appear before as many of these as he can. However, one man can do just so much — the human frame will stand just so much stress, and then it cracks up.

We just had a letter from Anne. . . . Incidentally, she reports (secretly) that when you come to see her, it is usually for some money. Remember that most Republicans are very severely criticizing the administration Democrats for "Big Spending." Republicans don't believe in financial deficits.

Eisenhower's neighbors and friends in Palm Desert had a premonition that his visit in 1968 would be his last. Organizers of the public events he attended added a little something extra to the ritual ceremonies and honors. Friends, led by Freeman Gosden, joined Eisenhower more frequently at the par three Seven Lakes Country Club, which was less tiring for the General than other golf courses. Eisenhower shared the premonition. In his diary, he revealed forebodings that his visits to California were "numbered." He made a record of doctor's visits and signs of his steadily declining health. In February, he chronicled the two events that brought his association with the desert to a storybook end:

Tuesday, February 6

Last Sunday I carried out my annual chore of presenting the Eisenhower trophy to the winner of the Bob Hope Classic. This year the winner was my good friend, Arnold Palmer. An unusual feature of the ceremony was a "salute" to me arranged by the bands of the several military posts in the area; there were Army, Navy, Marine and Air Force contingents in the band and aside from playing the different service songs, they played also the Star Spangled Banner. It was a very moving ceremony and one that for the first time in a good many years, brought tears to my eyes.

This morning the doctors visited me and seemed to feel that I was in pretty good condition. They decided there was no need for blood analysis or for a cardiogram today. Today George Allen has come in for one day's stay and I expect to play golf with him at 7 Lakes this afternoon and tomorrow morning. He leaves tomorrow afternoon.

Two days later, Granddad shot a hole-in-one. For the nation's leading amateur golfer, this achievement climaxed a lifetime of interest in the game. Photos appeared nationwide showing Granddad proudly displaying the ball with a wide grin under his floppy golf cap. In his diary, he recorded the event and the inevitable letdown following his thrill.

Wednesday, February 7

Yesterday I had a rather remarkable day at golf. Starting out with a number of errors on the first 3 holes, I settled down and began to play quite well. On No. 8, which is a short par 4, I had a nice drive, following which my wedge shot went into the hole for an eagle. Then, on No. 10, I made a nice birdie on a par 3 hole and on No. 13, another par 3, I made a hole-in-one — the first of my life. I ended the round with a birdie on No. 18. The three others in the foursome were Freeman Gosden, George Allen and [businessman] Leigh Battson. This was at Seven Lakes, which had fourteen par 3s and four par 4s.

This morning I played with the same foursome, except that Holmes Tuttle took the place of Leigh Battson. For the first time I got rather tired and made up my mind that tomorrow I would have no golf whatsoever.

Elsewhere his journal clearly indicates his weariness. In March, Mamie's annual vacation at the spa Main Chance was timed to coincide with the arrival of fourteen of Granddad's best friends from the east for a week of bridge and golf. For the seven days, Eisenhower proved that he had not lost his ability to frighten guests around a bridge table. But he was also obliged to confess to himself that he no longer possessed his former strength. He described the week:

Mamie has been in Main Chance for a week. I have telephoned her each evening and she obviously is feeling much better. . . . During the week I had a number of guests from the east who were here for bridge and golf. Cliff Roberts, George Allen, Clarence Schoo, Pete Kalmbach, Frank Willard, Sig Larmon, Slats Slater, Bill Robinson . . . Of these, neither Charlie Jones nor Al Gruenther could play golf, while John Murray and my good local friend, Freeman Gosden did not play bridge.

We had the entire crowd for a barbeque on Monday night and another one for those still here on Saturday night. In the meantime, Cliff Roberts gave a dinner at the Thunderbird on Wednesday and Leonard Firestone gave both a dinner on Thursday and a luncheon on Saturday. Finally, Justin Dart had the whole crowd for dinner at Pepitos, an Italian restaurant in Palm Desert, on Friday night.

As fond as I am of all those named, I must say that the week was rather wearing. I doubt that I shall ever try to have such a number of guests again.

THIS TOO SHALL PASS

On March 31, 1968, Lyndon Johnson, broken by the split within the Democratic Party over Vietnam, his falling popularity and near defeat in New Hampshire, and his projected defeat in the Wisconsin primary, spoke to the nation to announce a bombing halt north of the DMZ and his decision not to seek another term as president.

That day, my twentieth birthday, I was with the Nixons in Milwaukee at a jammed handshaking reception in a last-minute effort to get out the Wisconsin Republican primary vote. Usually Julie, Tricia, and I had our own schedule in the smaller towns, but we had all gone to Milwaukee for the last big rally of the primary. Rumors had already reached the Nixon camp about a major peace initiative planned by Johnson to quiet domestic criticism and to influence the vote, but no one had an inkling that he was going to remove himself from the presidential race.

Julie's campaign diary account of the day reads:

It is so ironic that this news came at the end of a happy and triumphant day for us, David's 20th birthday, the crowds in Milwaukee and the happy afterglow of

505

the trip home. . . .

We flew commercial to Wisconsin. In the car, Charlie McWhorter [former chairman of Young Republicans] said he wouldn't want to run against Bobby, ever. The crowd estimate at the reception or "hand shaker" as Daddy calls it was between 12–14,000 people. We shook hands with perhaps 3000 for 3 1/2 hours. The people were extraordinarily nice. So many brought their children. Many of the ladies were dressed in their best clothes. For a while, Tricia, David, and I greeted people in a downstairs room, so that those who could not fit into the main room would not go away disappointed. People seemed genuinely thrilled about our engagement. They all had prayers and wishes for M and D [Mother and Daddy]. "He's going to make it this time . . ."

We flew to Bradley Field in Mr. Parma's jet. . . . We had sandwiches on board and we ate David's birthday cake. . . . We talked about the campaign on the way back. Once during the flight, we turned out the lights in the jet to see the Aurora Borealis. We seemed to be very close to the stars. After the black, faint white light . . .

As Johnson delivered his speech to the nation, the Nixons and I were thirty-four thousand feet over northern Indiana. Nixon speculated that he expected a bombing halt in Johnson's televised address or a similar gesture that would pull the rug from under critics. For this reason, he had been reluctant so far in the campaign to be specific about actions he would take in Vietnam, pledging simply "to end the war and win the peace."

The Nixons' plane dropped Julie and me off at Bradley Field, Connecticut, the closest airport to the Smith and Amherst campuses, before continuing on to New York. From Bradley Field we drove the last forty minutes together back to school. We were tired, though satisfied after a hard day of campaigning. We gave passing thought to tuning in the car radio for a report on Johnson's speech, but decided we had had enough of the campaign for one day. After dropping Julie off at Smith, I returned to Amherst and a ghoulish spectacle. A bank of warm and humid air had settled over the Connecticut River valley, sending temperatures into the 60s and creating a summerlike evening. Every window blazed with light. The blast of stereo speakers, mingled with chanting and shrieks of joy created a cacophony of sound. Students were everywhere, dancing, clapping, and drinking.

My first interpretation of this incomprehensible scene was a hunch that classes had been canceled to protest whatever Johnson had said that evening. When I asked several friends what had happened, however, I learned that Johnson had withdrawn from the presidential campaign. Until that moment, I had assumed that all the stories about the President were true — that he was too tough to quit, and that, in wielding the power of the incumbency, he could not possibly be denied the nomination. I had taken it for granted that Johnson's nomination would make the task of winning in November easier. Suddenly the McCarthy-Kennedy wing of the Democratic Party was poised, ready to seize control of the party and to wash their hands of Johnson — and the war.

Dazed, I strode into my dorm, seized a phone, and dialed the Eisenhower home in Eldorado. If this did not move Granddad off dead center, nothing would.

The phone rang twice.

"Happy birthday, sweetie," Mamie answered gaily, recognizing my voice. "Your Granddad is going to say hi. The whole gang out here misses you so."

508

Granddad picked up a receiver and joined in wishing me a happy birthday. He reported that his bursitis was improving, and that he expected to be playing golf again soon. Right away, I brought up President Johnson's speech. I held the phone up to a window so that he could hear the pandemonium that had broken loose at Amherst. Returning to the conversation, I had questions and comments. I pointed out that the only Democrat currently in the field had repudiated the war. Democrats thus intended to escape political accountability for the conduct of their war. Would they succeed? Wasn't the path clear for Robert Kennedy? Johnson was admitting that his own policy had not worked. Did this mean the defeat of the Republican Party? The end of the world?

"Nonsense," Granddad replied.

"This too shall pass," Mamie added. She again wished me happy birthday and excused herself from the "men's talk."

For the next few minutes we argued about the speech. Granddad was unimpressed by the vehemence of my opinions, not prepared to "leap to conclusions," and not convinced Johnson's critics had been helped. A thought passed through my mind of how outraged everyone outside my window would be if

Granddad were right.

Granddad was least impressed by my analysis of Robert Kennedy's prospects. He dismissed Kennedy with a chilly story from his wide repertoire of historical biography, the history from *Plutarch's Lives* about a young Athenian named Alcibiades. He was a romantic figure — young and handsome, a fearless fighter and horseman, a gifted orator and scholar, adored by women, admired and envied by the men of Athens. Alcibiades' golden oratory dazzled the free population of Athens.

There arose loud clamors that he become dictator, which he encouraged. Alcibiades promised to save Athens from its enemies in exchange for total power. Half the population wanted to throw away their liberties and submit to the force of his personality. But the other half grew fearful of his pretensions. In the end, most Athenians became weary of him, and Alcibiades fled the city. Speaking metaphorically, Granddad's message was plain: he did not believe that the Kennedy campaign would have staying power.

But he had cause to wonder. The following night, he wrote a long analysis of Johnson's speech in his diary. He began by summarizing the points made in the President's speech, including his reiteration of American policy to achieve a settlement by negotiation and his order to halt bombing above the DMZ. Eisenhower regarded it as a "partial capitulation," at least "to the 'peace at any price' people in our own country." The most troublesome aspect of the speech, he wrote, was Johnson's announced withdrawal. He continued:

The inclusion of this statement seems to be almost a contradiction to his plea for a more unified America in attaining our limited objectives in Vietnam. His speech is virtually an effort to surrender to another the Presidential responsibilities in the conflict. The conclusion seems inescapable that though he is convinced of the worthiness of our purposes in Southeast Asia, he, himself, is unwilling to remain, personally, in the fight.

To me it seems obvious that the President is at war with himself and while trying vigorously to defend the actions and decision he had made in the past, and urging the nation to pursue these purposes regardless of cost, he wants to be excused from the burden of the office to which he was elected.

He made no mention of the leader

from his own Party who should now, in his stead, carry forward the effort. Indeed, I was left with the conclusion that the President had not truly analyzed the implications of his speech, as it affected both the country and himself.

Eisenhower continued for two more pages. In turning over in his mind why Johnson had chosen to remove himself from politics, Eisenhower satisfied himself on one point: if Johnson believed "that he was doing a service to the nation by trying thus to keep the Presidency out of partisan and divisive politics," he exhibited "some very confusing thinking." In short, Johnson had a duty to the nation if not to run then to stand by his policy in Vietnam, but he was doing neither. Eisenhower concluded: "I am besieged by papers and others to 'make a statement.' I am, and shall continue, refusing to say anything until I can convince myself of the true motivation of this performance."

Granddad never did comment publicly on Johnson's withdrawal. On April 8, Westmoreland once again visited him in the desert. On the 18th, Eisenhower met Johnson aboard Air Force One at March Air Force Base, near Riverside. The President and several aides briefed Eisenhower optimistically on the prospect of convincing the North Vietnamese to attend the peace conference in Paris. But Johnson's distracted manner betrayed his cheerful report. Gratitude for Johnson's gesture of unity had proven short-lived. Within days, the country reeled under another shock, the assassination of Martin Luther King, Jr., in Memphis. In the aftermath of the King assassination, there was rioting in 125 cities, exceeding the entire number of outbreaks in 1967. The most serious rioting occurred in Washington. Newspapers around the country carried front-page photographs of smoke rising behind the White House, symbolic of the pressures that had enveloped Johnson.

On April 23, Eisenhower's final journal entry of 1968 struck a somber note. He had not been feeling well and noted that his dependency on nitroglycerin pills meant a "steady deterioration in my heart muscle." Moving on to the shocking news of King and the riots, he recalled the unheeded predictions he had made in cabinet meetings during the late 1950s about the explosiveness of the racial situation in the North. He confessed that he was confused about Johnson's renunciation of the presidency. Talks were starting in Paris as a result of

Johnson's "generous" offer, which had given North Vietnamese leader Ho Chi Minh "every opportunity to negotiate." But he was no longer sure the President remained the tough, shrewd poker player Eisenhower had known in his White House days. Having seen Johnson twice recently, he had begun to grasp the personal toll the dissent, riots, and defections within his party had taken on the President.

On Monday, April 29, businessman Ken Norris and Freeman Gosden picked up Eisenhower at the house in Eldorado for the ride to Seven Lakes and a game of golf. Mamie greeted Norris and Gosden at the door in a dressing gown. She commented that Eisenhower seemed ill, and warned him not to play too hard.

"No, I'll play," Granddad replied irritably.

After nine holes, Gosden noticed that Eisenhower labored with every shot. He asked him if he would like to quit, but Eisenhower was determined to finish the eighteen holes. At the conclusion of the game, Norris, Gosden, and Eisenhower dropped by Norris's home to meet his wife. After brief introductions, Gosden and Eisenhower returned to Eldorado.

Several hours later, Gosden received a call

from Mamie. She evenly told him that Eisenhower had suffered an apparent heart attack. Freeman dressed hurriedly and ran the hundred yards to the Eisenhower home. He stopped short of the front door as several medics carried out Eisenhower on a stretcher. His arms were connected to bottles by intravenous tubes. Gosden wanted to say something, but Eisenhower appeared to be asleep as the result of an injection. Granddad was quickly transported to the intensive care unit at March Air Force Base. The diagnosis was a mild heart attack, and that he would recover, so the instructions the grandchildren received from Dad were "sit tight." But a planned two-week convalescence turned into four weeks and at the end of May, Granddad was flown to Washington and moved into the presidential suite in Ward Eight at Walter Reed. Doctors warned us at the outset of his ordeal that the prognosis was not good and that Granddad's chances of resuming an active life were less than even.

WARD EIGHT

Ward Eight at Walter Reed is, like the White House, part museum, part home, and a hub of activity. An austere portrait of George C. Marshall, who died there, greets all visitors as they step from the slow-moving hospital elevator into the reception area. Along the corridor, one passes several suites before entering the white-paneled double doors of the presidential suite. Inside, there is a large formal living room, which occupants use to greet dignitaries and family. In that room, Eisenhower and Winston Churchill had posed for photographs with terminally ill John Foster Dulles several days after Dulles resigned his position as secretary of state.

Owing to Eisenhower's frequent use of Ward Eight, the living room bore his stamp. It was decorated in Mamie's favorite greens, pinks, and tans, the colors of Gettysburg and Augusta. The room was comfortable and livable. Eisenhower's painting of Churchill, inspired by the famous photograph by Yousuf Karsh, dominated the room from the mantel over the fireplace. In it, Churchill wears a scowl, his left hand clasps a cigar, his right hand rests on a cane, and his jaw juts forward in defiance. Churchill's spirit lingers from the brief visit he made in 1959, a reminder to all those who occupy the suite to conquer grief and apprehension.

In Ward Eight, one senses the continuum of history that Eisenhower wrote about so frequently. Here the great become mortals, fragile humans who must submit to the care of doctors and surgeons to extend their lives. All patients are joined with each other in this struggle as old as time.

Ward Eight is not a place for tears or excitement. It is a pageant, a drama unfolding every day, a place where senators, generals, and presidents meet in hospital robes to trade stories and exchange gossip about the world outside. Each time we visited Granddad we were drawn into a nearby room to see another distinguished patient on the ward: Maine senator Margaret Chase Smith, admitted for a broken bone that caused her to miss the first roll call of her Senate career; Senator Richard Russell of Georgia, admitted with lung cancer; Mrs. William Westmoreland, in for a routine checkup; Senators Roman Hruska and Strom Thurmond, vital men in their seventies, in with the flu.

After Memorial Day, Ward Eight became a home for the Eisenhowers. Mamie moved a portion of her wardrobe, books, stationery, and a little television set into a small bedroom next to Granddad's suite. His room was stocked with his favorite books and photographs. His record collection in Gettysburg was packed and sent to Walter Reed. The Moaneys left Gettysburg to take up residence at their home on Georgia Avenue, conveniently located a few blocks north of the Walter Reed compound. General Schulz divided his time between the Gettysburg office, where all correspondence was answered, and the small room where the Secret Service had a command post at the end of the Ward Eight corridor.

We assumed that Granddad's convalescence in Walter Reed depressed him, that he longed desperately to leave the hospital and return to Gettysburg. But as his doctor General Leonard Heaton assured us, it is difficult to see matters through the eyes of a patient. In Walter Reed, Granddad felt secure. He was under the care of dozens of nurses, surgeons, and cardiologists. His vital signs were monitored constantly by an attendant who sat just beyond his view around the corner at the entrance to his bedroom. Like the desert, Walter Reed became a friend, extending his life.

Visiting him was wonderful and bewildering. He radiated joy and warmth, a hugging, clasping, happy appreciation of every visit. When possible, Granddad got out of bed with the aid of nurses and sat in an overstuffed chair next to a window with Venetian blinds screening the eastern side of the room from morning sunlight. When in particularly strong spirits, he dispensed with the nurse and asked one of us to help him. His emaciated arms would clasp strongly for balance as we walked from his bedside to the chair. In a clear voice, he would bark out orders not to rush him and to be careful.

With or without visitors, Granddad found ways to fill his daily routine with activity. The periodic tests performed by the medical staff became social events. He spent much of his day working crossword puzzles and playing cards with the nurses. Leonard Heaton dropped by the suite once a day for a talk. Together they would watch every golf tournament on television until Granddad's favorite, Arnold Palmer, was eliminated from the competition. He took visible pleasure in small things — a glass of scotch, a new record, a short personal visit.

Ward Eight was a safe shelter from the insanity and agitation of the world that summer. Mamie censored all the Vietnam and political news, and labored valiantly to keep politicians away from her husband's bedside. In fact, all bad news was withheld from Eisenhower on doctor's orders. On the night of June 4–5, a young Jordanian shot Robert Kennedy at the Ambassador Hotel in Los Angeles, moments after RFK had been declared the victor over Eugene McCarthy in the California primary. Kennedy died on June 6 but Eisenhower would not learn of it for more than seventy-two hours.

In May and June, peace negotiations in Paris quickly deadlocked over procedural issues. The news from Vietnam battlefields sounded increasingly grim. While editorials sermonized about the American propensity toward violence and the imminent demise of democracy, Eisenhower told his visitors that he thought the nation's ills would pass with time.

Lyndon Johnson quickly became one of Eisenhower's most frequent guests and doting friends. One could fill a short book with stories of the kindnesses, small and large, Johnson showered on Eisenhower. That summer, as Johnson's presidency passed into history and Vietnam wrecked his ambition to be the greatest and best-loved politician of his day in the mold of his hero Franklin Roosevelt, Johnson seemed drawn to the man who though perhaps not the greatest president, was regarded as the most loved.

Johnson's basket of flowers had been the first to arrive when Eisenhower checked into Walter Reed. During Eisenhower's slow convalescence in May, the President sent advisers and copies of his budget to the hospital for Eisenhower's perusal. He offered to staff Ward Eight with a full-time projectionist to run movies available through the White House film library. In July, Johnson proclaimed "Eisenhower Day" to be observed in the District of Columbia the week of October 14, Eisenhower's seventy-eighth birthday. He directed a steady stream of letters and messages of encouragement and admiration. In August, when Eisenhower's health worsened, the stream became a flood. In October, Johnson signed a bill appropriating public money for Eisenhower College.

Johnson's fleshy face seemed frozen in a permanent mold of despair and unspeakable sadness. In time, his visits became more solitary. Gone were the phalanxes of aides and generals. Johnson arrived and departed unobtrusively.

Granddad dictated short notes to Johnson. In one, he encouraged him to stand fast on the Paris negotiations. In another, he thanked Johnson for his thoughtfulness. In reply to one of Eisenhower's notes, Johnson wrote:

Thank you for your letter. Nothing occurs that brings me more assurance and cheer than the news I get about your continuing good progress.

I am sending you a picture showing how I spend my leisure time with a young man [his grandson, Lyn Nugent] whose main concern during these complex and uncertain days is making sure he gets enough to eat.

If you feel lonesome, and need a visit from a friend, just send word. I might even ask you to move over and make room for me too.

When alone, Granddad read. He had the usual stock of western pulp novels. He reread several of his favorite boyhood books, including *The White Company* by Arthur Conan Doyle, the short stories of O. Henry, the collected works of Rudyard Kipling, and Mark Twain's *A Connecticut Yankee in King Arthur's Court.* To gird himself for the lonely and frightening moments at Walter Reed, he memorized the prayer of St. Francis of Assisi:

Lord, make me an instrument of your
    peace,
Where there is hatred, let me sow love;
where there is injury, pardon;
where there is doubt, faith;

522

where there is despair, hope;
where there is darkness, light;
where there is sadness, joy;
O Divine Master, grant that I may not so
    much seek to be consoled as to
    console;
to be understood as to understand;
to be loved as to love.
For it is in giving that we receive;
it is in pardoning that we are pardoned;
and it is in dying that we are born to
    eternal life.

On each visit I made to his bedside, Granddad usually arranged for us to be alone for a while. I think we both knew that the end was approaching and that he would never leave Walter Reed, but he never conceded this fact in conversation. He seemed eager to know whether I was taking in stride the exposure and interest that was falling on me in the 1968 campaign, and if I was being diverted from work and studies that would be more important in the future. Julie and I were on the campaign trail almost nonstop; we would barnstorm through thirty states before it was all over. She had taken a semester off from Smith, but I had remained at Amherst, cutting more classes than Granddad would have liked, a detail I omitted when reporting to him. Granddad asked me to send him the articles and magazine stories that appeared about our campaign efforts and the texts of my talks. I was honorary chair of Youth for Nixon and Granddad was following my activities closely.

"Always take your job seriously," he said repeatedly, "but never yourself." The words were those of his mentor, Fox Conner. "The years ahead of you might be the most important of your life," Granddad told me. "Don't be afraid to reach above yourself, to associate yourself with people you know are better than you are in some respects — some call it apple polishing, but it's really the only way you learn anything in this world."

He had suggestions about the campaign. "The word these Republicans should be using is 'progressive,' " the most conservative man to be president in the twentieth century kept saying to me. The difference between Eisenhower and so-called conservative Republicans, I kept thinking as I watched him, was that with Eisenhower conservatism was something animated by a progressive and generous spirit, a desire to improve life. Although he considered the big issue in 1968 to be "law and order," he was careful to add that the party must not abandon its progressive character.

"THIS YEAR I CONSIDER AN EXCEPTION"

In June, following a huge win of 70 percent of the vote in the Oregon primary, where he had faced a tacit coalition of Reagan and Rockefeller, Nixon stood at the threshold of nomination. His opponents had claimed from the start that only by winning contested primaries could Nixon hope to erase his "loser's image" and prove himself worthy of a second chance at the presidency. Nixon had done this. He had won overwhelmingly in New Hampshire, Nebraska, Wisconsin, Indiana, and Oregon.

In shades of 1960, Nelson Rockefeller skirted most of the primaries and adopted many of the themes developed by the Democrats in the race. He chided Nixon for his lack of "specifics" on Vietnam, urging him to reveal his "secret plan" to end the war. He claimed that Nixon did not understand the problems of campus rioting and urban unrest, while Rockefeller, as governor of New York, did. Rockefeller charged Nixon with lack of fervor for civil rights. Following the assassination of Robert Kennedy, Rockefeller launched a nationwide tour in which he appealed to the supporters of the slain senator and positioned himself as the lone voice of compassion in the 1968 campaign.

In the weeks after Nixon's Oregon win, his momentum slowed. Rockefeller moved upward in nationwide polls. Although unwilling to go head to head with Nixon, Rockefeller tried to prove via the Gallup and Harris polls that he stood a better chance of winning the general election in November than did Nixon.

At Walter Reed, Mamie attempted to keep news of the Rockefeller campaign from her husband. But based on information that did reach him, Eisenhower felt that Rockefeller had gone back on his word by attacking Nixon personally, and he disapproved of Rockefellers courting antiwar forces. Eisenhower's 1967 Christmas salvo in which he had threatened to "stump the nation" against "peace at any price" candidates had been aimed at Rockefeller's surrogate George Romney, but as the convention approached, Rockefeller sounded like a man who would end the war by unilateral withdrawal of American troops.

Eisenhower had never entirely forgiven Rockefeller's embrace of the "missile gap" issue or his last-ditch effort before the

Republican National Convention in Chicago in 1960 to wreck the consensus Nixon had achieved within the party. Although the 1968 Rockefeller campaign claimed the support of many Eisenhower loyalists and wealthy friends, it also featured prominent critics of the Eisenhower years. Rockefeller's most trusted adviser was Emmet John Hughes, author of *The Ordeal of Power,* the most critical portrait of Dwight Eisenhower ever written by a former member of his staff. Eisenhower had actually pressured Doubleday to refuse to publish *Ordeal.* Rockefeller's foreign policy adviser was Henry Kissinger, well-known for his books on nuclear strategy and foreign policy published in the late 1950s, which were critical of Eisenhower's policies. Kissinger never concealed his lack of enthusiasm for the Eisenhower presidency.

In early June, Eisenhower reconsidered his rule of unbending neutrality in all pre-nomination races. He had come to view Nixon in an increasingly favorable and friendly light. Kevin McCann, a strong Nixon supporter, had kept the Nixon camp confidentially informed of Eisenhower's political thinking for almost a year. Back in May 1967, he had called Nixon's personal secretary Rose Mary Woods, after Eisenhower and Nixon had talked on the phone, to report that his boss felt "more kindly towards Nixon than ever." Nixon had been thoughtful enough to attend an exhibition of Eisenhower paintings opening at the Huntington Hartford Gallery in New York City.

Mamie's views were uncomplicated. The Nixon campaign was a family matter. An all-out supporter of the Nixons, Mamie kept a large glass bowl of Nixon buttons on the table next to her chair in her small bedroom at Walter Reed. Because she suffered from claustrophobia, she kept the door open and anyone passing by, staff and visitors alike, was hailed and handed a Nixon button. Sometimes this required visitors to be polite. For instance, Milton Eisenhower had strong ties to Nelson Rockefeller. Yet when Julie and I encountered Milton's homeward-bound family in the elevator leading to Ward Eight one evening, all of them were rather sheepishly wearing Nixon buttons. According to General Clay, "a day did not go by when Mamie did not ask her husband to support Nixon."

Bryce Harlow began dropping by Walter Reed regularly on behalf of the Nixon campaign to bolster Nixon's cause with the General. On June 12, Harlow drafted a long memorandum for Eisenhower's perusal in which he strongly recommended that Eisenhower erase any possible public doubts about his feelings toward Nixon by endorsing him prior to the convention. Before he could read Harlow's memo, however, Eisenhower suffered what was diagnosed as a mild heart attack. For three weeks, his visits were confined to immediate family.

On July 2, Kevin McCann visited Eisenhower in Walter Reed and showed him a newspaper column that claimed that according to "insiders," Eisenhower leaned strongly toward Nixon. On the phone with Rose Mary Woods, McCann reported that Eisenhower "was delighted." On July 12, Eisenhower appeared to be ready to issue an endorsement. Harlow's argument — that a preconvention endorsement would enhance and not detract from any support he could render a candidate in the fall elections — made increasing sense to him. He was eager to do something that would please the family. Mamie had announced her support publicly; Dad had become cochairman of "Citizens for Nixon" in Pennsylvania; and like Dad, Granddad had fallen in love with Julie. He kept a small photo of her by his bedside, and was fond of showing it to visitors. "Isn't that the picture of an angel," he once remarked to McCann.

On July 13, Eisenhower asked Harlow to assemble any material he could find on the Nixon campaign in order to review Nixon's position on the issues. On the 14th, Eisenhower met with Ray Bliss, chairman of the national Republican Party, to discuss plans for a scheduled televised appearance before the convention to be filmed from Ward Eight. Eisenhower sounded out Bliss about a preconvention endorsement. That afternoon, Harlow sent a message to Nixon through Rose Mary Woods reporting "things are moving apace on DDE," and informed her that Eisenhower wished to see him.

Nixon arrived in Washington the following morning. On the way to the hospital, Harlow recommended that Nixon "lay it on the line" with the General and ask him for his support outright. Although Nixon led in most delegate tallies, a Rockefeller-Reagan coalition was gathering steam. An Eisenhower endorsement would swing some momentum in Nixon's direction.

Nixon, however, found himself unable to ask Eisenhower face-to-face for his support. The two men had a long and friendly talk about the campaign, but did not discuss an endorsement. Instead, on the plane back to

New York, Nixon wrote his former boss a letter formalizing his request for help. He referred to an apparent agreement reached between Harlow and Eisenhower that the General would announce his support of Nixon before the balloting on August 6. He felt that this might be too late to render any assistance against the Rockefeller and Reagan forces that would have failed or succeeded by the time the convention opened. "In other words," he wrote, "we face the distinct possibility that in the public mind the decision would have been made before your endorsement was announced. . . ."

He concluded: "I hesitate to bring these additional facts up for consideration because I shall indeed be most grateful for your announcement of support whenever it comes. In view of our discussion, however, I felt that you should know of these possibilities since they bear on the critical question of the timing of your announcement and the relationship of that timing to the effect . . . on the voters in November."

A day later, Harlow reported to Woods that "things went quite well" regarding the letter, with all indications being that Eisenhower's endorsement will happen "in the next few days." Nixon and Eisenhower spoke by phone and discussed the mechanics of an endorsement. Nixon felt that the General should read it in person — if possible — to achieve the strongest impact.

On July 18, 1968, Eisenhower endorsed Nixon for the Republican nomination from the living room at Walter Reed. Seated in a wheelchair in front of cameras and microphones, he appeared thin and feeble, but his voice was strong and he smiled generously for the benefit of the cameras.

"Ever since I entered politics," he began, "in order to help maintain unity within the Republican Party, I have deliberately followed a policy of avoiding endorsement for any office, of one Republican candidate over another prior to his official selection by a primary or nominating convention."

He continued:

This year I consider an exception. The issues are so great, the times so confusing, that I have decided to break personal precedent. . . . I support Richard M. Nixon as my party's nominee. I do so not only because of my appreciation of the distinguished services he performed for this nation during my administration, but even more because of my admiration of his personal qualities: his intellect, acuity, decisiveness, warmth, and above all his integrity. I feel that the security, prosperity, and solvency of the United States and the cause of world peace will best be served by placing Dick Nixon in the White House in January, 1969. . . .

The reporters present asked the General whether his family had in any way influenced his decision. Specifically, they asked whether Julie or I had attempted to talk him into supporting Nixon. He replied with a twinkle, "I think they tried."

Within the week, a Gallup poll taken shortly after Eisenhower's endorsement was published showing that, for the first time in two years, Nixon ran stronger than Rockefeller against every Democratic hopeful in the field. Rockefeller's claim to be the GOP's only hope for winning in November was shaken, if not ruined. Julie, euphoric, wrote:

July 29 flew to Wash DC to attend Girls Nation reception. Michael McCarthy [son of Eugene McCarthy] also attended. Seemed like a nice shy boy. He was ill at ease. Felt sorry for him in the midst of all these rather aggressive "senators" of Girls Nation. David and I got excellent news notices the next day. . . . Then drove to Walter Reed to DDE and Mrs E. I've never enjoyed a visit with them more. They were so warm and seemed happy. General E commented on the ring (engagement) and kissed me. He seemed so pleased we are all thrilled with his endorsement and said that if it had really helped, he couldn't be a happier man. He looked very well. When I told him that Gary Weisband [a Secret Service agent assigned to Julie's detail] was from Abilene, Kansas, he wanted to meet him. Gary was so pleased — the General even liked David's hair. . . .

When we said goodbye to Mrs. E after leaving the General, she told us how sad she was that he would probably not be able to play golf any more. She also told us how she had told him what a good patient he had been and he replied that he guessed he wanted to live a little longer. Tears came to her eyes. She wants to keep him with her.

D and M were waiting for us when we got home . . . then we left for North Carolina. Daddy called to tell us about the Gallup poll results which showed him doing better than Rocky. We all concluded that Rocky was through.

"THE VICTORY IS YOURS, TOO"

By early August, Eisenhower's health appeared to be improving. On August 2, the Johnsons stopped by just before leaving for Texas and the LBJ Ranch. Lady Bird Johnson wrote in her diary:

Lyndon went directly in to see the General. Mrs. Eisenhower said to Lyndon, in the most graceful manner, "You'll leave your girl out here to talk to me, won't you?" . . . Mrs. Eisenhower was wearing a light, fluttery, green and blue summer dress. She was vivacious, cheerful, pretty — all good qualities in a woman. What a lucky man he is to have her constantly by his side! She said she stayed right with him all the time. "I know the General would worry so about me if I were out at the farm." She showed me her room. It was tiny, almost like a monk's cell, the only touch of luxury a soft, delicate, velvet coverlet. She said airily, "I brought my own comfort."

During our conversation, she expressed several times her desire to get free from "things." . . . I spoke up for any items of real family closeness for use in the little house in Denison where President Eisenhower was born, now a museum. And I told her how wonderful it was to me that they had turned over, in their lifetime, their home in Gettysburg to the National Park Service . . . then we talked of grandchildren, of movies — a thoroughly easy, pleasant, delightful hour.

On August 4, Eisenhower reiterated his endorsement of Richard Nixon when he spoke via closed circuit to the Republican National Convention. Dressed in a blue sport jacket and tanned by a sunlamp that had been wheeled into his suite that afternoon, Eisenhower delivered an upbeat greeting in which he urged the Republicans on to victory in the fall. Seated with Julie in the Nixon box at the convention center in Miami, I noted that the speech did not arouse an ovation from the delegates comparable to the one that had earlier greeted Barry Goldwater. But after six months of attending campaign events, I had grown used to the prevalent Republican criticisms of Eisenhower: that as president he had sided with Democrats on many of the party's gut issues, including McCarthyism, and that he had failed to dismantle the New

Deal. Much of the anti-Eisenhower sentiment had formed inalterably during his fight with Taft for the nomination. Taft's organization had succeeded in convincing a segment of the party that Eisenhower had been pro-Russian during the war, an ally of the Truman administration after the war, a dangerous internationalist, and a figurehead whose tenure had postponed the showdown between conservative and liberal thinking.

But Granddad's televised statement left a profound impression on the wider listening audience, prompting Hugh Sidey to write in *Life:*

It has been one of those mysteries of national life why all would-be Presidents . . . who have been frantically searching for some formula to catapult themselves to the heights of popularity have failed to study the example of Eisenhower. Perhaps in this age of contrivance it is too simple to be believed — decency, sincerity, and honesty. It shines out of Ike like a beacon . . . it illustrates anew that all the programs espoused and the bills passed and the billions spent are only a part of this thing of being President and maybe even the lesser part in a time of dispirited affluence.

At 6 A.M. the following day, Eisenhower suffered a heart attack that brought him to the threshold of death. The family was summoned to the hospital for the last visit. Unlike the previous six heart attacks, no muscle damage to the heart was evident. Rather, his heart went into ventricular fibrillations — wild pulsations that failed to pump blood. For eight days, teams of doctors and nurses labored around the clock through fourteen such attacks, each of which technically killed him. With the use of electrodes fastened to his chest, doctors electronically shocked his heart muscle back into rhythm and normal functioning. Granddad lost consciousness during each of these attacks, but upon being revived, he miraculously recovered his cognitive functions unimpaired.

The teamwork of the men and women assigned to save his life was inspiring. Night and day they labored like artists over a canvas, intervening against nature to extend Granddad's life. Over the several days, we were permitted visits of no longer than three to five minutes each.

He lay under a machine he called the

"bulldozer," his eyes black on account of the dilation of his pupils caused by the experimental drugs he had authorized. He was in too much pain to speak more than a word or two. His face was barely visible under the machine, which rose three feet above his bed — his entire body was laced with tubes and needles.

The doctors at Walter Reed began receiving letters protesting the extraordinary measures to preserve a single life when health care for the poor and indigent throughout the country was so inadequate. Walter Reed also received more than twenty offers from individuals willing to donate their hearts if Eisenhower could receive a transplant. These amazing offers were gratefully declined with the explanation that Eisenhower's physique could not tolerate a transplanted heart. Granddad was in pain, but the doctors reminded us that the pain was his decision.

"With him," General Heaton recalled, "you never killed hope." When Eisenhower was conscious, Heaton would stand by the bed and tease him about the golf strokes he would now get from his friends. With a breathless chuckle, Granddad would rasp, "and from you, Leonard."

Miraculously, he survived the fourteen attacks and began a long road back to recovery. For three weeks, he was restricted to sitting up along the side of his bed for three brief periods each day. He received several short visits from the family. For most of the day he lay on his back listening to records on the stereo, many of them previously donated to Walter Reed by John Foster Dulles. Mamie kept him supplied with his favorite show tunes, particularly anything written by Rodgers and Hammerstein. Granddad's favorite, played endlessly, was "Climb Every Mountain" from *The Sound of Music*.

While Eisenhower recuperated, the world changed again. The Soviets invaded Czechoslovakia; the Democrats nominated Vice President Hubert Humphrey amid raucous and at times violent antiwar protests outside their convention in Chicago; and Nixon, on the strength of his convention success, opened an early sixteen-point lead in the presidential race. Humphrey, in desperation, finally broke ranks with the Johnson administration's timetable in Vietnam with a speech in Salt Lake City on September 30, indicating his openness to pursuing a total bombing halt north of the 17th parallel. With the segregationist Wallace running as a third-party candidate and polling as high as 20 percent, the race began to tighten.

On Eisenhower's seventy-eighth birthday, October 14, Americans caught their final glimpse of the General. As part of "Eisenhower Week," the Army band stationed at Fort Myer was ordered to Walter Reed to serenade the Eisenhowers from below the windows of Ward Eight. Eisenhower had recovered sufficiently to observe the concert from a wheelchair. With the news that he would appear at the window, television and news photographers hastened to capture the moment on film. As the band began to play, Eisenhower appeared in his wheelchair waving a miniature five-star flag in thanks. Standing over him, Mamie joined in waving to the small crowd and the cameras below.

By late October, Nixon's large lead over Humphrey had evaporated, and the election was heading toward a climax reminiscent of 1960. By October 31, the tension was unbearable. That Halloween night, Lyndon Johnson intervened in the campaign with a speech announcing the cessation of bombing above the 17th parallel in Vietnam. In the words of a national reporter, "Johnson gave Nixon a trick and Humphrey a treat." Returning from a Madison Square Garden rally that had taken place during the speech, Nixon telephoned longtime adviser and Reagan lieutenant governor Bob Finch for a rapid analysis of its impact. "Well," Nixon began, "I suppose the best that can be said is that the worst is over." He paused anxiously: "Bob, how bad in your opinion was it?"

At Walter Reed, Leonard Heaton and Mamie prepared Eisenhower for Nixon's defeat. Julie and I had campaigned in California with the Nixons the last two days of the race and flew with them on election eve to New York to await the returns. The closeness of the vote meant no one could sleep. At 3 A.M. I left the family suite and went down to campaign manager John Mitchell's headquarters on the floor below to wait out the too-close-to-call vigil. I fell asleep on the floor around dawn and awoke around 8 A.M. to hear Mitchell on the phone with a high-ranking Democratic official in Chicago. The networks were refusing to call Illinois for Nixon. As in 1960, Cook County returns were being withheld until the Daley machine saw the numbers come in from Republican-leaning southern Illinois. But unlike 1960, the Nixon organization was prepared. Republicans this time were withholding Lake County in southern

Illinois. No amount of doctoring of returns in Cook County would swing Illinois against Nixon this year. I listened as Mitchell blandly set forth the facts by telephone, urging the Daley official to release Cook County and to be done with the suspense, which had mounted all evening over the Illinois outcome.

Meanwhile, Theodore White, author of *The Making of the President, 1960,* who was covering the election as a special correspondent for NBC News, accused John Connally, then Democratic governor of Texas, of voting irregularities in his state. Texas, White reminded Connally, was the scene of alleged vote fraud of such dimensions in 1960 as to taint the entire election. White asked Connally to explain why again in 1968 Harris County, a solidly Republican stronghold, was experiencing such difficulty with its voting machines. Before Connally could mount an effective reply, NBC interrupted to declare Illinois in the Nixon column, barely minutes after Mitchell's call to Chicago.

Nixon had long yearned for the moment when he would stand before Eisenhower as a true equal, bearing responsibility for the most complex job in the world. He achieved his goal on November 6 on his own. He had won against formidable odds: the hostility of many in the press corps; skepticism from the left and right wings of his party; the taint of two defeats; the lack of a political base; and lukewarm acceptance among the financiers of Republican Party politics.

That afternoon, Lyndon Johnson dispatched an Air Force cargo plane to transport the Nixon family to Washington for a stopover visit with Eisenhower before they made their way south to Key Biscayne and a vacation. Mamie greeted us with champagne. Julie and I preceded Nixon into Granddad's suite. Seeing us, he leaned up, hiding tubes running from his left arm under a sheet. He beamed with indescribable joy. Nixon, outside the door, fussed with his tie and his hair before presenting himself to his former boss. As he entered, Eisenhower feebly raised his arms in a boxer's salute. "Congratulations, Dick!" he exclaimed.

"The victory is yours, too, General," Nixon replied hoarsely. Eisenhower and Nixon clasped hands in greeting.

The nurses and doctors hovered nervously over the electronic monitor for signs of stress. Clearly, Granddad's feelings registered on the EKG. Julie and I were summoned out of the room, to leave Eisenhower and Nixon alone. Soon the Nixons were airborne, heading south in the November evening. I returned to Massachusetts aboard a commercial flight. At Walter Reed, the vigil resumed.

The election result temporarily improved Eisenhower's health. Tentative plans were drawn up for the installation of elevators at the Gettysburg office and on the farm to accommodate a wheelchair. Eisenhower also discussed the idea of moving into an apartment near Walter Reed as an outpatient. Mamie felt she could leave Ike's side more often and made plans to return to the farm for a few days. In the euphoria surrounding the election, one could imagine Eisenhower surviving even more heart attacks, becoming ambulatory and resuming his writing. In December and January, he began consulting tentatively with McCann on drafts for his planned book.

In this period, Eisenhower had ideas of becoming senior counsel ex officio to the Nixon administration. Bryce Harlow once commented that depending on your view of Nixon's presidency, Eisenhower's inability to fulfill this role was either fortunate or unfortunate. With Eisenhower to talk to,

Nixon might have avoided the trouble that brought him to grief. He might also have been inhibited from pursuing the creative initiatives he undertook in a détente with the Soviet Union and establishing relations with China. "In any event," Harlow recalled, "one thing is for sure — there would have never been a moment of peace. The General would have been breathing down his neck from start to finish."

Perhaps Nixon would have found a tactful way to ignore his former boss or would have found him an honorary position. Mamie recalls an incident that occurred a few months or so after Granddad's death. She was invited to stay overnight at the White House while in Washington to see friends. Sitting in the West Hall at cocktail hour, Mamie declined being placed in the Queen's Room as President Nixon suggested. She explained that she preferred to stay on the third floor where she could come and go without interfering. Nixon waved away her objections.

"Stay there," he said. "It's right for you."

"Oh, I'd rather stay upstairs, thanks," she replied.

"Mamie, stay there," he replied pleasantly. "I'm the President now."

At Thanksgiving, the Nixon and Eisenhower families gathered at Walter Reed. Granddad, visibly healthier, raised a small glass of champagne to the success of the new administration. In shifts, the family shared one course of the Thanksgiving dinner with Granddad at his bedside. Before and after dinner, Nixon and Eisenhower were locked in conversation concerning the organization of the executive branch. Predictably, Eisenhower expressed concern about the disuse of the NSC, the point of pride he had hurled at Kennedy in the aftermath of the Bay of Pigs. Among other things, Eisenhower pointed out that Kennedy's and Johnson's downgrading of a consultative body like the NSC had led to excessive personalization of the presidency.

Eisenhower lucidly observed that the theatrics of crisis and of presidential decision making had reached new heights during the 1960s. Every problem large and small seemed to bring out still photographs of a Lincolnesque president agonizing in his loneliness, silhouetted against the wintry South Lawn. Hovering aides were pictured with faces strained by tension and momentousness, whether pondering telephone calls from military control points or taking calls from legislative aides pushing some innocuous resolution. Americans were losing an appreciation for what mattered and what did not concerning presidential leadership. Too many vague hopes were being placed on the office.

GLORY

Julie and I decided to go forward with our wedding plans, scheduled for December 22. Granddad offered me one hundred dollars if I would cut my mop of curly hair into a neat military style. Just before the wedding, I got a light trim. It wasn't enough for Granddad and he didn't pay.

Julie and I were determined to have as private a wedding as possible. Instead of waiting a month to be married in the White House, we chose the Nixons' New York church, Marble Collegiate, and its pastor, our friend Dr. Norman Vincent Peale. The media was invited only to a photo opportunity at the Plaza hotel at the start of the wedding reception. NBC thoughtfully offered closed-circuit television to carry the ceremony live to Granddad's suite in Walter Reed. Unfortunately, because of technical problems the television transmission failed. Instead, Granddad and Mamie, who was bedridden because of an upper-respiratory infection, listened to the audio of the ceremony as it happened. Granddad and

Mamie sent a telegram expressing "abiding love to each member of both families. As the Spanish would say, *Vaya con Dios.*"

Both remained ill through Christmas, forcing them to skip opening Christmas packages together. Granddad began, at last, to yield to depression. Setback after setback seemed to retard his progress. With the excitement of the election over, he temporarily surrendered to the fact of his hopeless condition. He wrote several friends informing them that he would never again play golf. "My ambition," he told Slater, "is simply to mingle among friends once more."

In Florida one night after Christmas, I was awakened by a call from Walter Reed. Julie and I had been honeymooning for nearly a week. Granddad spoke distinctly on the other end. He had called to check and be sure the young marrieds were "still speaking." He confessed he was growing weary of the hospital, but said that he still clung to respectable odds of partial recovery.

During our long chat, Julie, listening at first, fell back asleep as we drifted from everyone's hopes for the new administration to my married future in Massachusetts. He was relieved that his grandchildren had survived the moral chaos of high school and college, and that we apparently retained a sense of responsibility despite the confusion and temptation confronting every young person these days. I reassured him that when my college deferment expired, I would enter military service. At 11 P.M., Granddad explained that he had been speaking in low tones to avoid detection by the attendant who monitored his heartbeat thirty feet away. "Past my bedtime," he concluded, saying good-bye.

To make sense out of his dreary circumstances, Eisenhower began a "hospital diary." In it, he planned to summarize the months spent in bed to date, the measures used to keep him alive, the personalities who cared for him, and the visits by outsiders. In doing so, he hoped to break the monotony, the blurring of night and day, the feeling of motionlessness he had in being confined to the same bed and the same room.

He began with an explanation:

I started this diary on January 14, the day that Sgt. Moaney and Delores gave it to me. Then I discovered that if I expected to write a hospital diary, I'd have to establish a background. This I tried to do on the pages designed for Jan

12–13, but next I discovered I'd under-estimated the space needed. While I had intended, on those pages, to give a summary of my sojourn in the hospital, I found this an impossible task within the space allotted. So now I shall try to do so here.

Meticulously, point by point, name by name, Eisenhower attempted to situate himself and to reconstruct his experience at Walter Reed. He recorded in technical language some of the extreme measures taken to spare his life. In grateful, matter-of-fact words, Eisenhower described his world and the people in it:

Walter Reed is a large hospital, something over 1200 beds. Moreover the Army Medical Corps is now quite large — and here are concentrated the Army's finest specialists. In surgery, these are Heaton (also the Commanding General of the Corps), Hughes, Bough, and Kempe (head and brain). Then there is Col. Moses, head of the Medical Department, and Col. Robert Hall, Chief Cardiologist. His assistants are several, the principal one being Lt. Col. Jules Bedynek. . . .

After profiling the doctors, Eisenhower turned to his favorite subject, the nurses:

Major Susanne Phillips, R.N., is the head nurse on my ward. The turnover in the medical corps is rapid, and the junior nurses on my ward are typical of the trend. Already transferred or discharged from my group of five (including Major Phillips) during the past eight months are Major Rolfe, Major Noorman, Captains Floates and Gurney, and Lt. Enderles. The only two nurses who have been with me throughout are Major Phillips and Captain Uhler.

Happily these two are among the finest nurses I've met. Highly qualified professionally, and possessed of a delicious sense of humor.

During my worst days in August, when as the doctors later told me they had no idea what might happen the next minute, these two seemed almost always on duty. Certainly they did much to keep up my spirits.

Will write later . . .

The same day he added, "Mamie, who has stayed close by my side for all these months, has gone to the farm. She left Monday the 13th."

Eisenhower gradually emerged from the doldrums. His entry on the 16th reads: "As usual, when I try to keep a diary, I have completely forgotten its existence. So I shall try to put down on the intervening days such items as I can recall. Visitor today — General Gruenther."

Meanwhile, the Gallup poll again named Dwight Eisenhower the "most admired American." The fourth time he gained that distinction while out of office.

In January, Eisenhower was temporarily transferred several doors down from the presidential suite to a room known as the "Pershing Suite," occupied by General Pershing during his long terminal illness in 1948. At first, Eisenhower's transfer was misunderstood. When informed, President-elect Nixon, suspecting that the hospital was letting down or losing interest, dispatched an aide from the transition office to find out the reasons. General Heaton explained that the presidential suite was long overdue for renovation and that General Eisenhower had cheerfully consented to the move.

Meanwhile, Nixon instructed his cabinet designees to pay courtesy calls on Eisenhower at Walter Reed. One by one old and new faces, many veterans of the Eisenhower administration, arrived daily to listen to Eisenhower's views on the function of the cabinet, the subcabinet, staff work, and national priorities. Each one arrived eager to lift Eisenhower's spirits, and one after another left amazed by his vitality and his keen interest in their jobs.

Personal friends, not persuaded by Eisenhower's brave optimism, dropped by to bid him farewell. Robert Anderson, Eisenhower's fragile though spirited secretary of the Treasury, chatted with his boss for forty-five minutes, which was fifteen minutes beyond the "absolute" time limit imposed by Eisenhower's doctors. As Anderson rose to leave, Eisenhower motioned him close.

"You are one of three men to ever disagree with me to my face," Eisenhower disclosed, clasping Anderson's hand.

Flattered, Anderson paused. "Mr. President, would you mind telling me who were the other two?"

"Never mind," Eisenhower replied. "Just know that you are one of the three."

In late January, Eisenhower received General Mark Wayne Clark. Like Eisenhower, Clark had been one of the "young men," in Marshall's words, who would run and win World War II. By an eyelash, Eisenhower and not Clark had been chosen to command OVERLORD, in charge of the greatest military operation in history, set on the path to immortality. Had Clark and not Eisenhower commanded the Normandy landings, perhaps their personal histories might have been reversed.

Clark buried his disappointment regarding OVERLORD, argued faithfully for a greater share of the military resources for his Italian theater, and led the triumphant Allied force into Rome the day before D-Day. In May 1945, he received the surrender of German armies on the Italian front.

Clark loved Eisenhower "like a brother" and regretted that they had been estranged briefly after a dispute over Clark's request to command a corps before the seizure of Tunis. For years, Clark relived the estrangement. To me, he revealed that many times he had awakened at night, dreaming he heard Ike's crisp voice over a phone ordering him "to keep your shirt on." Compounding the change in their friendship was Eisenhower's elevation to the presidency. Clark explained, "He had always been 'Ike.' Suddenly, it was 'Mr. President.'"

Now there was no point in rehashing wartime misunderstandings. Clark and

Eisenhower instead recalled their shared experience at West Point. Together they chuckled and fibbed about their cadet days, recalling the time Eisenhower had forced Clark to fall out at morning quarters after catching him trying to slip into formation late, and their weekends at the Thayer Hotel, where Clark's mother became a foster parent to many of the cadets. As Clark left at the prompting of doctors, Eisenhower called out to him, "Write a book about the things you and I did together, in North Africa — our decisions, Wayne." Clark promised he would.

On Inauguration Day, Julie and I were together again, twelve years after the first time, on the reviewing stand watching the military might of the United States parade before the President of the United States. In its coverage the day after the Nixon inauguration, the *Washington Post* reported that I looked pale and haggard, probably because I had pulled three all-nighters in order to finish several papers at Amherst.

After the inauguration, Julie and I went back to college. As frequently as we could, we flew to Washington to visit Granddad, often with Tricia. In the course of our visits, Granddad grew increasingly fond of Tricia. Granddad always had an eye for a pretty girl, and the blond, petite Tricia delighted him. With every announcement that Julie and I would visit the hospital, a request would come back through the Secret Service that we bring Tricia.

For that matter, Eisenhower appreciated all the women on Ward Eight. He enjoyed flirting and doted over the nurses like a kind of rich uncle. Suspicious of Eisenhower's magnetism with women, Mamie monitored the nurses like a hawk. Major Phillips, a slim, pert redhead, was Granddad's favorite. She aroused a slight jealousy in Mamie. Years later, Mamie recalled, "He was an old man, but after all he'd survived, you never knew."

On February 21, 1969, when Granddad learned it was Tricia's twenty-third birthday, he invited her to drop by. Several hours before she was to arrive, barium tests revealed that he might be suffering an acute recurrence of the ileitis condition he had had as president. The visit was canceled.

In the meantime, however, Granddad dispatched General Schulz to a flower shop to find an old-fashioned bouquet appropriate for a "beautiful gal." At four o'clock, Schulz arrived at the White House bearing a perfectly round arrangement of pink and white sweetheart roses laced with baby's breath and long pink streamers. Schulz had been ordered to deliver the flowers personally. Schulz located Tricia and Mrs. Nixon in the Yellow Oval Room on the second floor. He arrived agitated. At attention, he thrust the bouquet toward Tricia. Schulz officially pronounced: "Ma'am, I had a shaky morning. The General sent me back twice before he was satisfied with my choice. He wishes you a happy birthday."

Although Granddad's diary narrative is sketchy, its closing entries record a partial list of his activities:

Jan 17   Visitor. Sec. Designate Mitchell [Attorney general designee] . . . at 10:00 AM.
Governor Volpe [secretary-designate of transportation] came in about 3:00 PM.
Admiral Strauss a little later . . .

Jan 18   J.S.D.E. [John Eisenhower] visited about half an hour . . .

Jan 19   George Allen in the morning . . .
David and Julie came about noon (Mr. and Mrs. DDE II)
Tom Pappas [Greek-American busi-

nessman] came in also . . . then John and Barbie. Fine day.

Jan 20   Inauguration Day
Walter Annenberg came to see me.
It is planned to send him to Court of St. James as our Ambassador . . .

Jan 21   General Snyder came to see me briefly . . .
Then Mr. Shakespeare [Nixon's U.S. Information Agency appointee].
David, Julie and Tricia came in for a long talk. I love them all.

Jan 22   Charles Jones and Robert Anderson

Jan 23   David and Julie stopped by for an hour on way to farm . . . General Goodpaster and Dr. Kissinger . . . Mrs. Westmoreland dropped in about 5:30 to say goodbye . . .

Jan 24   Robert B. Mayo, Dir. of the Bureau of the Budget . . .
General Wayne Clark . . .

Jan 25   Justin Dart . . . George Champion . . .

Milton came in immediately afterward.

Eisenhower's final entry, at the end of January, reads:

> As usual, my diary has not even entered in my mind for 10 days. My last daily entry was the 16th. Boots Adams came in to see me at 10:30 AM.
>
> I have gone back over intervening days and gotten lists of my visitors and entered their names. Now, I shall probably go back and comment about their visits. . . . The doctors called to say Mamie's tests were O.K. I called to relay the news.

The hour was growing late. After one family visit, my mother tearfully asked us to forget what we were seeing at Walter Reed, to remember Dwight Eisenhower as we had known him in Gettysburg, as robust and active, committed to everything he undertook at the farm, to his friends, his family, his work, his painting. Of course we would remember that, I thought, but seeing him in Walter Reed was important, too. It rounded out the picture of a great man whose like we would not see again. Illness had stripped away the exteriors, exposing his spirit — serene, beautiful, and unafraid.

Two days after Tricia's birthday, General Heaton performed last-resort abdominal surgery on Eisenhower, estimating his chances of surviving the operation at less than even. Though the surgery was successful, the postoperative shock was the decisive turn in Eisenhower's health.

At first, he made gradual progress, and resumed seeing visitors. The family, hovering nearby, dispersed to go about its business. I had returned to Amherst and made plans to travel over spring break to Miami, Florida, where our singing group, the Zumbyes, had a week of bookings at hotels and clubs.

On the drive to Florida, my friends and I broke the trip with a brief stopover at the White House. Apparently the hospital had been attempting to reach me for several hours. Granddad was suffering congestive heart failure and would soon be gone. I was instructed to go on to Florida, and when the time drew near, transportation north would be available.

From the White House, we sped south through the night past Chancellorsville, Appomattox, Spotsylvania, Petersburg, and other battlefields dotting the outskirts of Richmond, where the Union armies slowly strangled the Confederacy. By dawn we were in South Carolina, then Augusta, then traveling south along Interstate 95 through Georgia, past Thomasville, the city awakening in green to a soft spring morning.

In places I-95 was incomplete, affording one a glimpse of rural Georgia's abandoned thatch huts mounted on stilts to escape run-off water, once family dwellings for thousands of black tenant farmers who had migrated north to the cities during the Depression. On the drive, I remembered how Granddad, Mamie, and the Moaneys had loved the South. At Augusta and Thomasville, the Eisenhowers had enjoyed the companionship of America's financial aristocracy and the astonishing beauty of springtime in the South. But a few miles away, the interstate highway system, pioneered by the Eisenhower administration, was slowly making inroads into Augusta-style feudalism, paving the way north to the outside world.

By evening of the second day, we approached Fort Lauderdale and the high-rise dwellings, fast food chains, and ribbons of commuter highways. Julie joined me in Miami just in time for the dreaded phone call from Walter Reed summoning us back to Washington.

The trip south had taken thirty-six hours

by car. As we flew north, the entire panorama of Georgia, South and North Carolina, and Virginia whisked under our window in less than three hours.

Meanwhile, a team of surgeons and cardiologists labored around the clock to arrest the deterioration of Eisenhower's condition. Throughout, his mind remained unimpaired by painkilling drugs and shock treatments. Every several hours, the doctors permitted him to receive a short visit.

In farewell, Eisenhower told his brother Milton that he had "always valued his counsel." He drew comfort from his last visit with Billy Graham, who, weeks before en route to South Vietnam for a visit with the troops, detoured to Walter Reed. Though Eisenhower did not know Graham well, he remained powerfully impressed by the evangelist's persuasive certainty about the mysteries of faith. At Eisenhower's request the previous fall, Graham had become an intermediary between Eisenhower and Nixon to heal what the General felt was a slight barrier that had grown up between the men during the campaign.

Eisenhower had greeted Graham with a question about heaven and a talk they had had fourteen years earlier in Gettysburg. Emotionally Graham repeated for Eisenhower what he had said to him before, reminding Eisenhower of God's promise of salvation, and the ways this promise is revealed in scripture. The two men shared a brief prayer.

Barely ten feet away, partitioned by the thin wall separating her room from Granddad's suite, Mamie sat dressed and alert for a moment's opportunity to slip in for a visit. She slept fitfully and never for more than an hour or two. When the doctors informed her that her husband was ready for a short visit, Mamie, denied all privacy, would hurry past the half dozen nurses and attendants monitoring every breath and pulse beat to a small chair at Granddad's bedside.

Eisenhower, because of his humble origins, or perhaps because of his past vulnerability with Ruby Norman, had long ago resolved never to reveal weakness to his wife. With her now, he refused to concede that he was failing. He tried, futilely, to persuade the doctors to withhold news from her about his situation and strictly forbade his wife to speak morbidly. Finally, he conceded. Prone, under the "bulldozer" life support machine and flanked by Heaton, Major Phillips, and several nurses, Eisenhower scolded her for any remorse about their life together. "Now Mamie," he growled, "don't forget that I have always loved you."

Moments before Julie and I arrived at the hospital, my father slipped into Granddad's room to report that the doctors had detected progress in the forty-eight hours since they had declared him hopeless. Granddad's eyes rolled in anguish. "I've had enough, John. Tell them to let me go."

I went into Granddad's room, bearing a new record my singing group had just cut for our tour of Miami. His head was barely visible under the maze of wires and the metal equipment. The room was dark and illuminated only by the bright colored dials and monitors, which cast a Christmas tree effect. Granddad's eyes were almost black, dilated by the darkness and by morphine. Tubes clearing away the fluid building in his chest kept him from speaking. His eyes flashed recognition, surprise, a trace of fear, and then happiness.

"Brought you a record," I said. He nodded slightly, then gazed hard at the stereo, an order to put it on.

I told him about our trip to Florida. "Julie's here," I reported. He glanced at the door. A doctor standing in a recess shook his head no. "She will drop by tonight," I added. I told him to listen for the fifth song

— my solo. I grabbed his hand, kissed him, and left.

Day and night merged. For hours, each time I slipped back into the room, the record played, automatically reloading and replaying, unnoticed by the team of surgeons in his suite.

Medical bulletins being issued from Walter Reed indicated that the end was near. For a year, senseless violent deaths and assassinations had plagued the nation. Americans had become conditioned to the cadence of tragedy: the gunshots from an unexpected corner, the sudden confusion, the hospital vigil, the television news specials, the presidential proclamations and commissions formed to investigate the causes of this brutality, the long funeral processions and eloquent memorial tributes, and the editorials about the chaos that threatened our way of life. Now the nation prepared for a death that made sense. A long suffering would end. A complete life, rich in its varied accomplishments, satisfactions, and triumphs, would be celebrated and not mourned. A person who had embodied attributes that propelled the country toward its position of postwar preeminence would leave the world stage.

That evening in the White House, with news of Eisenhower's imminent death, Nixon speechwriter Raymond Price began drafting a eulogy that the President would deliver at the Capitol Rotunda memorial service. The eulogy praised Dwight Eisenhower, like George Washington, as "First in War, First in Peace, and First in the Hearts of his Countrymen." This phrase in Price's draft would survive Nixon's editing, though Nixon would rewrite almost all the rest of it in his own words.

Senators Frank Church of Idaho and William Proxmire of Wisconsin, the latter a member of the Senate disarmament subcommittee, prepared statements reminding the American people that Eisenhower had warned against a military industrial complex. In keeping with his memory, both senators in the coming days would urge rejection of the proposed Anti-Ballistic Missile (ABM) project. In fact, several months earlier, Eisenhower had privately told President Nixon that he opposed the ABM project. Using one of his favorite analogies, Eisenhower compared the ABM to "Hadrian's wall." Drawing a lesson from history, Eisenhower had noted that building walls to keep invaders out never worked. Internally, it signaled a decline in confidence in social values and cohesion. Eventually, it invited invasion, he believed.

At the LBJ Ranch in Austin, Texas, a melancholy Lyndon Johnson drafted a statement beginning: "A giant of our age is gone." Four days later, he would stalk Eisenhower's funeral in Abilene like a ghost, barely noticed by many, eyes glistening in sorrow at the passing of a good friend.

In Independence, Missouri, Harry Truman wrote a statement conceding antagonism between himself and Eisenhower over the years. Nonetheless, Truman concluded, "I cannot forget his services to his country and to Western Civilization."

In Paris, Charles de Gaulle made plans to attend the funeral, selecting the uniform of the Free French to wear in honor of his and Eisenhower's service together during the war.

In England, Germany, and throughout the world, royalty and dictators alike prepared tributes to be placed in American embassies under a portrait of Eisenhower that would be hung in his memory.

The *New York Times* had twice endorsed Dwight Eisenhower for the presidency in his campaigns against Adlai Stevenson. But in the years since 1956, the *Times* had gradually adopted the view shared by most historians that Eisenhower's presidency had postponed needed action in redressing social injustice. For several years, the *Times* had recoiled at Eisenhower's support of Johnson's Vietnam policy. The editors drafted an affectionate but subdued tribute, calling Eisenhower "an understanding friend" but warning that "when history turns from the much-beloved man to the General and the President, it will naturally turn to a more complicated part of the Eisenhower story."

In Washington, the editors of the *Washington Post* tossed aside the complications in a generous tribute that captured the emotion of the hour:

It is difficult to deal separately with the "General" and the "President," regarding each without relation to the impact of the one image on the other. But it could be argued that "the General" is the greatest figure in American and world history. . . .

. . . [L]ong before his death, Dwight David Eisenhower entered the great gallery of authentic American folk heroes. There he will remain enshrined long after Americans of a new day no longer quite understand the secret of his legend, or the mystery of his myth. Never having seen that bright blue-eyed West Point cadet from Kansas, or the beaming and amiable father figure that became familiar to millions of citizens, the generations hereafter probably will never quite grasp the reasons why he became, and remained until he died, the most popular American of his generation.

Friday, March 28, 1969, dawned like a Sunday morning when as children we had climbed into itchy wool suits for church services and the large family meal at noon. With word from the hospital expected soon, I dressed hurriedly in my black pinstripe suit and Julie in a navy blue dress. The Secret Service drove us to Walter Reed, where we joined my parents, Mamie, and the Moaneys, who had gathered for coffee in the Ward Eight dining room.

Several minutes earlier, Granddad had requested relief from the life-sustaining "bulldozer." His attendants removed the tubings and the wire. His body, tortured but alive, finally rested free of the apparatus that had extended his life past the November election, our wedding, Dad's best-selling book on the Battle of the Bulge, *The Bitter Woods,* and his appointment by President Nixon to the ambassadorship in Belgium. An oxygen tube ran to Granddad's nose and a small electrode remained fastened on his chest to measure his heartbeat.

Free of the machine, Granddad asked Dr. Heaton and Dr. Hall to place pillows behind his back to seat him semi-upright. The Venetian shades were closed, permitting only small patches of the morning's sunlight to streak the wall above his head. The darkness hid his weakness and afforded him the dignity and privacy he wanted.

Tearfully, all of us in the room next door assured each other that Granddad's fondest wishes had been fulfilled. He had lived a long, happy life and the end of his suffering would be merciful.

At about noon, General Heaton walked into the room to inform my father that the moment had arrived. Dad motioned me into the hall, where he explained that Granddad expected the men of his family to join him in the suite as was traditional in the Doud and Eisenhower families. Dad offered to excuse me. "Perhaps this is something you do not want to see," he said emotionally. As he rushed off, I followed, driven by instinct.

Inside the suite, Leonard Heaton, my father, and I formed a line abreast at the foot of Granddad's bed and came to rigid attention. Granddad settled into unconsciousness, but the EKG registered the fact that he was still alive.

Mamie wandered in and out of the room and appeared to be whispering something into his unhearing ears. I stood in amazement. Granddad had passed beyond reach. Nothing more could ever be said. If he had thought of me in the past twenty-four hours, I thought frantically, I hoped he was satisfied that everything between us had been settled. His head tilted gently toward his right shoulder. His face was ashen white. A transparent but impenetrable shield seemed to partition him from everyone in the room.

At 12:35, surrounded by others as always, at peace and in the company of his doctors and his lineal heirs, Dwight Eisenhower died.

Outside the room, Mamie, my mother and sisters, Julie, and the Moaneys sobbed with relief. The Nixons arrived within minutes, dressed in black. Below the window, a military honor guard formed, reminding us of the inexorable ceremonies about to begin.

March 28, 1969, was a sunny spring day in Washington. Although it was a working day, Sixteenth Street leading from Walter Reed to the White House seemed oddly deserted. There were hardly any cars. We made our way rapidly back to the White House, pausing only for traffic lights.

The atmosphere in the city became bright, then festive. Bells tolled from every church. One could trace the progress of the news spreading like an expanding ripple through the federal bureaucracy as the flags were lowered to half staff, one at a time. I wanted to linger and to absorb the moment — the sunshine, the bells, and the flags.

I experienced a startling sense of independence and exhilaration, then loss. The pealing bells affirmed Dwight Eisenhower's greatness, the flags dipped deferentially. The brisk sunshine pointed to the road ahead. But I knew already that I would never be able to look forward, completely.

AFTERWORD

Within seven years of my grandfather's death, I decided to undertake a book about the life and times of Dwight Eisenhower. I began research in the summer of 1976, spending a month in Abilene, Kansas, at the Eisenhower Presidential Library examining documents, the first of five research trips to Abilene between 1976 and 1982. I then embarked on a long journey, mostly by car, to locate private collections about the Eisenhower years and to interview as many associates of Eisenhower as I could. I knew it was important to record firsthand stories about Eisenhower that might otherwise be lost and to interview the individuals who had stood by him in war and peace to gain their assessment of the events and issues that mattered most.

By late spring of 1977, I had paid calls on dozens of associates of Dwight Eisenhower, ranging from generals and cabinet officers to secretaries and personal friends. I met twice with General Omar Bradley, a West Point classmate of Eisenhower's who was his most trusted and important subordinate commander in Europe. I spent a day with General Mark Wayne Clark at the Citadel. I interviewed General Lawton Collins, whose VII Corps had spearheaded the Normandy breakout. Generals Lucius Clay and Alfred Gruenther met with me shortly before their deaths. I continued with Granddad's cabinet and White House associates, including Herbert Brownell, Robert Anderson, Arthur Burns, Sherman Adams, Harold Stassen, Jerry Stephens, and Bryce Harlow. My list of interview subjects included members of his personal staff and friends, people I had known as a child and teenager whose memories of Granddad were as vivid as my own.

The more I researched and conducted interviews, the more I came to realize that World War II was the central event of Granddad's career. He entered politics primarily to consolidate, on both the domestic and international fronts, the victory gained in World War II. I decided that to understand Dwight Eisenhower, I must begin my writing with his wartime command. *Eisenhower at War,* published in 1986, was the result. But as important as the war story is, I knew there was far more to Dwight Eisenhower's life. I had always intended to proceed with other books, including this one about his years in Gettysburg, when I knew him best.

In writing *Going Home to Glory,* I relied heavily on my personal recollections, which run seamlessly from my earliest memories as a child: the summer of 1951, which I spent with Granddad and Mamie in Paris, where he had assumed command of NATO, to his death, which coincided with my twenty-first birthday. The interviews I conducted and the papers I collected in my earlier research proved invaluable to this project.

I have long been indebted to all those who took the time to speak to me. Most of those interviewed in this book are gone, but I gratefully acknowledge their help nonetheless.

Kevin McCann, Granddad's speechwriter, assistant, and consultant on various books and articles, provided indispensable assistance. I interviewed Kevin many times both in Gettysburg and in Phoenix, where he retired in the late 1970s. Kevin provided important materials that I have used, including working drafts of *At Ease* with Granddad's notations in the margins and an unpublished diary that Granddad kept intermittently between early 1942 and late 1948 and gave to Kevin. Shortly before his death, Kevin presented the diary to Julie and me.

In the fall of 1976, I spent three days with Granddad's longtime friend Ellis Slater at the Lost Tree Village, a residential community at the northern tip of Palm Beach, Florida. Shortly after I arrived, he escorted me to a guest room where he had a file cabinet containing diary notes he had made since 1950 chronicling every contact, letter, and conversation with Dwight Eisenhower. One of the themes of his diary was that, like Dwight Eisenhower, Slater considered himself to be one of the "luckiest men" in history, having lived at the zenith of relative American prosperity and influence.

"I haven't looked at them in a long time," he told me with a sigh. He felt, however, that a historian would someday have use for these "notes," which I found to be remarkably detailed, unpretentious, and written in the direct, factual style of a businessman. Slater confided he had been wondering what he should do with the papers for some time. Should he give them to his grandchildren or make a bequest to a local library? I recommended that he bring in a historian to edit them for publication. In time, he would do so.

I met with General Lucius Clay in early 1977, several months before his death. Clay personified the business, financial, and military leadership of the United States in the 1940s and 1950s. He was also unique in that his professional association with Eisenhower spanned all the important phases of Eisenhower's military and political careers. With Clay, I discussed every aspect of their relationship, which dated back to service with General Douglas MacArthur in the Philippines. Clay's insights on Granddad's wartime service were invaluable and I relied heavily on them in the writing of *Eisenhower at War.* Clay was also able to shed important light on Eisenhower's decision to enter politics, on the selection of Earl Warren as chief justice, on Eisenhower's handling of Little Rock and the civil rights issue, and on many other political matters.

Freeman and Jane Gosden were Granddad and Mamie's most treasured friends in their years after the White House. Their many kindnesses and constant presence in Palm Desert made life for the Eisenhowers an unending pleasure. Freeman Gosden's wisdom and his legendary sense of humor enriched Granddad's retirement years. The interviews he granted me and Julie in late 1978 are among the most valuable we conducted. Jane is still a close friend, as are their children Craig and Linda.

I also called on two of the doctors who cared for Granddad in the White House and afterward. From 1945 onward, Granddad's health was precarious, especially after his 1955 heart attack. Physicians were omnipresent in the White House and at the farm, and medical professionals numbered among Granddad's closest associates and friends. Unfortunately, I was not able to interview "Doc" Snyder, the chief White House doctor. A full ten years older than Granddad, he retired in 1961 and died shortly thereafter. Doc Snyder's assistant, Walter Tkach, who became White House physician in the Nixon years, spent hours with Julie and me discussing the long afternoons he sat with Granddad while he painted during his mandatory midday rest. Tkach, one of the gentlest and most generous individuals we have ever known, was a fixture in the Eisenhower White House and an occasional guest at the farm. The same can be said of General Leonard Heaton, surgeon general of the United States, who attended Granddad during his major illnesses as president and supervised his treatment at Walter Reed from 1961 to 1969. I spent a full day with General Heaton at his home near Pinehurst, North Carolina, and came to understand better why this wise and thoughtful man enjoyed the trust and friendship of so many powerful men and women of his era.

Interviews with four ministers who were friends or served as pastors to Dwight and Mamie Eisenhower were key to this book. They helped illuminate Dwight Eisenhower's character and personal philosophy.

The Reverend Billy Graham burst into prominence in the late 1940s and was among those who urged Eisenhower to run for president in 1952. As president, Eisenhower frequently turned to Graham, the most popular southern religious figure in the country by 1956, for assistance and counsel in gaining compliance with the federal court decisions during the school crises of 1956–60. Most of my conversations with Graham centered on the desegregation issue, but, in rereading my notes, I see that Graham, above all others, emphasized the importance of Granddad's spirituality and character as elements of his leadership.

The Reverend Edward L. R. Elson was

minister of the National Presbyterian Church and later chaplain of the Senate. A formidable student of national and international affairs, Elson stressed the importance of Eisenhower's example as president in inspiring the revival of church attendance in the 1950s.

The Reverend James MacAskill of Gettysburg, described in some detail in this narrative, was also very generous with his time. After Granddad's death, MacAskill continued to enthrall Gettysburgians with his Sunday sermons, and he stayed close to Mamie.

Finally, there is a fourth churchman, the Reverend Dean Miller, pastor of the Palm Desert Community Presbyterian Church, where the Eisenhowers worshipped during the winter months they spent in California. At Mamie's suggestion, I contacted him and requested an interview, which was to be one of several Julie and I conducted in California and proved to be among the most valuable conversations we had. Dean Miller was able to describe Granddad's life in Palm Desert and his relationship with the Palm Desert community as no one else could. Like Graham, Elson, and MacAskill, he emphasized that Eisenhower was a military man and a Cold War statesman who maintained his optimism because of his faith in simple truths and his belief in the goodness of others.

Before our interviews with Dean Miller, Julie and I had met him just once, at Granddad's funeral in Abilene, on the blustery early spring morning of April 2, 1969. At Granddad's request, Miller played a major role in the service, which shepherded the family through a very difficult good-bye. Noting the appropriateness of Abilene as the site of Eisenhower's final resting place, Miller said, "Dwight Eisenhower was held in esteem as the first citizen of the world, but he was first a citizen of Abilene, Kansas." It was in Abilene that Dwight and his brothers had been blessed with strong and loving parents who imbued them with the values that enabled the six Eisenhower brothers to serve their nation: dedication to hard work, to education, and to the admonition of Micah "to do justice, and to love kindness and to walk humbly with your God."

I am particularly grateful to my family for their help. My grandmother, Mamie Doud Eisenhower, in countless conversations with Julie and me, regaled us with wonderful memories of her incredible fifty-three years of marriage, from San Antonio, Texas, to posts overseas to the White House and finally to Gettysburg, their first permanent home — and their favorite. Mamie's recollections were vivid reminders of the warmth and security of the Gettysburg farm and of the sense of adventure that permeated each year the Eisenhowers spent together.

I also had many talks with Milton Eisenhower at his home on the campus of Johns Hopkins University. Along with Dad, Milton was Granddad's most trusted friend. Milton, as the lone surviving Eisenhower brother, above all conveyed the sense of how far in life the six boys had traveled and the debt each felt to their parents, to Abilene, and to each other.

My father-in-law, President Richard Nixon, generously made available to Julie and me his diaries and notes covering his vice presidential years, his correspondence with Granddad, and handwritten and dictated notes covering 1961–68. We had long discussions about the Eisenhower years and about the Eisenhower-Nixon relationship in the 1960s.

My father knew Dwight Eisenhower best and is the living authority on every aspect of his life, having been at his father's side for most of the major events of Granddad's life. Dad's insights are fundamental to this narrative. It would be difficult to specify what is most important in all that he has taught me over the years.

I want to say special thanks to two members of my immediate family: my son Alex, whose expert research and editorial skills were key to producing this book; and Julie, my wife of forty-one years, whose help and support are evident on every page of *Going Home to Glory.*

Finally, I greatly appreciate the assistance of Robert Bender at Simon & Schuster whose editorial help made completion of this book possible, and our agent, Alan Nevins, who guided us to the remarkable team at Simon & Schuster.

My uncle Milton had a saying that while the young are impatient to change the world, those who are older wish to recapture the "golden days" of their youth. For me, the years covered in this book were indeed a golden time. I am grateful to have had the opportunity to revisit them, and to tell this story.

NOTES

Abbreviations

DDED: Dwight Eisenhower diaries (1961–69) housed at Eisenhower Presidential Library, Abilene, Kansas

DEP: David Eisenhower Papers, including 1962 European Trip Diary and schedules

EMC: Texts of Eisenhower's post-presidential speeches, posted online by the Eisenhower Memorial Commission

ENC: Eisenhower-Nixon correspondence, 1960–68

JSDE: John Eisenhower Gettysburg office memoranda, 1961–64

JFK: JFK Presidential Library and Museum online; Historical Resources: Speeches; John F. Kennedy Presidential Library telephone logs: Kennedy and Dwight D. Eisenhower: September 10, October 22 and 28, 1962

JNP: Julie Nixon Papers, 1968 Campaign Diary

KMP: Kevin McCann Papers, miscellaneous Dwight Eisenhower book drafts provided by Kevin McCann

LET: Author's personal correspondence with Dwight Eisenhower, 1962–68

MISC: Various documents and memoranda in author's possession

RNP: Richard Nixon Papers, handwritten speech notes, dictations, and meeting records, 1961–68

Surety Diary: Dwight D. Eisenhower diary, kept in National Surety Corporation Diary, 1942 (diary entries 1942–49)

Travel Guide: Dwight D. Eisenhower diary, kept in Executive Record and Travel Guide, 1964 (diary entries all dated in 1967)

PPP: Post-Presidential Papers, Eisenhower Presidential Library; Augusta–Walter Reed Series, which includes correspondence between Presidents Kennedy, Johnson, and Eisenhower and briefing by General Goodpaster and General Wheeler; Papers of C. D. Jackson

1. Gettysburg

"This is the greatest thing": Elise Scharf Fox interview.

"will end with his [Eisenhower's] administration": Time, January 6, 1961.

"scaffolds": Lyon, *Eisenhower: Portrait of the*

Hero, p. 820.

"very nice person": New York Times, January 20, 1961.

"lived in peace": Public Papers of the President 1960–1961, p. 915.

"military industrial complex": Ibid., p. 1038.

"wars of national liberation": Speech delivered January 6, 1961; Western press comments followed in mid-January. See *New York Times,* January 19, 1961.

"always consider": JFK, online speech text, January 9, 1961.

"a hazardous experience": JFK, online speech text, September 14, 1960.

"Only a few generations": JFK, online speech text, January 20, 1961.

"He is wrong in implying": Los Angeles Times, January 21, 1961.

"lean, lucid phrases": Time, January 27, 1961.

"crisis is always an opportunity": Nisbet, *Twilight of Authority,* p. 177.

"Wasn't it sad": Barbara Eisenhower interview.

"hit me like bricks": Milton Eisenhower interview.

"The world was coming to an end": Kevin McCann interview.

"Hi! I'm General Eisenhower": Elise Scharf Fox interview.

"Why are you talking to me": Ibid.

"I want him to see a happy people": Fox, *Hotel Gettysburg,* p. 112.

"Dear Dick and Pat": ENC, letter dated November 9, 1960.

Cuba's leading "banker": *Time,* April 7, 1961.

"fine fellow": John Eisenhower interview.

"nothing Eisenhower wants": General Ted Clifton interview.

"eccentric request": Ibid.

"Hold it up": Ibid.

"I worked all my life": John Eisenhower interview.

"eager to be tried": Schlesinger, *A Thousand Days,* p. 3. The phrase is from a poem by Robert Frost written for but not delivered at the Kennedy inaugural.

"great postponement": See introduction, *John Foster Dulles and the Diplomacy of the Cold War,* edited by Richard Immerman (Princeton: Princeton University Press, 1990).

"Mac [McGeorge Bundy] was presently": Schlesinger, *A Thousand Days,* p. 210.

"The S.O.B.": General Walter Tkach interview.

"Ike and I think": Truman Diary entry, July 25, 1947, quoted in *New York Times,* July 11, 2003.

"Astounding talk at the White House": Surety Diary, entry dated July 25, 1947.

"My amazing conversation": Ibid., entry dated December 31, 1947.

"January 1": Ibid., entry dated January 1, 1948.

"This house gave nine souls to the Confederacy": Allen, *Presidents Who Have Known Me*, p. 12.

By 1961, the Eisenhower farm: See Wolf and Weiland, *Ike: Gettysburg's Gentleman Farmer*, pp. 60–65.

"the Great Divide": Mamie Eisenhower interview.

filled a pinchpenny purse: Ibid.

"Complicating things": Ibid.

a hairdressing shop: Ibid.

"Though Ike was sentimental": Ibid.

1951 film titled: See *Angels in the Outfield*, Internet Movie Database, http://www.imdb.com/title/tt00432861.

on January 19: Ambrose, *Eisenhower: The President*, p. 615.

"invasion": Schlesinger, *A Thousand Days*, pp. 242, 256–57.

"infiltration" by night: Ibid.

"entirely Cuban affair": At Camp David, Kennedy explained to Eisenhower that the American hand was to be "concealed." See Ferrell, *The Eisenhower Diaries*, p. 387.

"wail of SOS's": Schlesinger, *A Thousand*

Days, p. 283.

At first glance: See Nelson, *The President Is at Camp David.*

"Eisenhower noted": MISC, transcript of interview with Dwight Eisenhower on subject of Kennedy and Cuba conducted by Dr. Malcom Moos, November 8, 1996.

"proven his complete unawareness of the job": DDE interview with Dr. Lewis Gerson, University of Connecticut, July 10, 1962; John Eisenhower papers, 1961–64.

The test of JCS opinion: Bryce Harlow interview.

"produce a corpse": Ibid.

"I could understand if he played": Schlesinger, *A Thousand Days,* p. 18.

"It was a delightful lunch": PPP, Augusta–Walter Reed Series.

"Dear Mr. President": Ibid.

"for the sake of history": JSDE, 1961.

"two skunks": Meeting with Fred Friendly, JSDE. In one of their meetings, Eisenhower related an amusing exchange with Kennedy during the transition on the subject of politicians and political campaigning. Eisenhower told Friendly that he had remarked to Kennedy that "any person positively seeking the Presidency is, by so doing, proving his unfitness for the job." According to Ike, Kennedy had

"taken this in good humor," adding "I know this is your opinion." Eisenhower had further told Kennedy that while supporting him on international questions, he reserved all rights to be critical of Democratic domestic policies. "I understand completely," Kennedy had said smiling.

"I don't answer criticism as such": JSDE.

"knowing when to quit": John Eisenhower interview.

"had a dream recently": JSDE; see also *Washington Post,* May 11, 1962.

"Who would ever have imagined": John Eisenhower interview.

The purpose of the meeting: JSDE, minutes of leadership meeting in Gettysburg, May 11, 1961. The phrase "above the battle" comes from the Maurice Stans interview — it reflects the consensus among Eisenhower's advisers who met with him that day. According to the minutes Dad kept, at the close of the meeting Eisenhower read a text of the speech he was planning to deliver at the National Armory on the 1st — to general nods of approval. In the actual speech delivered before more than five thousand Republicans, Eisenhower stressed bipartisanship in foreign policy and adherence to GOP principles in the coming debates on domestic policy. He urged Republicans to look forward, to emphasize the principles of fiscal responsibility, smaller government, and self-reliance, cautioning, "anyone in either party who resorts to irresponsibility when out of power does not deserve the responsibility of power." EMC, text of Eisenhower speech at National Armory, June 1, 1961.

"The passage of years has": Papers of Dwight D. Eisenhower, vol. 21, *Keeping the Peace*, p. 2258.

"Dear General": ENC, July 13 and 25, 1961.

Through former GOP national chairman Leonard Hall: Interview with Leonard Hall.

"In my own mind": ENC, September 11, 1961.

"excellent driver": New York Times, August 10, 1961.

"Years later, I attended": Red Patterson discussion, Anaheim Stadium, 1977.

"a record of personal experiences": Kevin McCann interview. Eisenhower reiterated his personal philosophy about memoir writing in "Afterthoughts," the last chapter of *Waging Peace,* p. 620.

"the intensity of feeling": John Eisenhower, *Strictly Personal,* p. 309.

"Well," Eisenhower reflected: JSDE.

"the brotherhood of man": Ibid.

"Small men made life very": Ibid.

"couldn't think of anything": John Eisenhower interview.

Pershing's obsession: Ibid.

"This does not pretend": Eisenhower, *Waging Peace*, Preface.

"In detail, the memorandum": MISC, document provided by Bryce Harlow.

"Young Turks": The anecdote was one of Granddad's favorites. I have reconstructed it from Granddad's telling of it in a speech delivered before the National Defense Executive Reserve Conference on November 14, 1957, as he attempted to stem the hysteria surrounding the news of the Soviet Sputnik. See *Public Papers of the President*, 1957, p. 817.

"In response to a question": JSDE.

2. New Horizons

slight shift of the Gulf Stream: Roberts, *The Story of the Augusta National Golf Club*, p. 200.

"Take him off my hands": Mamie Eisenhower interview.

Eisenhower's Barbeque Sauce: Russoli, *Ike the Cook*, p. 53.

"running the hand": Freeman Gosden interview.

"Go get him": Justin Dart interview.

"Why that old man George will live forever": Mamie Eisenhower interview.

"Well, I don't know": Ibid.

"Dear General": PPP, Name Files, Kennedy.

"Both Democratic candidates showed great": JSDE.

"President Eisenhower had given instructions": Ibid.

considered the matter closed: Washington Post, March 22, 1962.

"Dear Dick": ENC, September 5, 1961.

"outer space basketball": Lyon, *Eisenhower: Portrait of the Hero,* p. 803.

"no manned space program, period": Stans interview.

"He is still terribly unhappy": Slater, *The Ike I Knew,* p. 243.

"best expressed by someone without": General Clay interview.

"the convictions of responsible officials": Eisenhower, *Waging Peace,* p. 615.

"I could think of no better way": Ibid.

"What I have criticized": Ambrose, *Eisenhower: The President,* p. 641.

"One other thing": PPP, Name Files, Kennedy.

"Dear General": Ibid.

"We should plan our security": JSDE.

"no scruples about television at all": Ibid.

"presidents in order of greatness": New York

Times Magazine, July 29, 1962.

"He was greatly pleased that": Schlesinger, *A Thousand Days,* p. 675.

"The old man was wounded by the thing": John Eisenhower interview.

"I suppose this means I'll be Martin Van Buren": Ibid.

"would do anything to suck in": Washington Post, April 30, 1960.

"Ike, you can't do that": Mamie Eisenhower interview.

"The train from Copenhagen": DEP.

Eisenhower now regretted any implication: Time, August 10, 1962.

"I am before you solely as a witness": EMC, text dated July 31, 1962.

Schulz missed the ferry: DEP.

On August 5, I wrote: Ibid.

"I frankly do not see the need": Saturday Evening Post, quoted in New York Times, August 7, 1962.

"go to jail in a test case": Washington Post, June 1, 1962; *New York Times,* August 7, 1962.

"greatest disappointment": Newsweek, August 6, 1962.

"improving markedly": JFK; tape recording of DDE-JFK meeting of September 10, 1962.

"Dear David": LET, September 26, 1962.

had never been so strong: Public Papers of the President, 1958, p. 737.

"grab for power": EMC, speech text October 25, 1962.

"At my Inauguration": New York Times, September 21, 1962.

"fighting mad": Newsweek, October 22, 1962.

"Richard Nixon is one man": EMC, text of speech dated October 6, 1962.

That winter, in a meeting: JSDE.

Eisenhower's natural reaction: Abel, *The Missile Crisis,* p. 64.

In their phone conversation: JFK, library tape recording of DDE-JFK phone conversation dated October 22, 1962.

On the night of the 20th: MISC, Eisenhower memo for the record, October 22, 1962.

"They might": Ibid.

"We are, one and all": EMC, text of speech, October 25, 1962.

"What you say you will do": JFK, tape recording of DDE-JFK phone conversation October 28, 1962. In 1967, Dr. Malcolm Moos interviewed Eisenhower regarding his telephone conversations with Kennedy during the Cuban Missile Crisis. Recalling perhaps a conversation that was not recorded, Eisenhower said that he had suggested to Kennedy that Castro might have been dealt with after his 1961 decla-

ration in which the Cuban dictator affirmed he was a Marxist-Leninist. A copy of the transcript of the Eisenhower-Moos interview is in author's possession.

"There is no telling": LET, October 30, 1962.

"amusement": According to Schlesinger, Nixon's defeat "gave the White House a special fillip of entertainment." Schlesinger, *A Thousand Days,* p. 833.

"I've been wanting to write you": LET, February 4, 1963.

3. Changing Times

"climactic phase": New York Times, June 9, 1963.

"due date for freedom": New York Times, July 2, 1963.

"Negro problem": James Reston, *New York Times,* June 16, 1963.

"I have just received the news": DDED.

"with all deliberate speed": Herbert Brownell interview.

"simply needed Eisenhower": Lucius Clay interview.

boldest assertion of judicial supremacy: Krock, *Memoirs,* p. 303.

"dynamically": James MacAskill interview.

"It is proper and fitting": Text based on author's notes taken from tape of speech played for author by Reverend MacAskill.

"Define the steps": Clay interview.

"This is not a legal or legislative issue alone": JFK, online speech text, June 11, 1963.

"Dear Mr. President": PPP, Augusta–Walter Reed files, box 2.

"I did not quite understand": LET, May 20, 1964.

"You live in a defended island of freedom": JFK, online speech text, June 26, 1963.

"meant something more": Fred Friendly interview.

"Fred, this thing tomorrow at the cemetery": Friendly, *Due to Circumstances Beyond Our Control,* p. 130.

"Walter, this D-Day has a very special meaning for me": Ibid., p. 131.

Pete Jones's death had terminated: Nevins, *Gettysburg's Five Star Farmer,* p. 136.

On July 27, 1963: Wolf and Weiland, *Ike: Gettysburg's Gentleman Farmer,* p. 67.

"delight": John Eisenhower, *Strictly Personal,* p. 300.

"generally good": Ibid., p. 314.

"If we, without allies": Eisenhower, *Mandate for Change,* p. 354.

"The dilemma of finding a moral": Ibid., p. 374.

"While I had some second hand reports": Papers of Dwight D. Eisenhower, vol. 15, *The Middle Way,* p. 1033.

When Dad objected: John Eisenhower interview.

"He's Got the Whole World": Fox, *Hotel Gettysburg,* p. 119.

"True to democracy's basic principle": EMC, speech dated November 19, 1963.

"Next week, the whole family": LET, November 18, 1963.

"sense of shock and dismay": New York Times, November 23, 1963.

"We know what we did": Mamie Eisenhower interview.

"I've tried to make it crystal clear": Surety Diary, entry dated January 1, 1948.

"I humbly hope": Text of Johnson speech, November 27, 1963, on Americanrhetoric .com.

"the right people": White, *The Making of the President, 1964,* p. 106.

"I once heard that human minds": Ferrell, *The Eisenhower Diaries,* p. 271.

Critical Issues Council: Milton Eisenhower, *The President Is Calling,* p. 415.

"middle of the roader": JSDE.

"What the hell do you want!": John Eisenhower interview.

"I hope I am not revealing another secret": LET, May 26, 1964.

"all the potential": New York Times, May 25, 1964.

"transformed the California primary election": Reston in *New York Times,* June 1, 1964.

"a complete misinterpretation": New York Times, June 2, 1964.

Virginia awarded sixty-four delegates to Goldwater: White, *Making of the President, 1964,* p. 137.

"heard what he wanted to hear": John Eisenhower interview.

"about what I had expected": Ibid.

"deflated Scranton's trial balloon": New York Times, June 9, 1964.

"be part of a cabal to stop Goldwater": Ibid., June 12, 1964.

"suicidal self-destruction": White, *Making of the President, 1964,* pp. 146–47; *New York Times,* June 8, 1964.

"the TVA, Social Security": Los Angeles Times, June 9, 1964. Responding to an invitation by Governor James Rhodes of Ohio, Nixon attended the Governors' Conference for the purpose of huddling with GOP governors to plan strategy for the San Francisco convention. According to White's account, Nixon was anxious to gain Romney's entry into the race in hopes of stalemate and emerging as a compromise candidate in San Francisco. But Nixon's public statements before Cleveland and the notes he made en route

to the Governors' Conference leave little doubt that, certain of Goldwater's nomination, Nixon was hoping to broker a formula for party unity. RNP, Special Notes kept in Office and Used in Writing of Memoirs, 1975–78.

"the battle is over": Los Angeles Times, June 11, 1964.

"incomprehensible": New York Times, June 12, 1964.

"I reject the echoes so far": New York Times, June 13, 1964.

"In a letter to C. D. Jackson": Papers of C. D. Jackson, Box 51. Letter dated June 26, 1964.

His switching back and forth: Mamie Eisenhower interview.

"the pride of Abraham": Kevin McCann interview.

"The Love of Christ Controlleth All Men": Reverend Elson interview.

"by implication": John Eisenhower interview.

"Politics is particularly bewildering": Nevins, Gettysburg's Five Star Farmer, p. 106.

"Any foreign policy that this country adopts": Published text of Der Spiegel interview was reprinted in the July 9, 1964, issue of the New York Times. The Times published the unpublished portions of the interview two days later.

"You have too often casually prescribed nuclear war": White, *Making of the President, 1964,* p. 197.

"Some of you don't like to hear it": Ibid., p. 201.

"With the passage of this law": EMC, speech text dated July 14, 1964.

"those outside our family": Ibid.

"In the late afternoon on Tuesday": Slater, *The Ike I Knew,* p. 257.

"totally unfit, on the basis of his views and votes": *New York Times,* July 16, 1964.

"Anyone who joins us": Goldwater text posted on AmericanRhetoric.com.

overlooked his "personal choices": *New York Times,* July 17, 1964.

"He [Eisenhower] began the meeting": Nixon, *RN,* p. 261.

"The rest of the press conference": Ibid., p. 262.

"You know, before we had this meeting": Ibid., p. 262.

"The political situation beggars description": Papers of C. D. Jackson, Box 51, letter dated September 11, 1964.

"whether or not the American public": RNP, Harlow Memo, May 1964.

"a spoil sport and a divider": Nixon, *RN,* p. 263.

"The five converged on the hotel at dinner-

time": Elise Scharf Fox interview.

4. Elder Statesman

"Oh yes, you noticed": Averell Harriman interview.

"reconcile divergent views": From statement of purpose, American Assembly. According to Jacobs, "the entire premise of the American Assembly is that people with widely divergent interest, backgrounds, perspectives and training . . . can come together in a neutral place. Once together, they can work to find what it is they share, what they agree to . . . in a version — of not consensus — at least convergence on issues that matter to the American polity." Jacobs, *Dwight D. Eisenhower and the Founding of the American Assembly,* p. 58.

"The thousands who": New York Times, January 31, 1965.

"I hope I don't stammer": Interview with General Leonard Heaton.

"fulfillment": Anthony Lewis, *New York Times,* January 31, 1965.

"Sunset and evening star": EMC, speech text, January 30, 1965.

"would make a great mistake": Krock, *Memoirs,* p. 399.

"The situation in Vietnam": Pentagon Papers, Gravel Edition, vol. 3, p. 309.

"colossal mistake": Interview with Milton Eisenhower. In *The President Is Calling* (p. 202), Milton called intervention in Vietnam a "monumental error."

"I don't know whether he would have gone in or not": John Eisenhower interview.

"I think your policy of applying pressure": PPP, Augusta–Walter Reed Series.

"I have consistently said": Ibid.

"Laird Flunks as Historian": Higgins, *Philadelphia Inquirer,* July 28, 1965.

"demurred": *New York Times,* August 19, 1965.

"My Dear General": PPP, Augusta–Walter Reed Series.

"Dear Mr. President": Ibid.

"All the way over": Bryce Harlow interview.

"not going to be run out of a country": MISC, DDE, memorandum for the record regarding conversation with President Johnson at 10:30 A.M., July 2, 1965.

"must win": PPP, Augusta–Walter Reed Series, Goodpaster and Wheeler briefings. Eisenhower made the observation a number of times. General Eisenhower on June 16, 1965, told Goodpaster, "We have 'appealed to force,' and therefore we have got to win."

"If they do not respond": Ibid., briefing of

General Eisenhower dated January 4, 1966.

"For myself and the members of the family living with me": Papers of Dwight D. Eisenhower, vol. 14, *The Middle Way*, p. 298.

Years later, Tkach re-created for me: General Tkach interview.

"some people think the President's paintings": *New York Times*, July 6, 1959.

"What is it?": John Eisenhower interview. Incident is documented in Ann C. Whitman file at Eisenhower Presidential Library.

"In order to make the exercise": DDE letter to Donald Glew, Jr., dated January 27, 1959; *Papers of Dwight D. Eisenhower,* vol. 19, *The Middle Way*, p. 1319.

"rising and falling tide of civilizations": Eisenhower College Collection, essay by Frieda Kay Fall, p. 152.

"close friends": Slater, *The Ike I Knew*, p. 264.

"Why you old so-and-so": Rusty Brown interview.

"Until I saw that": Anne Eisenhower interview.

That winter he told Arthur Nevins: Wolf and Weiland, *Ike*, p. 78.

"The General had not seen the book": Slater, *The Ike I Knew*, p. 266.

"That evening Dad": John Eisenhower, *Strictly Personal*, p. 86.

"Afterthoughts": Eisenhower, *Waging Peace,* p. 655.

"Now you are signing up for the draft": LET, March 28, 1966.

"I am going to talk largely about 'character' ": LET, May 20, 1966.

"Suppose we liken the career": EMC, speech text, June 12, 1966.

"Remember": Anne Eisenhower interview.

"The great ideas of the West will continue": Eisenhower, *Waging Peace,* p. 658.

"a success," as Dad put it: John Eisenhower interview.

Parade *magazine's Rosalind Massow:* Parade, June 26, 1966.

"The one thing everyone needs is a purpose": Rusty Brown interview.

"General Omar Bradley": KMP.

"to bind up the wounds": Ambrose, *American Heritage,* p. 561.

"This evening we have been listening": Holt and Leyerzapf, *Eisenhower: The Prewar Diaries,* pp. 445–46.

"His highest praise": Rusty Brown interview.

Markoe was a legend in his time: For a sketch of Markoe's life story, see "Father Markoe: A Life on the Front Lines for Racial Equality" in *Window,* Creighton University, Winter 1995–96.

"He was ahead of his time": McCann interview.

"Lydia A.": Eisenhower, *At Ease,* p. 60.

"I hear you have a job lined up": LET, January 28, 1966.

"Personal–Confidential–Top Secret–Eyes Only": LET, June 13, 1966.

"Walking this morning": DDED, August 23, 1966.

"Nothing to report": Ibid., August 24, 1966.

"September 24": Ibid., September 24, 1966.

"September 27": Ibid., September 27, 1966.

"the moment we are assured privately": New York Times, September 23, 1966; ENC, October 4, 1966.

In a letter dated October 7: ENC, October 7, 1966.

In reply: ENC, October 13, 1966.

"Why don't you declare war?": John Eisenhower interview.

"October 12. Political campaign is apathetic": DDED.

"Around here there does not seem": DDED.

"November 8. Election Day": DDED, November 8, 1966.

"November 9. This morning": DDED, November 9, 1966.

"November 10. The Republican victory": DDED, November 10, 1966.

5. "Most Admired"

"Johnson," he noted, *"would be following the"*: Speech on March 8, 1967, quoted in *US News & World Report,* April 10, 1967.

"notwithstanding more cost": Lyndon Johnson, January 10, 1967, State of the Union address, www.infoplease.com/t/hist/state-of-the-union/180.html.

"the world has always": LET, October 5, 1967.

"Kevin, damnit," he would howl: Kevin McCann interview.

"Dr. Elson," he drawled, *"when I need comfort"*: Reverend Elson interview.

"November 23, 1963": MISC; DDE addendum to Notes for the President, November 23, 1963, titled "Memo of Subjects Covered Verbally with President and Which Were Not Made of the Record."

"We are, I think, talking about a chill": Rusty Brown interview.

"I had a little parade with tanks": PPP, Augusta–Walter Reed Series: Wheeler and Goodpaster briefings.

"I had always secretly hoped": LET, September 23, 1966.

"Of course I am delighted": LET, January 7, 1967.

"Of course, I am pleased to hear you speak": LET, August 30, 1967.

Dwight confessed the "blues": Papers of Ruby Norman Lucier, 1913–67. In *Ike the Soldier*, Merle Miller published several letters between Dwight Eisenhower and Gladys Harding (Brooks), who is also mentioned in *At Ease*. The letters, exchanged in the 1911–16 period, demonstrate a romantic relationship — Ike and Gladys dated during Ike's leave from West Point in the summer of 1913. But Ike reserved special mention for Ruby in *At Ease*, and their friendship lasted a lifetime. Both Ruby and Gladys were aspiring musicians who moved away from Abilene.

"San Antonio, Texas": Ibid.

He arranged for: Ibid.

"The family outside her hospital room": Ibid., letter from P. Lucier to DDE, dated November 3, 1967.

"endless war": PPP, Augusta–Walter Reed Series; phrase (or equivalent) appears in Goodpaster memoranda dated June 22, 1966, September 16, 1966, August 9, 1967.

"It is a long range discussion of Asia": ENC letter, dated August 5, 1967.

"assuming an expertise they do not possess": RNP, Special Notes kept in Office and Used in Writing of Memoirs, 1975–1978.

"the great temptation": Kenneth Crawford in

Newsweek, October 23, 1967.

"Dear David": LET, November 27, 1967.

"In your reply to my letter": LET, December 15, 1967.

"Under orders of Doctors": Travel Guide, November 10, 1967.

"October 25": Travel Guide, October 25, 1967.

"November 10": Travel Guide, November 10, 1967.

"I think you can overdo it": US News & World Report, December 11, 1967.

"Today Mamie and I": Travel Guide, November 27, 1967.

"Mary Jean's 12th birthday": Travel Guide, December 21, 1967.

"an obstacle to civil rights": Los Angeles Times, March 26, 1967.

Gallup poll: Article by Dr. George Gallup *in Los Angeles Times,* January 10, 1968.

6. Homeward Bound

actively oppose "any candidate": New York Times, December 25, 1967.

"as if they, and not the unsuccessful war effort": New York Times, December 26, 1967.

"Eisenhower Rides Again": Tom Wicker, *New York Times,* December 28, 1967.

"The General would not understand": Kevin McCann interview.

"Daddy mentioned that a June wedding": JNP.

"boundless nervous energy": New York Times, December 25, 1967.

Most enjoyable were visits from Coach John McKay: DDED.

"I told DDE that if things worked out": ENC memo, Rose Mary Woods to Richard Nixon, dated November 28, 1967.

"I quite agree with your statement": ENC, November 15, 1967.

"First of all, he [Eisenhower] keeps telling Reagan": ENC, memorandum of conversation by Bob Ellsworth, February 13, 1968.

"disquieting": Newsweek, February 26, 1968.

"The President is obviously rusty in golf": DDED.

"I admit that the conduct of the Presidency": LET, February 21, 1968.

"Last Sunday I carried out": DDED.

"Yesterday I had a rather remarkable day at golf": DDED.

"It is so ironic": JNP, dated March 31, 1968.

"partial capitulation": DDED.

"steady deterioration in my heart muscle": DDED.

"No, I'll play": Freeman Gosden interview.

"Thank you for your letter": PPP, Augusta–Walter Reed Series.

"more kindly towards Nixon than ever": ENC,

Rose Mary Woods memo, May 9, 1967.

"a day did not go by": Milton Eisenhower interview.

"things are moving apace on DDE": ENC, Bryce Harlow memo to Rose Mary Woods, July 14, 1968.

"lay it on the line": Ibid.

"In other words": ENC, Richard Nixon letter dated July 15, 1968.

"Ever since I entered politics": ENC, July 18, 1968.

"July 19 flew to Wash DC": JNP.

"Lyndon went directly in to see the General": Lady Bird Johnson, *A White House Diary*, pp. 699–700.

"It has been one of those mysteries": Sidey in *Life,* August 16, 1968.

Walter Reed also received more than twenty offers: Lyon, *Eisenhower: Portrait of the Hero,* p. 911.

"With him," General Heaton recalled, "you never killed hope": General Heaton interview.

"Johnson gave Nixon a trick and Humphrey a treat": Nixon, *RN,* p. 328.

"Well," Nixon began, "I suppose the": Author witnessed this exchange.

"In any event," Harlow recalled: Bryce Harlow interview.

"Stay there," he said: Mamie Eisenhower in-

terview.

Eisenhower lucidly observed: Richard Nixon interview.

"abiding love to each member of both families": LET, December 22, 1968.

"My ambition": Slater interview.

"I started this diary": DDED, January 14, 1969.

"As usual, when I try to keep a diary": Ibid., January 16, 1969.

"Never mind," Eisenhower replied: Robert Anderson interview.

"like a brother": General Mark Wayne Clark interview.

"He was an old man, but after all he'd survived": Mamie Eisenhower interview.

"Visitor. Sec. Designate Mitchell": DDED, January 17, 1969.

"J.S.D.E. [John Eisenhower] visited": Ibid., January 18, 1969.

"George Allen in the morning": Ibid., January 19, 1969.

"Inauguration Day": Ibid., January 20, 1969.

"General Snyder came to see me briefly": Ibid., January 21, 1969.

"Charles Jones and Robert Anderson": Ibid., January 22, 1969.

"David and Julie stopped by for an hour": Ibid., January 23, 1969.

"Robert B. Mayo": Ibid., January 24, 1969.

"Justin Dart": Ibid., January 25, 1969.

"As usual, my diary has not even entered": January 28, 1969.

He drew comfort: Billy Graham interview, covered also in Graham, *Just as I Am,* p. 204.

"Now Mamie": General Heaton interview.

"First in War, First in Peace": New York Times, March 29, 1969.

"A giant of our age is gone": Ibid.

"I cannot forget his services to his country": Ibid.

"when history turns": Ibid.

"It is difficult to deal separately": Washington Post, March 29, 1969.

BIBLIOGRAPHY

Unpublished Online Materials and Unpublished Materials in Author's Custody

Author's personal correspondence with Dwight Eisenhower, 1962–68

David Eisenhower Papers, including 1962 European Trip Diary and schedules

Dwight D. Eisenhower diary, kept in Executive Record and Travel Guide, 1964 (diary entries all dated in 1967)

Dwight D. Eisenhower diary, kept in National Surety Corporation Diary, 1942 (diary entries 1942–49)

Eisenhower-Nixon correspondence, 1960–68

JFK Presidential Library and Museum online; Historical Resources: Speeches; John F. Kennedy Presidential Library telephone logs: Kennedy and Dwight D. Eisenhower: September 10, October 22 and 28, 1962

John Eisenhower Gettysburg office memoranda, 1961–64

Julie Nixon Papers, 1968 Campaign Diary

Kevin McCann Papers, Miscellaneous Dwight Eisenhower book drafts provided by Kevin McCann

Richard Nixon Papers, handwritten speech notes, dictations, and meeting records, 1961–68

Texts of Eisenhower's post-presidential speeches posted online by the Eisenhower Memorial Commission

Various documents and memoranda in author's possession

Unpublished Material in Dwight D. Eisenhower Library

Dwight Eisenhower diaries (1961–69) housed at Eisenhower Presidential Library, Abilene, Kansas

Papers of Ruby Norman Lucier, Eisenhower Presidential Library, Abilene, Kansas

Post-Presidential Papers, Eisenhower Presidential Library

Augusta–Walter Reed Series, which includes correspondence between Presidents Kennedy, Johnson, and Eisenhower and briefing by General Goodpaster and General Wheeler

Papers of C. D. Jackson

Select Bibliography of Published Works

Abel, Elie. *The Missile Crisis.* New York: Bantam, 1966.

Allen, Craig. *Eisenhower and the Mass Media.* Chapel Hill: University of North Carolina Press, 1993.

Allen, George. *Presidents Who Have Known Me.* New York: Simon & Schuster, 1960.

Ambrose, Stephen E. *American Heritage New History of World War II.* New York: Viking Penguin, 1997.

————. *Eisenhower: Soldier and President.* New York: Touchstone, 1990.

————. *Eisenhower: The President.* New York: Simon & Schuster, 1984.

Clifford, Clark. *Counsel to the President.* New York: Random House, 1991.

Davis, Kenneth. *The Eisenhower College Collection: The Paintings of Dwight D. Eisenhower.* Los Angeles: Nash, 1972.

Duram, James C. *A Moderate Among Extremists: Dwight D. Eisenhower and the School Desegregation Crisis.* Chicago: Nelson-Hall, 1980.

Dwight David Eisenhower: Memorial Tributes in Congress. Washington, D.C.: U.S. Government Printing Office, 1970.

Eisenhower, David. *Eisenhower at War*

1943–1945. New York: Random House, 1986.

Eisenhower, Dwight D. *At Ease: Stories I Tell to Friends.* Garden City, N.Y.: Doubleday, 1967.

———. *In Review.* Garden City, N.Y.: Doubleday, 1969.

———. *Mandate for Change.* Garden City, N.Y.: Doubleday, 1963.

———. *The Papers of Dwight D. Eisenhower.* 21 vols. Baltimore: Johns Hopkins University Press, 1970–2001.

———. *Public Papers of the President: Dwight Eisenhower 1957.* Washington, D.C.: U.S. Government Printing Office, 1958.

———. *Public Papers of the President: Dwight Eisenhower 1960–1961.* Washington, D.C.: U.S. Government Printing Office, 1961.

———. *Waging Peace.* Garden City, N.Y.: Doubleday, 1965.

Eisenhower, John S. D. *General Ike: A Personal Reminiscence.* New York: Free Press, 2003.

———. *Strictly Personal.* Garden City, N.Y.: Doubleday, 1974.

Eisenhower, Julie Nixon. *Pat Nixon: The*

Untold Story. New York: Simon & Schuster, 1986.

Eisenhower, Milton S. *The President Is Calling.* Garden City, N.Y.: Doubleday, 1974.

Eisenhower, Susan. *Mrs. Ike.* New York: Farrar, Straus & Giroux, 1996.

Elson, Edward L. R. *Wide Was His Parish.* Wheaton, Ill.: Tyndale House, 1986.

Fairlie, Henry. *The Kennedy Promise.* Garden City, N.Y.: Doubleday, 1973.

Ferrell, Robert. *The Eisenhower Diaries.* New York: Norton, 1981.

Fox, Elise Scharf. *Hotel Gettysburg.* Gettysburg, Pa.: Downtown Gettysburg, 1988.

Friendly, Fred W. *Due to Circumstances Beyond Our Control.* New York: Vintage, 1968.

Gould, Lewis L. *Grand Old Party: A History of the Republicans.* New York: Random House, 2003.

Graham, Billy. *Just As I Am.* New York: HarperCollins, 1997.

Gravel, Mike. *The Pentagon Papers: The Senator Gravel Edition: The Defense Department History of US Decision Making on Vietnam, Volume III.* Boston: Beacon, 1971.

Holt, Daniel, and James W. Leyerzapf. *Eisenhower: The Prewar Diaries and Selected Papers, 1905–1946.* Baltimore: Johns

Hopkins University Press, 1998.

Jacobs, Travis Beal. *Dwight D. Eisenhower and the Founding of the American Assembly.* New York: American Assembly, Columbia University, 2004.

Jamieson, Kathleen Hall. *Packaging the Presidency.* 3rd ed. New York: Oxford University Press, 1996.

Johnson, Lady Bird. *A White House Diary.* New York: Holt, Rinehart & Winston, 1970.

Johnson, Lyndon. *The Vantage Point.* New York: Holt, Rinehart & Winston, 1971.

Karnow, Stanley. *Vietnam: A History.* New York: Viking, 1983.

Krock, Arthur. *In the Nation 1932–1966.* New York: McGraw-Hill, 1966.

———. *Memoirs.* New York: Funk & Wagnalls, 1968.

Lyon, Peter. *Eisenhower: Portrait of the Hero.* Boston: Little, Brown, 1974.

Miller, Merle. *Ike the Soldier: As They Knew Him.* New York: G. P. Putnam's Sons, 1987.

Morin, Relman. *Dwight David Eisenhower: A Gauge of Greatness: An Associated Press Biography.* New York: Associated Press, 1969.

Nelson, Dale W. *The President Is at Camp*

David. Syracuse, N.Y.: Syracuse University Press, 1995.

Nevins, Brigadier General Arthur S. *Gettysburg's Five Star Farmer.* New York: Carlton, 1977.

Nichols, David A. *A Matter of Justice: Eisenhower and the Beginning of the Civil Rights Revolution.* New York: Simon & Schuster, 2007.

Nisbet, Robert. *Twilight of Authority.* New York: Oxford University Press, 1975.

Nixon, Richard. *RN: The Memoirs of Richard Nixon.* New York: Grosset & Dunlap, 1978.

Pipes, Kasey S. *Ike's Final Battle: The Road to Little Rock and the Challenge of Equality.* New York: Midpoint Trade Books, 2007.

Roberts, Clifford. *The Story of the Augusta National Golf Club.* Garden City, N.Y.: Doubleday, 1976.

Rostow, Walt W. *The Diffusion of Power.* New York: Macmillan, 1972.

Russoli, Edward, and Candace Russoli. *Ike the Cook.* Allentown, Pa.: Benedettini, 1990.

Schlesinger, Arthur M., Jr. *A Thousand Days.* Boston: Houghton Mifflin, 1965.

Sheehan, Neil. *The Pentagon Papers.* New York: Bantam, 1971.

Slater, Ellis D. *The Ike I Knew.* Baltimore:

Ellis D. Slater Trust, 1980.

Smith, Malcolm E. *John F. Kennedy's 13 Great Mistakes in the White House.* Smithson, N.Y.: Suffolk House, 1980.

Smith, Merriman. *Merriman Smith's Book of Presidents.* Ed. Timothy G. Smith. New York: Norton, 1972.

Thernstrom, Stephan, and Abigail Thernstrom. *America in Black and White.* New York: Simon & Schuster, 1997.

Thompson, Robert. *No Exit from Vietnam.* New York: David McKay, 1969.

Westmoreland, General William C. *A Soldier's Report.* New York: Dell, 1976.

White, Theodore H. *The Making of the President, 1964.* New York: Atheneum, 1965.

———. *The Making of the President, 1968.* New York: Atheneum, 1969.

Wolf, Stanley R., and Audrey (Wolf) Weiland. *Ike: Gettysburg's Gentleman Farmer.* Getrysburg, Pa.: Thomas, 2008.

Selected Interviews

Governor Sherman Adams, March 1977.

Secretary of the Treasury Robert Anderson, February 1977.

Leonore Annenberg

Rusty Brown, August 1976.

Attorney General Herbert Brownell, March 1977.

General Mark Wayne Clark, March 1977.

General Lucius Clay, February 1977.

General Ted Clifton, March 1977.

Justin Dart, August 1976.

Anne Eisenhower

Barbara Eisenhower-Foltz

John Eisenhower

Mamie Doud Eisenhower

Mary Jean Eisenhower

Milton S. Eisenhower

Susan Eisenhower

Reverend Edward L. R. Elson, March 1977.

Alfred "Fred" Friendly, October 1992.

Freeman Gosden, August 1976.

Reverend Billy Graham, August 1976.

General Alfred Gruenther, February 1977.

Leonard Hall, October 1976.

Bryce Harlow, October 1976.

Ambassador Averell Harriman, January 1977.

General Leonard Heaton, March 1977.

Reverend James MacAskill, October 1976.

Kevin McCann

Reverend Dean Miller, August 1976.

Delores Moaney

Aksel Nielsen, August 1976.

Patricia Ryan Nixon

President Richard M. Nixon

Clifford Roberts, August 1976.
Elise Scharf Fox, October 1976.
Peggy Scharf, October 1976.
Ellis ("Slats") Slater, March 1977.
Maurice Stans, December 1979.
General Walter Tkach, March 1977.
Ann C. Whitman, February 1977.
Rose Mary Woods

ABOUT THE AUTHORS

David Eisenhower is director of the Institute for Public Service at the Annenberg School of Communications at the University of Pennsylvania.

Julie Nixon Eisenhower is the younger daughter of President Richard M. Nixon and author of the bestselling *Pat Nixon: The Untold Story* and *Special People.* The Eisenhowers live in suburban Philadelphia.

The employees of Thorndike Press hope you have enjoyed this Large Print book. All our Thorndike, Wheeler, and Kennebec Large Print titles are designed for easy reading, and all our books are made to last. Other Thorndike Press Large Print books are available at your library, through selected bookstores, or directly from us.

For information about titles, please call:
(800) 223-1244

or visit our Web site at:
http://gale.cengage.com/thorndike

To share your comments, please write:
Publisher
Thorndike Press
295 Kennedy Memorial Drive
Waterville, ME 04901